T0381981

HISTORY

OF

CITIES

IN

MAPS

Published by Collins
An imprint of HarperCollins Publishers
Westerhill Road, Bishopbriggs, Glasgow G64 2QT
www.harpercollins.co.uk

HarperCollins Publishers
Macken House, 39/40 Mayor Street Upper, Dublin 1, D01 C9W8, Ireland

First edition 2024
© HarperCollins Publishers 2024
Text © Philip Parker 2024
Maps © see Acknowledgements on p224

A catalogue record for this book is available from the British Library

ISBN 978-0-00-867181-5

10 9 8 7 6 5 4 3 2 1

Printed in India

If you would like to comment on any aspect of this book,
please contact us at the above address or online.
e-mail: **collins.reference@harpercollins.co.uk**

collins.co.uk

HISTORY
OF
CITIES
IN
MAPS

Philip Parker

Contents

Québec City

Chicago

Boston

New York

Washington, DC

Los Angeles

Tenochtitlán/
Mexico City

Stock

Amsterdam

Edinburgh

Manchester

Dublin

Ham

Liverpool

London

Prag

Paris

Vie

Palman

Venice

Florence

Rom

Madrid

Lisbon

Lagos

Bogotá

Cusco

Brasília

Rio de Janeiro

St Petersburg

Moscow

Kyiv

Constantinople

Priene

Nicosia

Damascus

Baghdad   Isfahan

Jerusalem

andria

Cairo   Babylon

Dubai

Delhi

Mohenjo-daro

Dharavi
Mumbai

Beijing

Seoul

Kyoto

Tokyo

Chang'an

Oceanix
Busan

Nagasaki

Chongqing

Jakarta

Town

Adelaide   Sydney

Christchurch

"Houses make a town, but citizens a city."

The Social Contract

Jean-Jacques Rousseau, 1762

Introduction

The history of mankind is the history of the city. It is no accident that cities and writing both appeared in Egypt and Mesopotamia at about the same time around 4000BC, as societies grew large enough and complex enough to require record-keeping. Cities, therefore, can speak to us from the past, and if there is one constant citizen in all of them it is the scribe, the archivist, the historian or the novelist who documents the momentous events in its rise, grandeur or decline. And the cartographer, who charts the physical aspect of the city in maps, plans and panoramas, providing us with some sense of how the city looked, its layout, growth and organisation.

History of Cities in Maps looks at the development of the places where over half of us now live (a proportion expected to reach nearly 70 per cent by 2050), presenting maps of over 60 of the greatest cities in world history, each of which illustrates a key moment in the development of urban life. For some it is a technical innovation, such as the invention of sewerage in Mohenjo-daro (in what is now Pakistan), for others, reflections of military might (such as ancient Rome) or wealth gained through trade (as in China's Chang'an) or the bringing of artificial light to the city (which London

pioneered in 1807). They range in time from 2500BC – the height of Mohenjo-daro – to the present day, a span of over four-and-a-half millennia, and include three cities that have disappeared completely (Babylon, Priene and Mohenjo-daro), three which were almost totally reshaped on the ruins of the old (Tenochtitlán, Cusco and Chang'an), one which has yet to be built, and a large majority that have grown, either over centuries or mere decades, to their present form.

But how did it all begin, and what constitutes a city (as opposed to a town or village)? The first faint stirrings of urbanism happened around 9000BC when the development of agriculture encouraged people to become more sedentary, as they needed to be close to the crops and herds they were tending, and as they created surpluses which could allow society the luxury of specialists such as potters or priests. By around 7,000 years ago the process had advanced far enough to produce small walled towns such as Jericho in today's West Bank and Çatalhöyük on Turkey's Anatolian Plateau, where around 10,000 people lived in a dense cluster of cube-like mud-brick houses. Living off farming and a trade in obsidian, volcanic glass

The fresco found on a wall at Çatalhöyük shows a grid of rectangles (at the bottom) representing the settlement's houses, with a faint red triangle at the top left depicting the nearby volcano of Nemrut Dağ erupting.

from nearby Nemrut Dağ, they also left the world's first town plan on a fresco which depicts the volcano's eruption.

Yet Çatalhöyük was not quite a city. Over time, the determining factors of city status have included size (though at the start of urban history, a population of around 20,000 seems to have counted as a city, whereas now that would be generally regarded as a very small town), the possession of a cathedral (a parochial British definition), the granting of some kind of municipal charter, or merely possessing enough political clout to claim the title unchallenged.

The reality is a little more intangible. Cities have always been places to which incomers have been drawn because they see a social or economic advantage in doing so: medieval Germany had an expression, *Stadtluft macht frei* ("city air frees you"), referring to the belief that serfs would be liberated of their obligation after living for a year and a day in a city. Once in urban areas, people created networks, of family members, of patron–client relationships, of groups of artisans that gave city life a multiplier effect: innovations and trends that would simply die out in villages were spread and disseminated in the creative cauldron of a city.

Allied to networks is trade, the lifeblood of many cities, acting both as markets through which goods both vital and exotic flowed, and as vast reservoirs of consumption,

sucking in food and materials from the surrounding countryside. When the Spanish conquistadors came across the vast Aztec marketplace in Tlatelolco near Tenochtitlán in 1519, they were struck by the huge range of goods available to the 60,000 people who frequented it each day: from precious stones to exotic bird feathers, jaguar skins, honey paste, firewood and beans.

Cities, too, are generally characterised by monumental public buildings, though a few, such as Mohenjo-daro, seem to lack these. But the bulk have grand buildings, such as Rome with its Colosseum, Moscow's St Basil's Cathedral or Isfahan's Shah Mosque. Cities provide public services of some kind: even in the legendary squalor of medieval European cities, efforts were made to keep the streets clean, and Imperial Rome had its (somewhat ineffective) fire services. These are generally run by a city authority to some extent independent of the national ruler, their powers often (and particularly in the earlier European cities) laid down by charter.

An efficiently run city placed squarely on trade routes, and with a growing population, becomes a store of wealth that excites the jealousy of others. Most early cities, therefore had walls (and again, Mohenjo-daro is an exception) which long kept them constrained within their bounds. Attacks by others are one of the main challenges cities have faced

The Codex Sigüenza map was created in the indigenous tradition some time after the Spanish conquest of 1519–21. It shows important locations in the migration of the Mexica people from their traditional homeland of Aztlán to the spot where an eagle perched on a cactus holding a snake marked the future site of Tenochtitlán (see page 40).

throughout history: the sack of Baghdad by the Mongols in 1258, in which tens of thousands were killed and the last Abbasid caliph trampled to death inside a rolled-up carpet, is just one example of the scores of assaults suffered by almost every city described in this book. Disease is the second main challenge cities have faced. In the pre-modern period, epidemics of infectious diseases were an ever-present challenge, with the Black Death pandemic of 1347–50 – which killed around a third of the population of Europe and the Middle East, and more in some urban areas – the most notable.

Acquiring their daily bread has been a third challenge for the citizens of most cities over time: simply feeding the city has required a hinterland many times the footprint of the urban area itself, as, divorced from their rural past, city-dwellers' ability to feed themselves unaided has been limited. Failure on the part of the city authorities to achieve this has often led to disorder; the discontents of city-folk are manifold, and riots are a constant feature in the annals of cities over time (though few as unexpected as the deaths of 22 people in New York in 1849 over a theatre performance).

Cities have been shaped by all these forces: money, war, the successes and failures of urban and national governments to provide for them and develop them, and the shifting vagaries of global economic balances. Nothing, though, has stopped the onward march of urban life, as the millions who lived in cities in 2000BC have been surpassed by the billions who did so in AD2000. There are serious challenges posed by the acceleration of the rate of growth experienced by cities in recent decades. Levels of pollution have increased, with implications for the health of the residents, while in many cities the proportion of people living in informal districts, or slums, has increased, with little access to public services like health, education or even clean water. Climate instability, which has made life for rural dwellers even harder, and the civil wars and insurgencies that plague many developing countries, have pushed more people into cities, creating even more problems for the municipal authorities already struggling to cope. And the emergence of Covid-19 in 2019–20 has shown that the blight of epidemic diseases is not a thing of the past and can strike even cities in rich, industrialised countries with a devastating toll of death and disruption.

Yet despite it all the ranks of the more than four billion city dwellers continue to swell, and that surge shows no signs of diminishing. The history of mankind may have been the history of the city, but it seems sure that the city will be mankind's future.

The projection of how the artificial city of Oceanix Busan might look shows how its component hexagonal models tessellate to form a larger urban network (see page 222).

Cities Get Healthy

Mohenjo-daro, c 2500BC

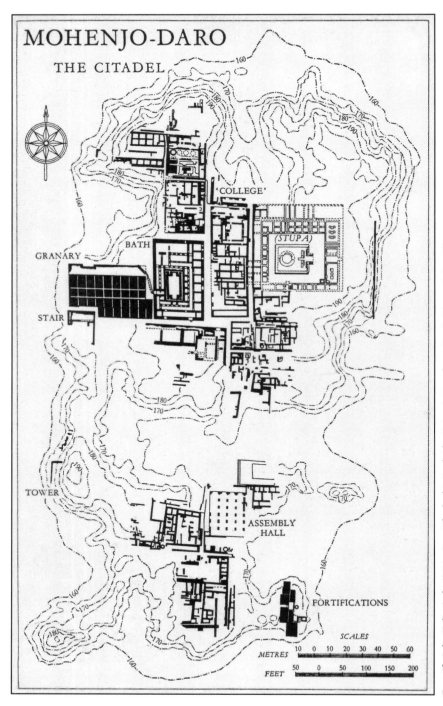

From *The Indus Civilization* by Sir Mortimer Wheeler / © Cambridge University Press / reproduced with permission of the Licensor through PLSclear / Australian National University Archives: Basham Collection, ANUA 682-35. Mohenjo-daro: plans of Mohenjo-Daro citadel, heights in feet above sea level, 1968

People need water and people produce waste, large quantities of it. The million inhabitants of Imperial Rome at its height in the 1st century AD are estimated to have created around 450 tonnes in weight of excrement each day, much of it finding its way into the less-than-pristine waters of the River Tiber. The history of cities is in large part the story of their management, or in many cases mismanagement, of the business of providing their citizens with water, and the safe disposal of waste.

The plan shows the earliest city to crack the problem, two thousand years before the Romans built their grand covered sewer, the Cloaca Maxima (so pleased were they with it that they even had a dedicated goddess for sewage, Cloacina). Mohenjo-daro, in Sindh in Pakistan, was founded around 2500BC at the height of the Indus Valley Civilisation, which constituted a string of similar cities (notably Harappa, Lothal and Dholavira), whose level of urban organisation far surpassed contemporary rivals in Egypt, Mesopotamia and China. The plan, from the report on the 1945 excavations by the British archaeologist Mortimer Wheeler, shows the "Citadel", one of the most prominent features of the site, an artificial hill some 7 to 15 metres (23 to 50 feet) high on which the largest of the city's structures were built.

The grid pattern evident on the map already indicates a planned settlement: the lower city to the east of the citadel is a dizzying grid of blocks covering around 385 by 225 metres (420 by 250 yards), subdivided by lanes, some of them dog-legged, possibly as a protection against the wind. One of the most striking features on the Citadel is the Great Bath (labelled as "Bath" on the plan), a huge water tank, around 12 by 7 metres (40 by 23 feet) in area, and 2.4 metres (8 feet) deep, proofed against leakages with a layer of bitumen, and accessed by wide staircases to the north and south.

The exact function of the tank is unclear – as for many of the city's buildings – but it most probably had some role in purification rituals, and it is evident that to keep it filled with water required sophisticated plumbing. This, Mohenjo-daro had in abundance. More than 700 wells have been discovered in the city, most brick-lined to strengthen them, and largely around a metre (3.25 feet) in diameter, although one giant is double that size. Leading from the main residences is something even more extraordinary: a citywide network of covered drains to supply fresh water and take away wastewater. Many houses had rooms connected to the system, which seem to have been private bathing chambers. Some of these were on an upper storey, requiring even more complex plumbing. The system was well maintained, too; small piles of grey-green sand at the edges of the sewers suggest they were regularly scoured to avoid becoming blocked up.

The Citadel had other grand structures, labelled on Wheeler's map as the "Granary" (though none of the finds there support this attribution) and the "College" which, it is theorised, was some kind of hostel for priests, though its 71-by-25-metre (323-by-82-foot) bulk could have housed hundreds of residents. The ambiguity is typical of Mohenjo-daro, aggravated by our inability to decipher its writing system, which appears on hundreds of clay seals, impressed with images of animals (oxen, buffalo and an Indus "unicorn", which is the most common, but may represent a mythical creature) and script symbols in an unknown language.

Despite all attempts to break its code, the Indus Valley script remains stubbornly opaque. As a result, key aspects of Mohenjo-daro's culture remain a mystery. The city has none of the palaces, or indeed the temples, found in most other large urban settlements in the ancient world. Despite the labelling of one of the most striking sculptures found on the site – a soapstone statue of a man with pierced earlobes, a ribbon headband and a trefoil pattern cloak – as the "Priest king", there is no evidence the city was ruled by priests, or indeed of any hierarchy at all. Some arrowheads and clay ball missiles have been found, but there is no sign of a warrior class, nor much in the way of defences; the city had no walls, and only a few guard-towers.

There clearly was some form of guiding organisation. The maintenance of the sewer system tells us that, as well as the regularity of the measures discovered, which are all based on the weight of a black-and-red *ratti* seed (around 13.7 grams or half an ounce) in multiples of 2, 4, 8 and 16. The city also traded extensively – some of its seals have been found in Mesopotamia, and its merchants seem to have acquired turquoise from Afghanistan, jade from Tibet or Myanmar and copper from Mesopotamia. The community, too, was strong enough to survive several floods from the Indus river that ran alongside the city. By 1700BC, though, the site was abandoned: one theory suggests that a final devastating flood made it uninhabitable, others that the shifting of the course of the Indus, which now runs around a kilometre (0.6 miles) away, made the balance between water and life untenable.

Deserted, the city's structures collapsed, though a Buddhist stupa was built atop the Citadel in the 2nd century AD. The decay was aggravated by the rising of the water table beneath, the brick remains of Mohenjo-daro sucking in salt, which crystallised and then caused the bricks to simply crumble away in heavy rain. It also made investigating the earlier stages of the city's development almost impossible: the final excavations in 1965 pumped enough water out to dig 10 metres down, but then the archaeologists' trench flooded and collapsed. Just as water gave the city life, and was harnessed by the inhabitants to create possibly the ancient world's cleanest city, so water destroyed it and continues to frustrate attempts to fully understand it.

City of the Tower

Babylon, c 600BC

The map overleaf, by the distinguished French Benedictine scholar Antoine Calmet (1672–1757), is dominated by the Tower of Babel, the most famous feature of one of the ancient world's most famous cities. Appearing in Calmet's *Historical and Critical Dictionary of the Bible* (1722–28), a work somewhat less popular than his later treatise on Hungarian vampires and revenants, it is largely based on an account by the 5th-century BC Greek historian Herodotus, writing when the city was still partially intact.

The Tower, or as it really was, the ziggurat of Etemenanki, the "House of the Foundation of Heaven and Earth", is symbolic of Babylon's image problem, lambasted by Biblical prophets like Micah and Jeremiah who were forever predicting its downfall, and characterised in the New Testament Book of Revelations as "the whore of Babylon". The animus against the city derived from its role as the place of exile of the Jewish people after Jerusalem's destruction by Babylon's greatest ruler, Nebuchadnezzar, in 587BC, an event that fatally damaged the city's subsequent reputation.

When Nebuchadnezzar came to the Babylonian throne in 604BC, the city was already 17 centuries old. First recorded around 2300BC, it remained a small, unassuming place under the sway of the Akkadians, Gutians and the Third Dynasty of Ur until Sumuabum, an Amorite from Syria, established an independent kingdom there around 1894BC. Little is known about this "Old Babylonian" phase of the city's existence, although the sixth ruler of the dynasty, a certain Hammurabi (reigned 1792–1750BC), achieved enduring fame as the author of the world's first substantial law-code, whose retributive penalties included severing the hand of a physician who caused the death of a noble patient. Hammurabi carved out a Babylonian empire in Mesopotamia, conquering previously mighty cities such as Ur, Nippur and Lagash, but his achievement was ephemeral. His son Samsu-iluna failed to hold the empire together and for the next thousand years Babylon was ruled by a succession of Hittites, Kassites, Akkadians and Assyrians.

Babylon retained a memory of its former greatness, and its relations with its foreign masters was fractious. In 689BC, the Assyrian ruler Sennacherib sacked it after a revolt and deported the whole population. Three generations later, however, Assyrian power was fraying, and a local magnate, Nabopolassar (reigned 625–605BC) seized power in Babylon and then, together with his Median and Scythian allies, sacked Nineveh, the Assyrian capital, in 612BC.

As Babylon began the most glorious phase in its history, Nabopolassar's son Nebuchadnezzar II created the Babylon that Herodotus described, and that the first full excavation by the German archaeologist Robert Koldewey uncovered in 1898. He campaigned in Egypt, against the Lydians and the Kingdom of Judah, whose capital Jerusalem he stormed in 587BC, deporting most of its population back to Babylon. In between, Nebuchadnezzar built. At the end of the period, Babylon, with 200,000 inhabitants, was the world's largest city, and its most magnificent.

The city was surrounded by a triple set of baked brick walls up to 8 metres (26 feet) thick, protected by a moat and studded with defensive towers. The city was entered by one of eight ceremonial gates dedicated to Babylonian deities, such as Sin, the moon god, Enlil the sky god, and the city's patron deity, Marduk. The most splendid was in the north, dedicated to Ishtar, the love goddess, and decorated with a polychrome glazed frieze of dragons. Leading from this was a grand ceremonial avenue, the *Aibur-shabu* ("the enemy shall never pass"), along which statues of the gods were processed during the annual New Year Festival dedicated to Marduk and which was flanked by walls adorned with over 100 glazed-brick friezes of lions. To the west of the Processional Way lay the three palaces of Nebuchadnezzar. The southernmost had five great courtyards, in the third of which was sited the great throne of the king himself. Excavators found the remains of ancient wells in the palace, which suggested that it might have been the location of the fabled Hanging Gardens of Babylon, one of the Seven Wonders of the Ancient World, an extravagant oasis of greenery on a set of artificial tiers of which, sadly, all other trace has vanished.

Further along the Aibur-shabu lay the centrepiece of the city, the Esagila, the shrine complex of Marduk himself, and beside it the Etemenanki, whose base, a 90-metre (300-foot) square, rose to a similar height on eight tiered levels. At its very apex, Herodotus claims, was a shrine holding a table made with 22 tonnes of gold. The Babylonians themselves believed the tip of the ziggurat was where the Earth touched the heavens, and the story of the Tower of Babel, in which God punishes them by fracturing their previously universal language into a myriad of competing tongues both indicates awe at the size of the building and reflects the population of Babylon, made up in large part of other peoples forcibly transplanted there, such as the Jewish inhabitants.

The fate of the real Babylon mirrors that of the Tower. Nebuchadnezzar's reign ended darkly, as he spent his final years sequestered in the palace, convinced that he was possessed by a demon. After his death in 562BC, his successors proved short-lived until finally, Nabonidus, a former general, took power in 555BC. His reign proved a disaster. The son of a priestess of the god Sin at Harran (now in southeastern Turkey), he devoted enormous resources to her temple, and then in 552BC moved the court, for reasons which are unclear, to the oasis of Tayma in northwestern Arabia. In his absence, the New Year Festival could not be conducted, and the revolts, the outbreaks of plague, the famines and the soaring prices that afflicted Babylonia, were all blamed on this neglect. When Cyrus of Persia attacked the city in 539BC, there was little will to resist and Babylon quickly surrendered.

Although it remained an important religious centre, Babylon was now just a provincial capital in the Achaemenid Persian Empire. Once more subject to foreign masters, its importance dwindled, and although Alexander the Great planned to make it the capital of his vast empire, his premature death there in 323BC meant Babylon's downward slide continued. In 275BC, Seleucus I Nicator, one of Alexander's successors, deported most of the city's population and cannibalised its buildings to construct his own new capital at Seleucia-on-the-Tigris. By the 19th century, all that was left of the once mighty city, of the towering ziggurat and of the Hanging Gardens, were a few mounds and piles of mouldering bricks. That, and its reputation for licentiousness and the account by Herodotus that enabled a French monk to sketch an image of the city, over two millennia after its heyday.

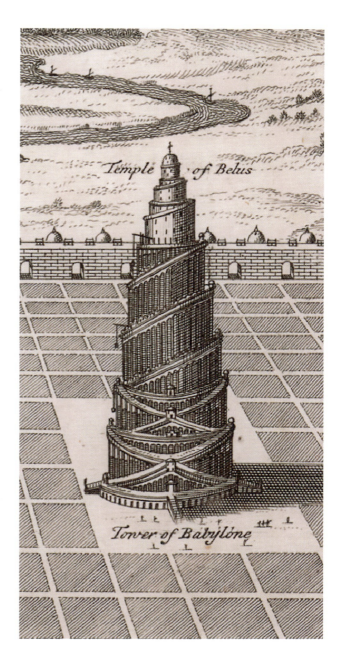

The Kings Palace

Gardens made upon Arches

West

A PLAN OF THE CITY OF BABYLON ACCOR

Temple of Belus

Palace of Simerenis

Tower of Babylone

Obelisk

East

Theatre of Dreams

Athens, c 400BC

For centuries, Athens was seen as the archetype of the ancient city. Constitutional, scientific and literary ideas took root there that would spread and be echoed down into the modern era. It was the theatre both of dreams, where democracy first developed over 2,500 years ago, and of nightmares, where it collapsed scarcely a century later.

The map overleaf, by the English architect William Barnard Clarke, was drafted in 1832 for the Society for the Diffusion of Useful Knowledge, a body established by Henry Brougham, champion of public education, opponent of the trade in enslaved people, and later British Lord Chancellor, who believed that "the progress of improvement among the People is chiefly obstructed by the want of Elementary works … written in a plain manner … and published at a low price". The Society's map of ancient Greece lay close to the heart of this project and was its most popular, selling over 30,000 copies. This companion map of Athens encapsulates a landscape that both resonated with 19th-century politicians' self-image as champions of liberty, and is a palimpsest of the city's dizzy rise to glory and heady fall from grace.

Athens was something of a late developer. The citadel – or Acropolis – had been occupied since Neolithic times up to 7,000 years ago, providing an easily defensible refuge whose internal spring meant attackers could not cut off its water supply. Great defensive Cyclopean walls were thrown up around 1400BC, giving rise to the legend that the city had been founded by the hero Theseus, helped by the goddess Athena who gave it the gift of the olive tree (much to the chagrin of Poseidon, who had wanted to be the city's patron). Yet the Athenians did not participate in the early jostling for power among the infant Greek city states, nor join the colonising voyages around the Mediterranean in the 8th century BC.

A period of retraction followed, but by the mid-7th century BC the Athenians had absorbed the rest of Attica, crucially giving them a larger hinterland, a greater number of citizens, and so a wider pool of military recruits than any other state. The aristocratic rule which replaced the old monarchy aggravated social tensions, and in 594BC Solon began a radical revision of the way Athens was ruled. The old council of the Areopagus, meeting on the hill of that name and dominated by the *Eupatridae* (which translates as "sons of good fathers"), was replaced by a new Council of 400, based at the *Bouleuterion* (Council House) to the north. Poorer, free Athenians were given the right for the first time to vote in an assembly that gathered on the Pnyx Hill. For good measure, Solon also banned enslavement for debtors and broke up large, landed estates.

The experiment soon foundered as the aristocrats fought back, and the new rights were temporarily rolled back under Peisistratos, who ruled from 546BC as tyrant – in Greek thought not necessarily a bad ruler, merely a non-royal one. He, and his sons Hippias and Hipparchus, began the transformation of Athens. The old wooden shrines on the Acropolis were replaced by stone temples. To the northwest a new *agora*, or marketplace, was established, a large open square which became the political, judicial and religious hub of the city. Then, in 508–507BC, Kleisthenes overthrew Hippias and injected new life into Athenian politics by enlarging the Council (to 500), making it the decision-making body that decided on the business of the Assembly and establishing a system of election to public office by lots. Democracy, "government by the people", it seemed, was here to stay.

It was the sense of having a stake in the city that made its citizens – who were only 15,000 out of a total ten times that number when women, foreigners and enslaved people were counted – fight so hard and overcome two Persian invasions that swept over Greece in 492 and 480BC. Part of the cost was the forced evacuation of Athens, as the Persian army of Xerxes captured and razed it to the ground. The compensation, after Xerxes was humiliatingly defeated in the naval battle of Salamis, was the remodelling of the city by Pericles and his successors. The Long Walls were built to the Athenian port of Piraeus, allowing it to receive supplies even when under siege. The temples of the Acropolis rose again. Its centrepiece, the Parthenon, in resplendent white marble from Mount Pentelicus to the north of the city, was begun in 447BC. Richly decorated with friezes that told the city's foundation myths, it housed a massive gold and ivory statue of Athena, about 10 metres (33 feet) high, crafted by the master sculptor Phidias.

All this was financed by silver mines at Laurion and the dues paid by members of the Delian League, a crypto-empire presided over with ruthless efficiency by the Athenians. Resentment at their subversion of the freedom the other Greek cities thought they had preserved finally led to the Peloponnesian War against Athens's arch-rival Sparta between 431BC and 404BC. The ultimate Athenian defeat led its democracy to collapse and to brief rule by the "Thirty Tyrants". But even after democracy's restoration, Athens was never the same again, living under the shadow of the growing power of Thebes and then conquered by Macedonia in 338BC.

New buildings were still erected – the Temple of Athena Nike in 425BC, and an auditorium built on the Pnyx in the 330s BC. After that, monuments were bestowed on Athens more in memory of its greatness than as a token of its power, which had long since ebbed away. By 146BC, all of Greece had come under Roman rule, which was destined to last nearly 16 centuries. The emperor Hadrian (reigned AD117–138), an inveterate philhellene, gifted Athens a library and an aqueduct, and pushed through the completion of the Temple of Olympian Zeus begun over 600 years earlier, adding to it the self-aggrandising inscription: "This is the city of Hadrian".

Instead, Athens became known for its philosophers and orators, who thought and talked when it was no longer possible to build, live freely or conquer. Already the homeland of pioneering historians such as Herodotus and Thucydides, and playwrights such as Euripides, Sophocles and Aristophanes (whose *The Clouds* lampoons the great philosopher Socrates), the city now added Plato (c 425–348BC), his pupil Aristotle (384–322BC) and the orator Demosthenes (384–322BC) to its roll of distinguished citizens. A reputation for philosophical excellence continued even after attacks by the Germanic barbarians – notably the Heruls in AD267 – and imperial retrenchment caused its population to dwindle. Then, in 529, Emperor Justinian forbade the teaching of philosophy by pagan teachers, extinguishing the tradition. Even then, and through long years of twilight, when the city suffered attacks by Slavs, domination by a procession of western adventurers (including Venetians and Catalans), Turkish conquest and then the final re-emergence as capital of an independent Greek nation in 1832, the echo of its ephemeral greatness continued to resound. Once a city has achieved the status of a dream, it is hard for reality ever again to intrude.

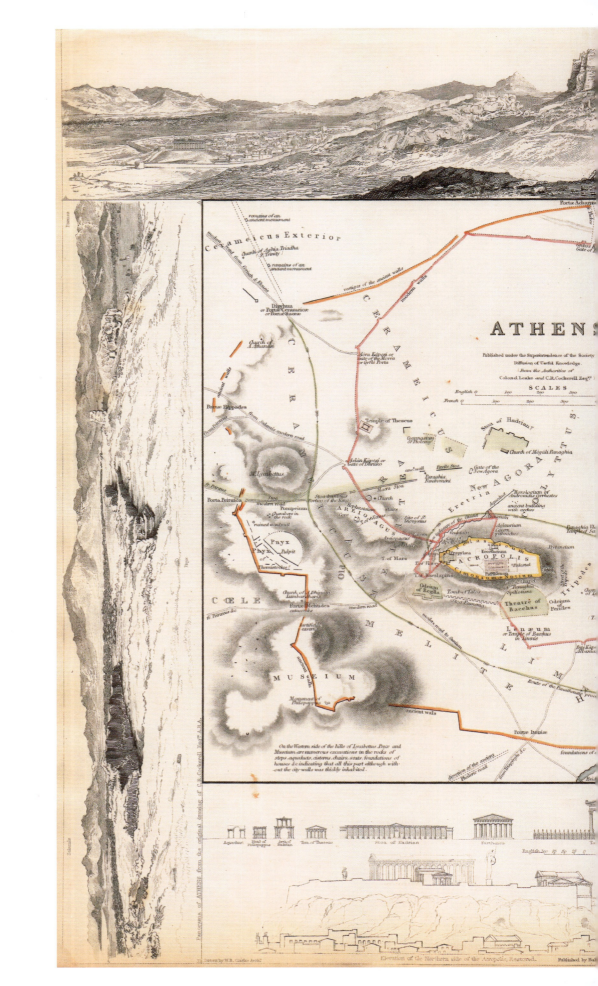

ATHENS

Published under the Superintendence of the Society

Diffusion of Useful Knowledge

(From the Authorities of

Colonel Leake and C.R. Cockerell Esq.)

SCALES

English 0   100   200   300

French 0   100   200   300

Ceramicus Exterior

remains of an
ancient monument

Church of Aghia Triadha
S. Trinity

remains of an
ancient monument

vestiges of the ancient walls

modern walls

Diphum
or Portæ Cerameicæ
or Portæ Sacræ

Church of
A. Athanas

Agra Kâposi or
Gate of the Morea
or Gyftà Porta

C E R A M E I C U S

Portæ Hippades

Temple of Theseus

Stoa of Hadrian?

Gymnasium
of Ptolemy

Church of Megáli Panaghía

L Y C A B E T T U S

Iskli Kâposi or
Gate of Dhrakos

anct wall

Recile Stoa

Gate of the
New Agora

Diraghia
Inidoveuni

Horologium of
Andronicus Cyrrhestes

ancient building
with arches

New AGORA

Portæ Peiraicæ

St. Lycabettus

Stoa

modern road

Stoa basilicus
Portico of the King

Pompeium

Chambers in
the rock

ruined windmill

A R E I O P A G U S

Eretria

Panaghia Vl.
Templnet Set.

Aglaurium
Cavern
of Aglauros

Prytaneum

Pnyx

Pulpit

Pnyx

Themistocles

T of Mars

Propylæa

ACROPOLIS

Pedestal

Parthenon

Cimonium Wall

Erechtheum

Tripoles

Temple of Æsculapius

Odeium
of Regilla

C Œ L E

Church of Dhmitri
Lumbardhari

Portæ Melitides
catacombs

modern road

Tombs of Talos

Stoa Eumena

Panaghia
Spiliotissa

Theatre of
Bacchus

Odeium
of Pericles

M
E
L
I
T
E

artificial
cavern

Lenæum
or Temple of Bacchus
in Limnis

M U S E I U M

ancient walls

Route of the Panathenaic proces

Monument of
Philopappus

ancient walls

Portæ Ropiæ

On the Western side of the hills of Lycabettus Pnyx and
Museum are numerous excavations in the rocks of
steps aqueducts, cisterns chairs, seats, foundations of
houses &c indicating that all this part although without the city-walls was thickly inhabited.

Direction of the ancient
Phaleric road

from Diogenis &c

Drawn by W.B. Clarke Archt.

Elevation of the Northern side of the Acropolis, Restored.

Published by Bald

Aqueduct   Head of
Philopappus   Arch of
Hadrian   Tem of Theseus   Stoa of Hadrian   Parthenon

English 10 20 30 40 50

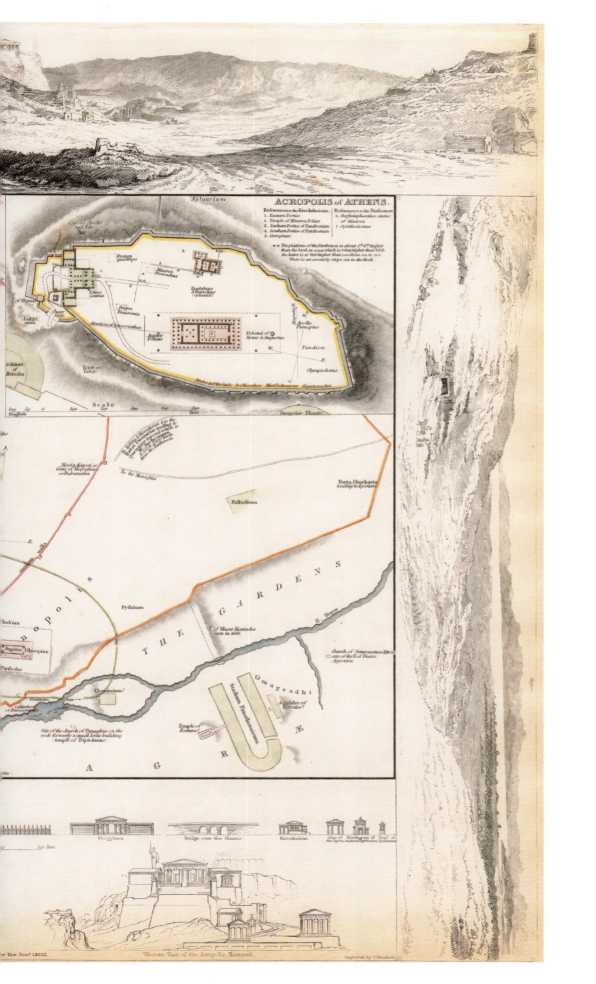

ACROPOLIS of ATHENS.

References to the Erechtheum.
1. Eastern Portico
2. Temple of Minerva Polias
3. Northern Portico of Pandrosium
4. Southern Portico of Pandrosium
5. Caryopium

References to the Parthenon.
6. Chryselephantine statue of Minerva
7. Opisthodomus

The platform of the Parthenon is about 5 ft 6 in higher than the level at a.a.a. which is 9 feet higher than b.b.b. the latter is 20 feet higher than c.c.c. from c.c. to a.a. There is an ascent by steps cut in the Rock

Aglaurium

Cave of Apollo and Pan

Brazen quadriga

Minerva Promachus

Erechtheus & Cecrops (colossal)

Venus Leaena

Diana Brauronia

Jupiter Polias

Pedestal of Rome & Augustus

Apollo Panopius

Pandion

Olympiodorus

Station of Chaeretinthus

T. of Themis

Asclepium

Pluto Gold

Tomb or Talos

Dionysiac Theatre

Statue dedicated to Marathon M[...]

Scale
100 50 0   100   200   300   400   500
English   feet

Mevia Kæpen or Gate of Meleghian or Diomæum

To the Mesoghia

Eastern Mausoleum & c. the heroes proceeded leading to Omophia by which they were let in the Erechtheum

Porta Diocharis leading to Lyceum

Palladium

ACROPOLIS

THE GARDENS

Pythium

Church of Stauromenos Hieros site of the T. of Diana Agrotera

Hadrian

Jupiter Olympius

Paribolus

R. Ilissus

T of Muse Ilissiades seen in 1676

Omagradhi

Eleusinium

Southern Panathenaicum

Sepulchre of Herodes

Temple of Fortune

AGRÆ

Site of the church of Panaghia on the rock formerly a small Ionic building temple of Triptolemus

Fountain

Callirhoe or Enneacrunus

Propylæa

Bridge over the Ilissus

Erechtheum

Planning the Town

Priene, c 350BC

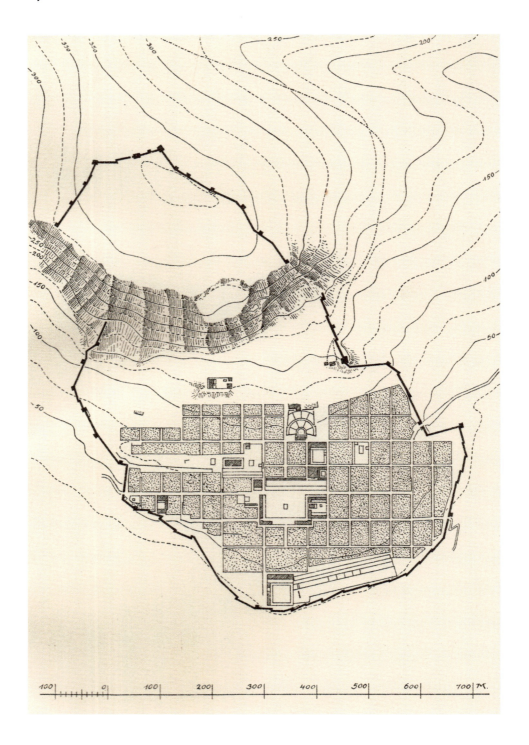

The plan is a monument to town planning, a discipline that was slow to emerge from the crowded welter of temples, palaces, markets and hovels that characterised the earliest cities. The map of Priene, from the Baltic German archaeologist Armin von Gerkan's *Griechische Städteanlagen* ("Greek City Plans", 1924) shows a town artfully laid out in rectangular blocks, a huge challenge against the backdrop of Mount Mycale, on whose lower slopes the city precariously perches.

The orthogonal grid pattern of criss-crossing north–south and east–west roads – characteristic of many cities founded in the burst of colonising zeal that spread Greek settlers across the Mediterranean from the 8th century BC – came to be called "Hippodamian". It was named for Hippodamos of Miletos, born around 500BC, to whom its application at Piraeus, Miletos (both refoundations, the latter after the Persians destroyed it in 494BC) and Rhodes was attributed. Although Aristotle says that Hippodamos devised "the division of cities", this was part of the general philosophical speculation about what constituted the ideal city: Aristotle himself advised health should be privileged so that "a city which fronts the east and receives the winds that blow from thence is esteemed most healthful", while his master Plato was more dogmatic, saying ten miles from the coast, with a good harbour, a modest level of prosperity (so as not to attract too many foreigners) and the precise number of 5,040 households should be the rule.

Hippodamos cannot have planned all the cities ascribed to him – he would have been over 90 by the time Rhodes was founded in 408BC – but he did take part in the establishment of Thurii in southern Italy in 443BC. It was a kind of panhellenic utopia, settled by colonists from all over Greece, which explicitly promoted literacy and had a certain star quality, with the historian Herodotus joining Hippodamos among the first settlers.

The orthogonal grid was not original to Hippodamos; examples are found as early as the workmen's settlement at Tell el-Amarna in Egypt around 1350BC, and the reshaping of Babylon by Nebuchadnezzar around 600BC (see page 14). Possibly under the influence of such eastern models, the Greeks began to use grid patterns in the late 8th century BC for cities such as Megara Hyblaea in Sicily and Smyrna (after its destruction by an earthquake). Such early examples are only partial, but by the 5th century BC the system was fully developed, as at Akragas in Sicily after 479BC, where the philosopher Empedocles said his fellow citizens "eat as if they were to die tomorrow, and build as if they were never to die". Priene, too, was a refoundation, its population moved to the new site in the mid-4th century after its old harbour silted up. It shows the full application of the "Hippodamian grid", with clearly defined areas for public

buildings clustered in the centre, such as the semicircular theatre and the agora, the political and social heart of the city. The six main streets and 15 cross streets divide the city up into about 80 blocks, just over half of which were dedicated for private housing. Laying out the city was a challenge. The steepness of Mycale's 600-metre (650-yard) slopes gave the citizens a stunning view but made their daily life somewhat vertiginous; some of the streets are made up of flights of steps, the only practical way to get around. At Priene's apex was the Temple of Athena Polias ("Athena of the City"), in which Alexander the Great took a particular interest, paying for its construction around 334BC. The work was carried out by Pytheos, also the architect of the Mausoleum of Halicarnassos, one of the Seven Wonders of the Ancient World.

By the 2nd century AD Priene's new harbour had silted up, too, beginning a slide into oblivion that ended with its total abandonment around 1300. By then, though, the grid idea had spread. Alexander the Great used it for his numerous foundations, notably Alexandria in Egypt, and the Romans took it with a will. Although Rome itself grew too big to be tamed and gridded, the new towns which were laid out for military veterans, first in Italy and then in the new conquests, were planned by *agrimensores* (surveyors) on a standard template, with the east–west roads (or *decumani*) being crossed by a series of north–south avenues (or *cardines*). Taurinum (Turin), Mediolanum (Milan) and Ariminum (Rimini) were all laid out in squares around 2,400 by 2,400 Roman feet, each divided into 100 lots (or *centuriae*), and the practice spread as far afield as Thamugadi, deep in the Algerian desert.

The Roman east adapted the basic plan with the addition of colonnaded streets, beginning with that built by Herod the Great at Antioch around 10BC, and still visible today in the stunning ruinscapes of Gerasa (Jerash) in Jordan and Palmyra in Syria. Yet here, at the end of antiquity, the Hippodamian plan met its nemesis, as stalls and houses encroached on the neat order of the city plans, transforming agoras into souks and orderly grids into chaotic mazes. In Europe, too, medieval cities became known less for their grand avenues than for their narrow labyrinthine lanes. Hippodamos, though, would have his vindication. When town planning revived as an art in the 18th century, it was to his vision that they turned. When New York was relaid out in 1811, it was on the grid pattern that is so characteristic of the city today, and the founders of Adelaide (1836, see page 162), Canberra (1913) and Brasília (1960, see page 200) all resorted to the grid. Priene may be deserted now, a destination in modern-day western Turkey for archaeologically minded tourists, but its influence resonates into the 21st century.

Hero City

Alexandria, 331BC & 1910

Alexandria began with a dream. It helped for the future prospects of the city that the dreamer was a world conqueror, the Macedonian military genius Alexander the Great. He was inspired, legend has it, by a vision of the great poet Homer, who, while Alexander was taking a rest from his conquest of Egypt in 331BC, appeared to quote his own *Odyssey*, mentioning Pharos, an "island in the surging sea" where the Greek king Menelaus had been becalmed on his way back from the siege of Troy. Not a man to hesitate, Alexander ordered the place to be located and decreed a new city be built there, on the site of a former Egyptian fishing settlement named Rhakotis. It is a reconstruction of this splendid Hellenistic foundation that is shown in the first map overleaf, published in the 1889 edition of the *Imperial Bible Dictionary* by the Reverend Patrick Fairbairn, a Scottish Free Church minister and renowned biblical scholar. Sandwiched between entries on Alexander of Cyrene (whose father Simon carried Christ's cross on the way to the crucifixion) and Allegory, the Alexandria map shows the first, and most enduring, of Alexander's foundations: he was a prolific establisher of cities, founding as many as twenty in his quest to implant Greek culture in his new empire, with the most far-flung being Alexandria Eschate ("the furthest") in modern Tajikistan, complete with a theatre that could seat up to 6,000 spectators.

Alexandria almost died at birth, as Alexander is said to have sketched out his vision of a royal city, with a natural harbour and causeway linking the mainland to the Pharos island, using grains of barley, the only material available. A flock of seabirds swooped down and gobbled up his plan, but a quick-thinking soothsayer declared that the omen was not bad, as it signified that the new city would feed the whole world.

The design of the city was entrusted to the architect Dinocrates, who laid out an orthodox grid shape bisected by the Canopic Way – a 30-metre- (100-foot-) wide central spine alongside which the main buildings of the city, notably the royal palace, were to lie – and a cross street, with the entrances to the city, the Gate of the Moon and the Gate of the Sun, at the north and south ends respectively. Alexander only stayed a few months longer, departing before any real progress had been made and so never saw

his dream become reality. It was left to Ptolemy I Soter – one of the squabbling Macedonian generals who disputed Alexander's heritage – and his successors to add the Heptastadion, the 1,250-metre- (0.75-mile-) long causeway to the Pharos island, and the two most famous buildings of the city.

The Pharos Lighthouse, which soared to over 135 metres (443 feet) high, had three levels: the first was square (with a military barracks), the second octagonal (with stalls to sell trinkets to the tourists who came to visit in ancient times), and the third the cylindrical section on which sat the burning fire or mirror array (accounts vary) that guided ships into the Great Harbour – which was large enough for 1,200 ships – for over a thousand years.

Built under the first Ptolemy, the lighthouse, accorded the accolade of one of the Seven Wonders of the World, was outdone in prestige by the Mouseion, the institute of scholarship established during the reign of Ptolemy II (284–246BC) in the royal palace compound. Attached to it was a library, which in time grew to house as many as 500,000 scrolls, the largest repository of knowledge in the ancient world. The lure of such a trove attracted – as Ptolemy surely intended – the intellectual superstars of the late Greek world. Its second head was the poet Apollonius of Rhodes (who composed an epic on Jason and the Argonauts), who was succeeded by Eratosthenes of Cyrene, a polymathic genius, among whose accomplishments was the first reasonably accurate estimate of the circumference of the Earth. The Mouseion and Library counted among their other luminaries Euclid, the father of geometry; Hero, who invented a very early form of steam engine; and the astronomer Ptolemy, whose model of the solar system remained iron orthodoxy until overturned by Copernicus a millennium and a half later.

By their time, Alexandria had acquired another prestigious building, the Soma or tomb of its founder, whose body, much as his empire, had become the subject of bickering between his heirs after his death in Babylon in 323BC. Ptolemy I hijacked the royal corpse on its way back to Macedon, and it was eventually interred in a mausoleum right at the heart of the city, complete with life-size statue of Alexander. Unlike other cities founded by heroes –

Mycenae by Perseus, the gorgon slayer; Thebes by Cadmus; Pontevedra in Spain by Teucer, one of the Greek leaders in the siege of Troy; and Rome by Romulus – Alexandria thus acquired the very real body of its indisputably non-mythical founder. It did not look after it well, nor did its other signature buildings survive the test of time. By the Middle Ages nobody was quite sure where the Soma had been – though one tradition has it that the Mosque of Nabi Daniel incorporated Alexander's tomb.

The library was the first to crumble. Already neglected by the 1st century BC, it is said to have been severely damaged when Julius Caesar besieged it in 47BC, and after Egypt was definitively incorporated into the Roman empire in 30BC, its prestige waned. The coming of Christianity – although it provided a bonanza for religious speculation, with thinkers such as Origen (c AD185–c 252) laying the basis of much of the early Church's orthodoxy – did little for the Mouseion's traditional role. An invasion by the armies of the Syrian queen Zenobia of Palmyra in 270 dealt it a further blow, and, though a satellite library staggered on in the Serapeum, a temple of a hybrid Egyptian-Greek cult, it ceased to operate in 391 after Emperor Theodosius I ordered a clampdown on residual pagan institutions.

The Pharos fared slightly better, although trade stagnated as the Roman Empire contracted and the Arab conquest of Alexandria in 640 cut it off from its traditional markets. The city's architecture was reshaped as mosques replaced churches, but its trade inexorably declined. A revival in the 13th century as Venetian and Genoese traders penetrated the eastern Mediterranean was but a temporary reprieve, as the pioneering by Portuguese navigators of a separate sea route to India via the Cape of Good Hope shut off even this conduit. The renowned traveller Ibn Battuta found the lighthouse partially ruined in 1326, following a series of earthquakes, and in 1477 the Mamluk sultan Qait Bey ordered its stones to be used to construct a fort, which still sits on the promontory once occupied by the Pharos.

By the late 18th century, Alexandria had shrunk almost to the state of the fishing village from which Alexander had developed it: the population, which had reached over 500,000 under the Ptolemies, was now scarcely 10,000. Restoration came from an unlikely source: the invasion in 1798 by Napoleon, who fancied himself following in Alexander's footsteps. The brief French, and then British, occupation allowed Muhammad Ali, notionally the viceroy of the ruling Ottomans, to throw off Turkish rule and establish the first independent Egyptian state for over 1,800 years. The building of the Al-Mahmudiyyah Canal in 1818–20 gave the city an outlet to the Nile, and then the opening of the Suez Canal in 1869, although nearly bankrupting the country, provided a new route for the cotton that had become an important cash crop from the 1820s.

A new occupation – this time by the British, who bombarded Alexandria in 1882 following protests against increasing European domination of the Egyptian government – led to a renewed influx of outsiders. Alexandria's avenues once again resounded to the sound of the Greek language; the renowned poet Constantine Cavafy was born and worked there, and the city acquired a slew of neo-classical and art nouveau buildings. It became a fashionable haunt of European writers, such as EM Forster, who served with the British Red Cross there and wrote a guidebook to the city, and Lawrence Durrell, who celebrated the city in his *Alexandria Quartet*, and called it the "capital of Memory".

The 1952 revolution that ultimately brought Gamal Abdel Nasser to power saw a pivot back towards Egypt's Arab and Muslim heritage and a thinning of the cosmopolitanism that had characterised it since Ptolemaic times, when around a third of the population was Jewish, concentrated in the Delta quarter (its five districts were, less than imaginatively, named for the first letters of the Greek alphabet). Yet Alexandria still remains one of the great cities of the Mediterranean, the largest along its coastline, and, with nearly 6 million inhabitants, the fourth biggest city in the Arab world. Although little now survives from its original foundation – a few blocks have been found since the 1990s in the harbour, submerged by earthquakes and a devastating tsunami that struck in AD365 – the topography that attracted Alexander is still there.

The 1910 Spanish map of Alexandria on page 27 shows a city that, two millennia on, has broken the bounds of its classical predecessor, but with the site of the Pharos, and the great sweep of the harbour, still visible. Alexander's dream is still alive.

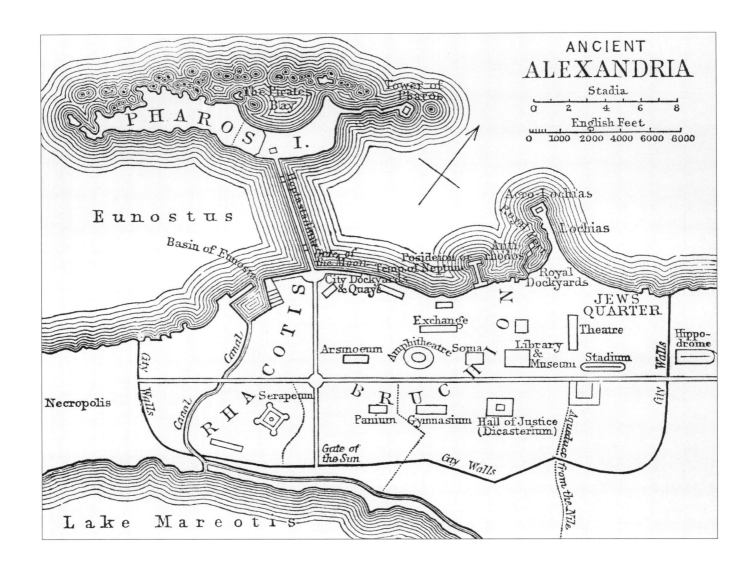

ANCIENT
ALEXANDRIA

Stadia

0 2 4 6 8

English Feet

0 1000 2000 4000 6000 8000

PHAROS I.

The Pirate Bay

Tower of Pharos

Eunostus

Basin of Eunostus

Heptastadium

Gate of the Moon

Acro Lochias

Lochias

Royal Port

Anti rhodos

Posideium or Temp. of Neptune

Royal Dockyards

City Dockyards & Quays

JEWS QUARTER

Canal

RHACOTIS

Exchange

Arsinoeum

Amphitheatre

Soma

BRUCHION

Library & Museum

Theatre

Stadium

City Walls

Hippo-drome

Necropolis

Canal

Serapeum

Panium

Gymnasium

Hall of Justice (Dicasterium)

Gate of the Sun

City Walls

Aqueduct from the Nile

City Walls

Lake Mareotis

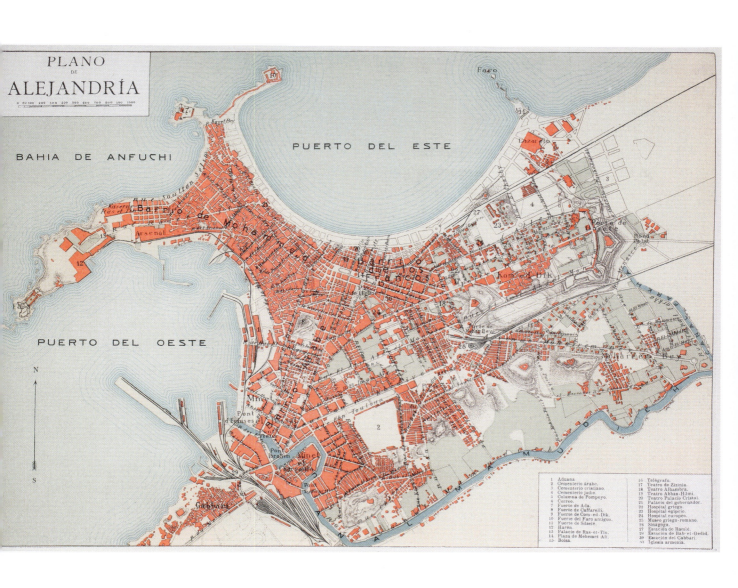

PLANO
DE
ALEJANDRÍA

BAHIA DE ANFUCHI

PUERTO DEL ESTE

Faro

Lazareto

Barrio de Mohamed

Barrios
de los
Francos

Ramleh

Kom-el-Dik

PUERTO DEL OESTE

N

S

Minet-el-Bassal

Pont d'Ecluses

Pont Ibrahim

Minet-el-Chincristia

Gabbari

Arsenal

Ras el Tin

Ras-et-Tin

Toulon

Mahmud-Bey

MAHMUDIEH CANAL

1	Aduana.	16 Telégrafo.
2	Cementerio árabe.	17 Teatro de Zizinia.
3	Cementerio cristiano.	18 Teatro Alhambra.
4	Cementerio judío.	19 Teatro Abbas-Hilmi.
5	Columna de Pompeyo.	20 Teatro Palacio Cristal.
6	Correo.	21 Palacio del gobernador.
7	Fuerte de Ada.	22 Hospital griego.
8	Fuerte de Caffarelli.	23 Hospital egipcio.
9	Fuerte de Com-ed-Dik.	24 Hospital europeo.
10	Fuerte del Faro antiguo.	25 Museo griego-romano.
11	Fuerte de Silseie.	26 Sinagoga.
12	Harén.	27 Estación de Ramle.
13	Palacio de Ras-et-Tin.	28 Estación de Bab-el-Gedid.
14	Plaza de Mehemet Alí.	29 Estación del Gabbari.
15	Bolsa.	30 Iglesia armenia.

The Eternal City

Rome, AD203

For its inhabitants, Rome was the eternal city. Its not-quite-eternal career in reality spanned the 1,229 years from its traditional founding date in 753BC, through seven kings, over a thousand consuls and around 90 emperors (plus dozens of usurpers) until the deposition of Romulus Augustulus, a youth who was the last Western Roman emperor, in AD476.

For all the vagueness of its foundation (it probably really sprang up from the amalgamation around 800BC of several settlements on what would become the seven hills of the later city) and the ignominy of its fall (by then the largely powerless emperors had abandoned it for the safety of marsh-girt Ravenna), Rome was magnificent. It was the first city in history to exceed a million inhabitants, who jostled, thronged, fought and shouted in its chaotic streets; the satirical poet Juvenal acidly commented that in Rome it required money to sleep.

Rome was also the first town to have a proper city map, the *Forma Romae Urbis*, an 18-by-13-metre- (60-by-45-foot-) colossus on 150 marble slabs which covered a wall of the city's Temple of Peace. The section shown here includes the Septizodium, a monumental façade to the palace of the emperor Septimius Severus, which it is known was erected in 203 or later, and which helps date the map to between then and the end of Septimius's reign in 211. Highly detailed, including even internal features of buildings (though not, curiously, the River Tiber), it was probably more a statement of imperial power than a practical route finder, since someone standing on the floor level of the Temple could not possibly have made out any details of the sections near the ceiling.

Almost nothing remains of the very earliest phases of the city, though a grotto found deep beneath the Palatine Hill in 2007 could be the Lupercal, the shrine commemorating the city's foundation by Romulus (in an act of fratricide that was to be repeated with monotonous regularity as Roman emperors murdered their relatives; Septimius's son Caracalla murdering his brother Geta less than a year after their father's death). The earliest structures in the Forum, the economic, religious and social heart of the city, were later extensively remodelled but included the most venerable: the Temple of Capitoline Jupiter, as well as the old Senate House, from which the aristocratic senate ruled the city by decree after the fall of the monarchy in 509BC. In the Forum, too, were set the Twelve Tables, the

first codified Roman law, created in 449BC; the originals were destroyed when the Gauls took the city in 387BC, though fragments remain of its somewhat harsh edicts (the singing of satirical songs deemed offensive to another was punishable by death). It was also the site of another antique monument, the Lapis Niger, a black volcanic stone protected by taboos, whose original purpose even the Romans had forgotten, but which may have been a symbolic gateway to the underworld.

By the time Rome's population reached a million around 133BC, its size had caused almost insoluble social tensions between the patrician upper classes and the plebeian masses, resulting in the clubbing to death of their great champion Tiberius Gracchus, with 300 of his supporters, and a gradual slide into civil war. The streets of Rome became a battleground between the champions of the various factions, only finally resolved when Julius Caesar defeated all his rivals and took on the title of dictator, before then being murdered on the steps of the Senate House in 44BC.

Caesar had given the city a new Forum, and an adopted son, Octavian, who, after a further round in the civil war, became the first emperor, Augustus, in 27BC. The monumentalisation of the city accelerated under the early empire: Augustus boasted that he had found a city of brick and left one of marble; his many restorations included the Temple of Saturn, the Treasury, the Temple of Concord, as well as the building of the *Ara Pacis* (Altar of Peace) and a grand mausoleum to contain his remains. His successors' family lives were as sanguinary as the civil war had been. Caligula (reigned AD37–41), narcissistic and unstable, was murdered by the Praetorian Guard, while Nero (reigned 54–68) murdered his mother and wife, and then caused the death of his mistress-turned-second wife Poppaea Sabina by kicking her in the stomach while pregnant. When a fire broke out in central Rome, Nero took advantage of the devastation to build himself a grand new palace, the Domus Aurea, on the ruins, complete with a colossal golden statue of himself.

The palace itself eventually succumbed to fire; the *insulae*, the slum-like multistorey wooden dwellings in which the city's poor lived were notoriously combustible. But the statue gave its name to one of Rome's iconic monuments, the Colosseum, completed in AD80 under Titus (reigned 79–81), as an amphitheatre in which to hold spectacular

beast hunts and gladiatorial combats. The 60,000 spectators enjoyed 100 days of inaugural games and from then, until the early 5th century, the politically ambitious in Rome were forced to pay the massive cost of such spectacles in order to gain favour. It was one part of the imperial strategy of "bread and circuses" to keep the masses loyal; the Circus Maximus, the city's horse-racing stadium, first built in 329BC and accommodating up to 150,000 spectators, is on the left portion of the *Forma Romae Urbis* fragment. The other part was the *annona*, the imperial dole instituted under Julius Caesar, which gave 33 kilograms of free grain to 150,000 male inhabitants of the city (and by the reign of Septimius was replaced with bread).

To generate such huge quantities of grain, and of the olive oil and wine the populace of Rome consumed, required constant imports from other portions of the empire, so great that the shattered remains of amphorae created the Monte Testaccio, an artificial mound a kilometre in circumference made entirely of pottery sherds.

Under later emperors, the frenetic pace of building slowed. Trajan (reigned 98–117) constructed the *Mercatus Traiani* (Markets of Trajan) and a 38-metre- (125-foot-) high column adorned with a cartoon-like spiral of frieze commemorating his victories over the Dacians. After a pause in the mid-3rd century – when the empire almost fell apart as military pretenders arose on the frontier, rarely lasting more than a year or two, and not infrequently never making it to Rome at all – Diocletian (reigned 284–305), who ended the chaos, gave the city its largest bathing establishment, the Baths of Diocletian, in which hundreds of clients could luxuriate in alternating hot and cold pools, dreaming of the height of empire.

By then the emperor Aurelian (reigned 270–275) had given Rome a new wall, much of whose 19-kilometre (12-mile) circuit can still be seen, to replace the antiquated 6th-century BC defences traditionally attributed to Servius Tullius, the sixth king (a fragment of which survives in the unlikely setting of a McDonald's restaurant in the city's Termini railway station). It would need them, as the empire and Italy came under increasing pressure from Germanic tribes breaching the frontier. In 410 the city was sacked by Alaric's Goths, and then in 455 more violently by Genseric's Vandals. By then Rome's pretensions to be an imperial city were purely theoretical; though the shadow cast by the idea of empire would be a long one (with Constantinople and Moscow having pretensions to be its heir, and the imperial ambitions of Paris and London being modelled on it). Imperial no more, eternal it remained.

A Tale of Two Plans

Baghdad, 762

The Round City of Baghdad, shown in this artistic recreation by Edmund Sandars, was one of the wonders of the medieval Islamic world. Appearing in Sir Tatton Benvenuto Mark Sykes's *The Caliphs' Last Heritage* (1915), an account of the British diplomat's travels in the region while posted to the Ottoman court at İstanbul, it shows a city that time, and several brutal sackings, had erased centuries before.

Baghdad arose from the Abbasid caliphs' need for a new capital to replace Damascus, the chief city of the Umayyads whom they overthrew in 750. Its location, suggested to the caliph al-Mansur by a group of Nestorian Christian monks, allowed easy access to Iran, Syria and Egypt, the principal provinces of the Islamic Empire over which the Abbasids now held sway. But the city became far more than that, its round shape symbolising its place at the very centre of the empire. Al-Mansur was deeply involved in its planning; he is said to have soaked cotton balls in naphtha, which were then set alight to produce a plan of the city literally burnt into the ground.

Building began on the fertile west bank of the Tigris in 762, and it is said the workforce – of architects, carpenters, masons and labourers – exceeded 100,000 people. The caliph cannibalised ruins from around the empire, taking five iron gates from the city of Wasit in southeastern Iraq. Four of them went to adorn the double walls of his new foundation: Kufa Gate to the southwest; Basra Gate to the southeast; Khurasan Gate to the northeast; and the Syria Gate to the northwest. From each of these a wide avenue led to another circular wall in which the fifth gate was set. Inside lay the sumptuous Palace of the Green Dome, topped by a gigantic 35-metre (115-foot) dome.

The palace is visible at the centre of Sandars' plan, and next to it the Great Mosque which was to be the religious heart of the city. Besides this are a scattering of other mosques and palaces to serve other members of the caliphal family, plus houses for their servants and government offices. The city was inaugurated officially at 2pm on July 30, 762, a time and date revealed as auspicious after careful scrutiny of horoscopes, but al-Mansur only took up residence four years later. The Round City soon acquired suburbs, as merchants, scholars, soldiers and the merely ambitious flocked to it, swelling its population to a million, the largest in the Islamic World. Yet the caliph himself soon tired of the Round City and, in 775, he decamped to the al-Khuld ("eternity") palace he had built just outside the Khurasan gate. This became the nucleus of the Rusafa district, an entirely new caliphal complex in competition with the Round City. The city reached further heights of splendour under the Caliph Haroun al-Rashid (reigned 786–809), whose patronage of scholars brought additional prestige to a city already overflowing with wealth. Despite a bloody civil war that devastated the city after his death, Baghdad recovered its stride under al-Ma'mun (reigned 813–33). The new caliph established the Bayt al-Hikma, or House of Wisdom, as a centre for the translation of Latin, Greek and Persian manuscripts into Arabic, making works by Euclid, Aristotle, Plato and Galen available to scholars and sparking a golden age in Islamic science.

Baghdad stuttered again in 836, when al-Mutasim moved the capital north to Samarra, and by the time the caliphs returned in 892 the population had fallen by half. Although the Abbasid Caliphate staggered on for over three-and-a-half centuries, an ever-shrinking empire was mirrored by a slow decline in the city (although the building in 1233 of the Mustansiriya, sometimes claimed to be the world's oldest university, continued its tradition of scholarly excellence). Then, in 1258 disaster struck, as the Mongol armies of Hulagu Khan pulverised the city's crumbling walls with state-of-the-art siege engines and then brutally sacked it. Among the 200,000 dead were the caliph al-Musta'sim, trampled to death wrapped in a carpet to avoid shedding his blood. Any chance of recovery was snuffed out by a further sacking in 1401 by Tamerlane, another Mongol warlord, and for the next 500 years Baghdad was a provincial city of little political importance.

That was until Mark Sykes devised a plan, a diplomatic piece of double-dealing concocted with the French diplomat François Georges Picot to carve up the Arabic-speaking provinces of the Ottoman Empire following the First World War into spheres of influence dominated by France and Britain. The Sykes-Picot plan, drafted in secret in 1916, provoked outrage when its contents became known and, although never fully implemented, it resulted in the

birth of the separate countries of Iraq (under the sway of Britain) and Syria (under that of France). Much that has transpired in the region since then has flowed from the plan and the scars it left. The Hashemite monarchy of Iraq fell in 1958 to be replaced by a republic, then ten years later by the Ba'athist regime, headed from 1979 by Saddam Hussein, whose overthrow in 2003 during the US-led coalition invasion of Iraq unleashed a complex web of insurgency and civil war that left Baghdad once again devastated. The Round City documented in Sykes's book was long gone, but the impact of his other plan continues to reverberate around the region.

City of the Silk Road

Chang'an, c 800

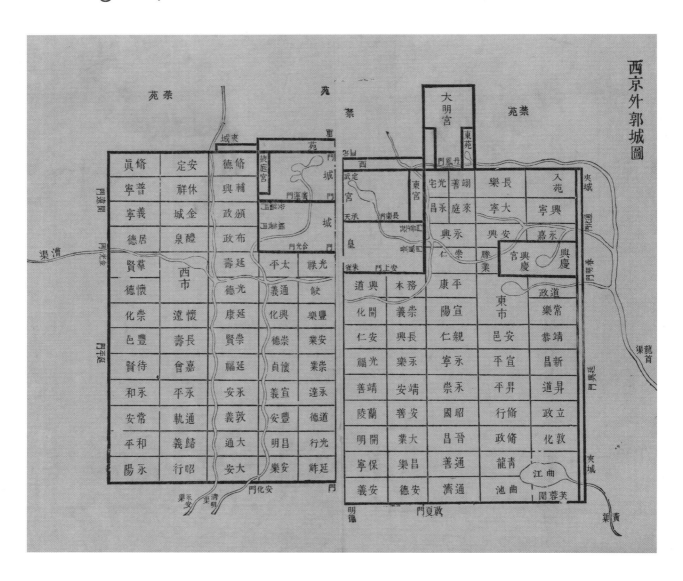

Silk was the oil of the ancient world, bringing enormous wealth to the one country, China, that was (until the 6th century AD) able to produce it. Transporting it westwards and southwards was the Silk Road, a series of routes that acted as an international trading superhighway, carrying goods, people and ideas in either direction for well over a millennium. And at its head stood Chang'an, a city whose population reached over a million during its zenith in the 8th century, and which acted as capital to ten imperial dynasties.

The map shows the city at this peak during the Tang (AD618–907), its square shape topped by the imperial palace in the auspicious position to the north. Drafted by the scholar Xu Song (1781–1848) for his *Tang liang jing chengfang kao* ("Study of the walled cities and wards of the two Tang capitals"), it was part of a concerted effort during the Qing period to recover elements of China's past at a time of increasing pressure from western European powers.

Chang'an itself long preceded the Silk Road, beginning as a Neolithic village of the Yangshao culture about 4000BC and eventually becoming the capital of the Zhou dynasty around 1050BC. But it was the massive expansion of China's borders under the Han dynasty that both created the Silk Road and made Chang'an's fortune. Already enlarged by Qin Shi Huangdi, the first emperor, from 221BC, it was enriched even further under Han Emperor Gaozu (reigned 202–195BC), who imported 145,000 labourers to build his lavish Changle Palace. Subsequent Han rulers embellished it further, with Wudi (reigned 141–87BC) creating a huge boating lake for pageants and a menagerie that boasted a rhinoceros. But it was the extension of China's borders into Central Asia in the late 2nd century BC, absorbing desert oases such as Dunhuang, that made it possible for traders to travel from Chang'an all the way to the Mediterranean in relative peace.

Down this corridor the silk flowed, and in the opposite direction came people, so that Chang'an found itself with an eclectic mix of Muslim traders, Nestorian Christians, and above all Buddhist scholars, as the religion percolated northwards from its Indian homeland. Most importantly, though, silver went eastwards, causing the Roman naturalist Pliny the Elder to complain in the late 70s AD that the trade was costing the Roman Empire 100 million sesterces a year and risked bankrupting it.

The three centuries that followed the fall of the Han in AD220 were dark times for Chang'an, as successive waves of invaders from the north sacked the city. A revival came under the Sui, who restored China's unity, and in 582 refounded Chang'an (which they called Daxing). Their successors, the Tang, brought Chang'an to greater heights, as the 108 wards into which the city's grid divided it became filled with houses and two huge markets, including the Eastern, where all of the exotica of the Silk Road could be found, including spices, rare hardwoods and gemstones. A vast new palace, the Palace of Long-Lived Benevolence was built on the northern edge of the city. Guarded by 12-metre- (39-foot-) high walls, the complex included vast audience halls and the offices of the imperial bureaucracy.

Merchants thronged the crowded streets – as many as 10,000 foreigners may have been resident – and the city was a religious hotchpotch, with a Zoroastrian temple erected in the 620s and several churches for the Nestorians, a heretical variant of Christianity. There were a dozen Daoist shrines and scores of Buddhist shrines, notably the Big Wild Goose Pagoda, a soaring 64-metre- (210-foot) high edifice constructed in 652 to contain the collection of precious Buddhist texts brought back from India by the pilgrim-monk Xuanzang.

Prosperity, though, had its price. The Tang government became corrupt, dominated by a clique of eunuchs. The city was sacked in 756 by the rebel general An Lushan, and then again during a rebellion in 880. The Tang, long moribund, finally fell in 907, and Taizu, the first emperor of the Liang, who succeeded them, had Chang'an literally dismantled, employing 20,000 carpenters to take down its monuments and rebuild versions of them in his new capital at Luoyang.

Chang'an's ruins mouldered, the riches of the Silk Road were diverted elsewhere, and only the weeds prospered until the Ming dynasty partially rebuilt it in the late 14th century as a minor provincial centre, complete with a new circuit of city walls and a Bell and Drum Tower which dominated the little city and from which the curfew was sounded each night.

The Silk Road seized up after the Mongol Empire's fragmentation into competing khanates in the late 13th century left Central Asia's trade routes prey once more to raiders, and then the growth of the Ottoman Empire from the 14th century sealed off its western reaches. For Chang'an (renamed Xi'an during the Ming dynasty), revival came with the discovery of the tomb of Qin Shi Huangdi in 1974, with its extraordinary trove of over 7,000 terracotta warriors that is one of China's leading tourist attractions. And for the Silk Road, a new era began in 2013, when the Chinese government announced its Belt and Road Initiative, a huge project to create a new trading superhighway linking 150 countries with Chinese-built infrastructure. Once more, a Silk Road buzzes with traders, and Chang'an, crowded with foreigners, prospers.

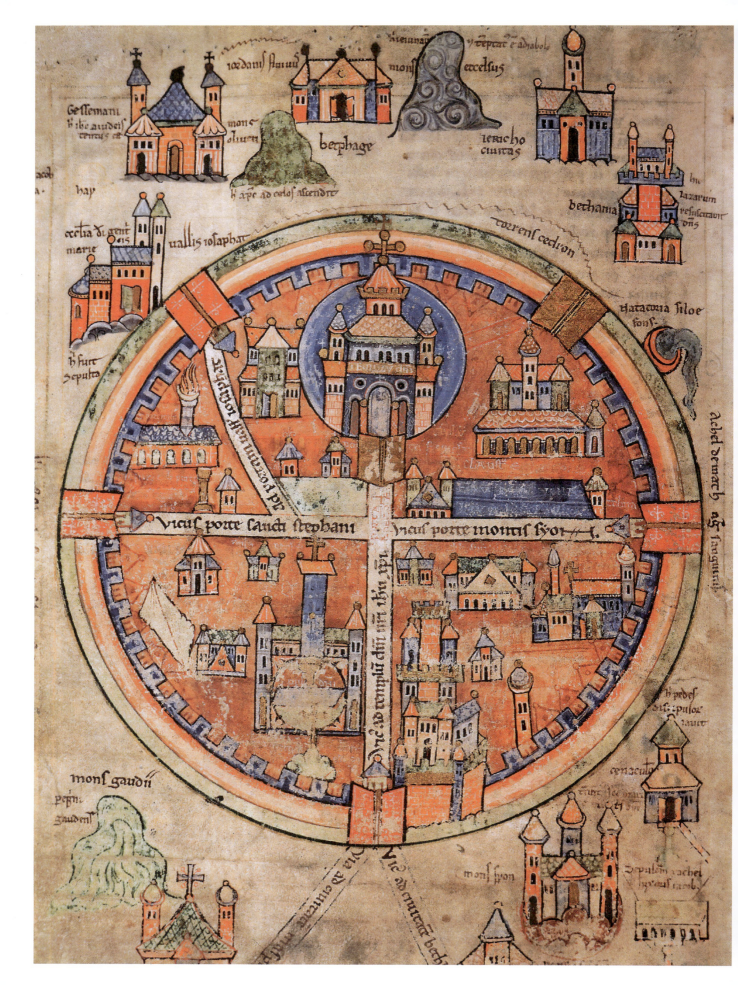

Holy City

Jerusalem, c 1100

There are many cities regarded as holy to the adherents of particular faiths, among them Amritsar to Sikhs, Ayodhya to Hindus, Bodh Gaya to Buddhists, and Rome to Roman Catholics. Jerusalem, though, is unique, since it is considered holy by the faithful of three religions. Its contested status – it is Judaism's most sacred site, for Christians the backdrop for significant events of the New Testament, and Islam's third most holy city – has historically brought it more woe than blessing, and more often armies of conquest than peaceful pilgrims.

The map, which was included in a bound manuscript of the *Historia hierosolymitana* ("History of Jerusalem"), generally attributed to Robert the Monk (c 1055–1122), Abbot of Saint-Rémi near Reims, shows the city during a period of Christian dominance, shortly after its capture by Crusaders in 1099. Its focus is firmly on locations of importance in Christ's life: the large structure at the top, "The Temple of the Lord", is the site of the former Jewish Temple. The large building in the southwest is the Church of the Holy Sepulchre, believed to contain the burial place of Christ, while among the other places shown are the Tomb of Mary, the Mount of Olives and "Solomon's Temple" (now the site of the Al-Aqsa Mosque).

By the main city gate to the east lies the Gihon spring, which attracted Jerusalem's first inhabitants to build a hilltop settlement on a site of otherwise little strategic importance around 3000BC. By 1000BC, its Canaanite inhabitants displaced by the Israelite king David, Jerusalem began its long career as the prime focus of Jewish religious culture. The Temple built around 50 years later by David's successor Solomon became Judaism's most holy site, and its destruction by the Babylonian king Nebuchadnezzar in 587 or 586BC and the exile of its population to Babylon was a disaster seared into Jewish consciousness for millennia.

Although the Jews were allowed to return by Cyrus of Persia in 539BC, the Persian occupation was followed by the conquest by Alexander the Great in 331BC. One of his Seleucid successors, Antiochus IV Epiphanes, outlawed Jewish religious practices in 164BC, leading to a revolt by the Jewish leader Judas Maccabeus and a century-long restoration of independence. Intermittent Roman rule from 63BC was followed by a more definitive occupation from 4BC and, following a Jewish revolt in AD66, the destruction of Herod the Great's rebuilt Temple. These trials, and their complete exclusion from the city by Emperor Hadrian in 135, only served to solidify the central position of Jerusalem in Jewish eyes. Yet by the 4th century another vision of the Holy City arose to compete with the Jewish one, as Christianity became the official religion of the Roman Empire, and large Christian basilicas were erected in Jerusalem, such as the Church of the Holy Sepulchre, consecrated in 335.

This, in turn was overlaid by an Islamic conception of the city after the Muslim armies of the Caliph Umar captured it in 638. As the place from where the Prophet Muhammad was believed to have ascended to heaven, the city was provided with a complement of mosques (notably the Dome of the Rock, built on the Temple Mount in 691–92) and madrasas during the nearly thirteen centuries of Muslim rule. This was not uninterrupted: the Christian army of the First Crusade stormed the city in July 1099, unleashing a further round of physical bloodletting as they slaughtered thousands of Muslims and local Christians. Once again mosques were converted to churches, and madrasas to pilgrim hostels, until the wheel of faith turned again, when Saladin reclaimed the city for Islam in 1187.

Despite brief periods of Crusader reoccupation in the early 13th century, Jerusalem was to remain under Muslim rule until the 19th, gradually bursting out of the claustrophobic confines of the Old City as its population increased and Jewish migrants founded new settlements on the urban fringes. Steadily, the Jewish population grew, from around 3,000 in the 1830s, to nearly ten times that number by the end of the century. The British, who secured a League of Nations Mandate over Palestine in 1919 after the collapse of the Ottoman Empire, struggled to balance the interest of Jerusalem's Muslim inhabitants and its growing Jewish population, and in 1948 walked away, leaving the newly proclaimed Jewish State of Israel to fight a series of wars with its Arab Muslim neighbours, in large part over who had a right to all or part of the city.

The violence and tension have continued ever since, whether over rights of access to holy sites or the simple right to live in the Old City. Nine hundred years after Robert the Monk's work, there continue to be bitterly contested visions of the city's status. His map acts as a warning that the translation of a symbol into physical reality may only be achieved at a terrible human cost.

Eternal Capital

Constantinople, 1422

Constantinople, today's İstanbul, is a city whose importance few have denied throughout its long history. Taking its name from the Roman emperor Constantine who founded it in AD330 on the site of the pre-existing Greek settlement of Byzantium, its modest nicknames have included the Latin *Nova Roma* (New Rome), the Greek *Basileuousa* (Queen of Cities) and the Old Norse *Miklgard* (Great Fort). Capital of an empire for 1,593 years – a record for any city – it hosted 92 Roman emperors and 30 Ottoman Turkish sultans before the transfer of the seat of the new Turkish Republic to Ankara in 1923 ended its reign.

The map, by the Florentine Franciscan monk and geographer Cristoforo Buondelmonte – who travelled extensively in the region in the 1420s – is a copy of an original dating from around that time and is the last detailed portrayal of Constantinople before its conquest by the Ottoman sultan Mehmed II in 1453. It shows a city both blessed and cursed by its topography, lying astride the trade routes from Asia Minor into Europe and from the Mediterranean through to the Black Sea. The projecting triangle of the city's main quarters dominates the waterways of the Bosporus to the south and east, and the Golden Horn to the north, girdled by the imposing triple line of the Theodosian Walls – whose 12-metre-high and 6-metre-thick inner wall had helped protect it from all overland attacks since the 5th century – and the rather lower and more vulnerable sea walls.

Yet by Buondelmonte's time, the city was a head without a body. Having had over half a million inhabitants in the mid-6th century (making it one of the world's largest cities at the time), by the 1450s its population had dwindled to just 25,000, rattling around in a landscape of ancient ruins and ornate medieval churches. These are said to have housed an impressive collection of relics and sacred paraphernalia, including the axe with which Noah built the ark, a basket of leftovers from the Feeding of the Five Thousand, and the body parts of no fewer than 476 saints.

The most splendid church of all was Hagia Sophia, built in the 530s by Anthemius of Tralles and Isidore of Miletos after its predecessor burnt down, and long the headquarters of the Orthodox Patriarchs, who vied with Rome's Popes for spiritual supremacy in the Christian world. Its dome prominent on the map, it sits beside the Hippodrome racetrack, where charioteers could win fame and fabulous fortunes while the partisans of the Green and Blue teams cheered and brawled. Once, in AD532, the two united

in a spasm of collective anger after Emperor Justinian condemned several of their leaders to death. In the ensuing riots, they nearly forced him from the throne, only to be subdued in a massacre that cost 30,000 lives.

Such moments of extreme political instability were rare, though emperors such as Michael III, a drunkard who rode chariots in the Hippodrome in the 850s, hardly helped. More dangerous were those ever-present scourges of the medieval city: plague and fire. The pestilence first struck in Justinian's reign, wiping out almost half the city's population, and afterwards with monotonous regularity, killing 55,000 people in just four weeks in 1492, and recurring as recently as 1812. Fires were distressingly frequent – in one, in 1693, much of the city centre was burnt, only for a fresh conflagration to wipe out most of the rest just days later.

It was outsiders, though, who posed the greatest peril. The city was besieged at least 13 times by Avars, Persians, Arabs, Bulgars, Pechenegs, and Seljuk and Ottoman Turks. Its walls failed it only once before the Ottoman conquest, when the Christian arm of the Fourth Crusade, notional allies, took advantage of a succession dispute and stormed the city in 1204. They neglected to install their supposed Byzantine candidate for the throne, and instead looted the city and carved up the empire between them.

Even though a Greek emperor was restored in 1261, the Byzantine city never recovered its stride. Already too dependent on "Latins" – Venetian, Pisan and Genoese traders, the latter establishing their own virtually independent colony in Pera across the Golden Horn (its tower unmistakable on the map and still standing today) – its territory gradually shrank in the face of Turkish advances, to a rump beyond the wall and a few outlying fragments. Sultan Mehmed II put an end to its agony in May 1453, with the aid of a Hungarian gunsmith named Orban, whose cannon – having been rejected by the Byzantines on grounds of cost – played a key role in shredding the walls and putting an end to a defiant yet hopeless resistance.

The city's fall, paradoxically, led to a new rise. Mehmed made it his capital – now popularly, if not officially, called İstanbul – and built a new citadel, the Yedikule, just outside the Theodosian Walls, as well as mosques, religious schools, hammams and the sumptuous Topkapı palace. Helped by the forced transfer of 5,000 households, the city's population

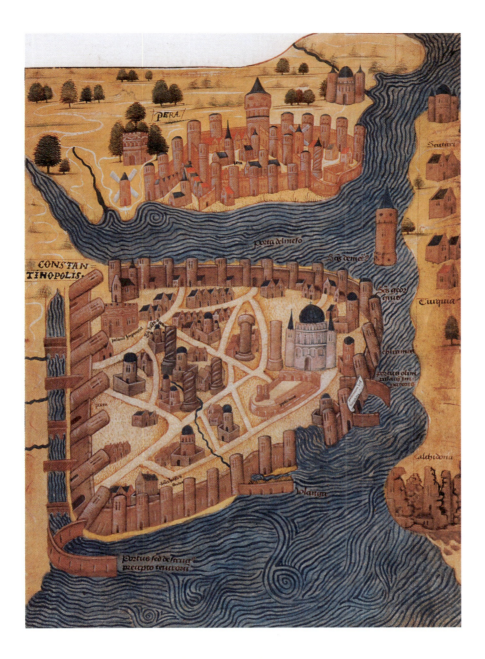

surged, doubling by 1480, when a census revealed around a quarter were still Greek Christians (though a strictly enforced dress code meant they had to wear black slippers, while Armenian Christians wore violet, and only Muslims could wear yellow). Under Suleiman the Magnificent (1520–66), the master builder Sinan adorned İstanbul with mosques of staggering elegance, making it once more worthy of the title Queen of Cities. Thereafter the capital's energy ebbed, and the sultans neglected it; in 1703 the populace rioted to force the ruler's return from Edirne.

The 19th century brought new efforts at reform, with the railway – eventually forming the eastern terminus of the famed Orient Express – reaching the city in the 1870s, and electric lighting being introduced in 1914. But by then the old Ottoman system was brittle in the face of the challenges of modernity, and a combination of Arab nationalism, Greek revanchism and an unwise dalliance with Germany in the First World War brought it down. And while Kemal Atatürk saved the core of the empire as the modern Republic of Turkey, it was Ankara he chose as his capital in 1923, not İstanbul. Although no longer the seat of government, the city has had a posthumous revenge of sorts: one of the key political centres of gravity of Turkey, it is also its premier tourist attraction and, with 16 million inhabitants, is by far Europe's largest city.

Between the Classics and Christianity

Rome, 1474

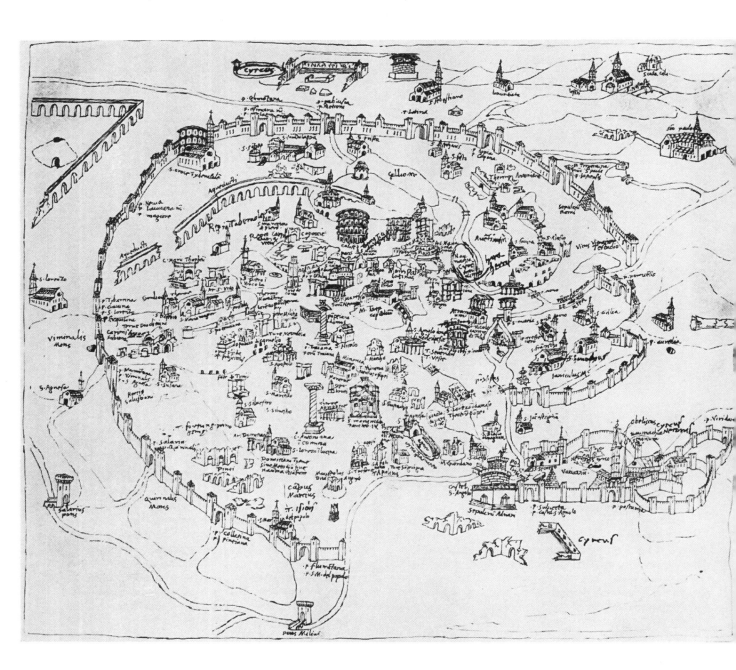

The 1474 map, by the Venetian cartographer Alessandro Strozzi, shows a city reborn. The power of Rome's image was so strong through the ages that it spawned imitators, notably Constantinople, the "Second Rome" inaugurated by Emperor Constantine in AD330. Yet, for all its former power as an imperial city, Rome had experienced several near-deaths before its revival during the Renaissance – which literally means "rebirth" – catapulted it once more into the ranks of Europe's great cities.

The map displays the interest in Roman antiquities so typical of Renaissance scholars: it may even draw from the *Descriptio Urbis Romae* (1433) by the architect and humanist Leon Battista Alberti, which catalogued all that was left of the city's ancient splendours. Strozzi shows Trajan's Column and the Colosseum amid a wealth of other remains including the Temples of Peace and of Concord, and the Baths of Diocletian. Yet he also includes traces of a previous transformation of Rome, from pagan city to Christian, showing dozens of churches, including Sant'Apollonius, San Giovanni in Laterano, and, at the base of the map, the bulk of Old St Peter's Basilica.

The toleration of Christianity by Constantine in 313 began the change – which the Bishops of Rome exploited, together with aura lent them by the martyrdom of St Peter in the city – to establish a spiritual dominance over the Church. The construction of grand basilicas accelerated the process, beginning with St Peter's, the first version of which was complete by 329. Many were built around old Roman ruins, or with the use of their tumbled stones.

After the collapse of the western Empire in 476, Rome suffered centuries of trial during which efforts by the eastern Roman Emperors to wrest back control from the Germanic Goths who had captured it, only resulted in further devastation: in 537 the destruction of the aqueducts serving the city permanently reduced Rome's capacity to sustain a large citizenry. From about 600,000 in the 5th century, the population sank to around 30,000 in the 9th.

Although notionally a semi-independent duchy loosely attached to the eastern Empire, Rome was largely left alone (though Emperor Constans II did visit in 663, staying long enough to make off with cartloads of its surviving statuary). Beleaguered by Lombards and the plaything of the Frankish rulers – the greatest of whom, Charlemagne, came in 800 to receive the prestigious accolade of a Papal coronation – Rome became lawless, fought over by rival families from the hundreds of fortified towers which sprouted. In 897 a mob even exhumed the body of Pope Formosus, which they put on trial for violation of canon law. Found guilty, he suffered the further posthumous indignity of having his fingers cut off.

Although 11th- and 12th-century Popes restored a modicum of order, the departure of the Papacy into exile in Avignon in 1309 heralded a new nadir, as the population slipped below 30,000. Only the return of the Papacy in 1377 and the definitive re-establishment of Rome as the sole Papal seat in 1420 brought renewed hope. It was fortunate that this coincided with an epoch when scholars such as Lorenzo Valla (c 1407–57) were seeking to recover the knowledge of the ancients – though his exposure of the Donation of Constantine, a document which purported to give legal basis to the Papacy's claims over Central Italy, can hardly have endeared him to his Papal patron Nicholas V.

Renaissance Popes and the artists and architects they employed created much of the Rome which enthralled visitors in subsequent centuries, including the Sistine Chapel, commissioned by Sixtus IV (1471–84), which boasts the handiwork of Botticelli, Perugino, Ghirlandaio and, most famously, Michelangelo, who painted its ceiling frescoes between 1508 and 1512 under the papal patronage of Julius II.

Rome's new dawn soon proved short-lived. In 1494 Charles VIII of France invaded Italy, intervening in the spiralling conflicts between Italian city-states such as Milan and Venice, and by year's end was besieging Rome. Although Pope Alexander VI weathered the storm by barricading himself in the Castel Sant'Angelo, the scale of his nepotism on behalf of his Borgia relations, and the money-raising this required, in part by selling indulgences as a free pass out of purgatory, helped spark the Reformation. Europe was torn by religious tumult and wars of religion, during which German mercenaries in the employ of the Holy Roman Emperor Charles V – a Catholic, but no friend of the Papacy – brutally sacked Rome in May 1527. The city was devastated, and the secular ambitions of the Papacy shattered. Although the Catholic Church recovered ground after the reforms of the Council of Trent (1545–63) began a slow restoration of its position, Rome once again reverted to a city that lived largely off its memories.

There were still grand artistic projects, such as the Trevi Fountain, completed in 1762, but the Papacy was increasingly powerless against outsiders: in 1809 the city was annexed by Napoleon's troops, and a short-lived Republic in 1849 toppled Papal power completely. Even after its restoration 17 months later, theocratic rule over Rome had only two decades to run: in 1870, troops of the newly unified state of Italy overran it and the following year the city was declared the national capital. Two thousand six hundred and twenty-four years after its legendary foundation by Romulus, Rome was born once again.

From Marsh to Megalopolis

Tenochtitlán, 1524 & Mexico City, 2024

The map overleaf shows a city on the cusp of a transformation. Tenochtitlán, the metropolis of the Aztec Empire that had been founded by the Mexica people in 1325, was just about to fall into the hands of Spanish conquistadores, who would then remodel it into the capital of their colonial empire in the Americas. The map was printed in 1524 to illustrate a letter written by Hernán Cortés, principal agent of the city's destruction, to his sovereign Charles V, the Holy Roman Emperor and King of Spain. It portrays the city at the height of its power, its dense cluster of buildings on an island in Lake Texcoco dominated by the pyramid-like Templo Mayor – the cartographer even marks the *tzompantli* or skull rack where the severed heads of sacrificial victims were put on public display – and connected to the surrounding shoreline by three radial causeways, with bridges that could be removed to deter attackers.

Tenochtitlán was far from an ancient city when Cortés arrived at the head of a motley band of 700 Spanish adventurers and thousands of indigenous allies. Indeed, its foundation held little promise of its future glory, as the Mexica people, who had migrated around 1200 from a fabled homeland named Aztlán ("the place of the herons") were for over a century a marginalised tribe, derided by the overlords in whose lands they were permitted to settle, a situation not helped by a marriage alliance with the lord of Culhuacan which foundered when they flayed his daughter alive as a sacrifice to the war god Huitzilopochtli. Finally, in 1325 they followed the directions of that deity to found a new city on a spot where they saw an eagle seated on a prickly pear cactus eating a snake. They called their new home Tenochtitlán, from the words in Nahuatl (the Mexica language) for rock (*tetl*) and cactus (*nochtli*), and its position on a marshy island on Lake Texcoco offered them temporary respite from their erstwhile persecutors. Gradually, and by dint of deft diplomacy leavened with ruthless aggression, they built a powerful alliance with the cities of Tetzcoco and Tlacopan, and together conquered the rest of the lakeside cities. Then, under the leadership of a succession of able *tlatoani* (or emperors) they expanded outwards into the Valley of Mexico.

The city they built was one intimately tied to water, from the causeways to the aqueduct that brought water from the nearby spring of Chapultepec and the *chinampas* or floating fields reclaimed from the swamp, which fed its burgeoning population. Tenochtitlán was laid out on a grid pattern, criss-crossed by canals, in which the fastest means of transportation was by canoe. Its four zones were further divided into 20 districts, each home to a *calpulli* or kinship group, part of a rigorous hierarchy in which the *pipiltin* or nobles lorded it over the *macehualtin* or commoners, who had strict controls on their dress and had to restrict their houses to a single storey. Every district had its own marketplace, with the largest being in Tenochtitlán's neighbouring sister city of Tlatelolco, where goods from all over the Aztec Empire – whose cities bartered security for hefty annual tribute to the emperor – could be found. When the Spanish arrived in 1519, they were awed by this: twice the size, one account said, of the entire city of Salamanca and large enough to contain 60,000 people. There they could find, as well as a panoply of live goods such as parrots, eagles, hawks and doves, a dizzying array of ceramics, precious quetzal feathers, jaguar hides, jade and the cotton blankets and cacao beans which served as currency.

More striking still were the temples, to Quetzalcoatl, the feathered-serpent god, whose prophesied return some associated with the coming of Cortés and his men, and, in the very centre of the city, the great platform on top of which soared the pyramid temples of Huitzilopochtli and Tlaloc, the rain god. The first was reached by a set of red steps symbolising blood, and the second by a blue flight of stairs representing water. The human sacrifices the priest made there, the Mexica believed, were essential to keep the sun moving in the sky.

At first treated cordially by the tlatoani Moctezuma II, the Spanish relations with the Aztecs soon soured. Cortés was forced to flee Tenochtitlán during the night of June 30, 1520, *La Noche Triste* ("Night of Sorrow"), when many of the Spanish perished, but he returned the following May, and laid siege to the city. The fighting was brutal: a small fleet of Spanish brigantines was launched into the lake to see off the Aztec war canoes, the aqueduct was cut and gradually the city starved. Raids across the causeway took small parts of Tenochtitlán, which the Aztec warriors recaptured each night. After almost three months, though, they were exhausted and their leader Cuauhtémoc – Moctezuma having been murdered by the Spanish the previous year – surrendered.

Its warriors slaughtered and much of the population – at its height over 200,000 – dead of starvation or smallpox,

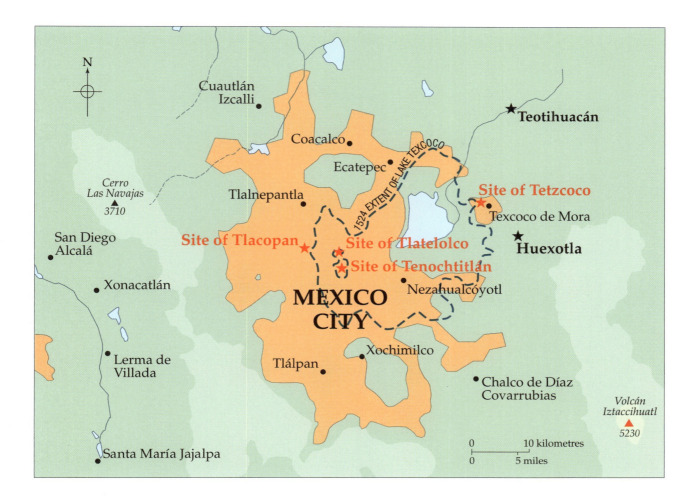

Tenochtitlán hovered between two worlds. The Mexica were excluded from the city's central thirteen blocks, now the exclusive preserve of the Spanish, but they were allowed two municipal councils to represent them in the rest. Then, in 1538, the Spanish viceroy Antonio de Mendoza ordered the destruction of the Templo Mayor and other temples. Down came the Palace of Moctezuma, with its zoo of exotic animals, and in place of the old central market, the Zócalo, the square at the heart of the modern city, was laid out. Gradually, the cityscape became populated with convents, monasteries and churches, including the cathedral, which, though begun in 1573, was only finally consecrated in 1667. Large parts of Lake Texcoco, whose former extent is shown on the map above, were drained to shape what became known as Mexico City. This land reclamation had disastrous consequences, with especially destructive floods in 1607 and 1629 (the weight of the city's buildings on the unstable lakebed beneath is still causing it to subside by about 50cm (20 inches) a year).

By the late 1700s, the population had recovered to around 100,000, with the grandeur of its aristocratic residences moving the German naturalist Alexander von Humboldt, who visited Mexico in 1803–04, to call it the "city of palaces". Setbacks such as a typhoid epidemic in 1737 could not halt the remorseless growth, as newcomers flocked in from the countryside. The secularisation of most church property in 1856 opened up sections of the centre for development and under the long rule of President Porfirio Díaz, street lighting, gas, electricity and the railway came to what was now the capital of the independent Republic of Mexico. By 1921, the city's population had reached 600,000 and was spreading in all directions, as far as Tacuba (the site of Tlacopan) in the west by 1929 and then in the 1930s past the Chapultepec Forest. In 1956 it acquired its first skyscraper, with the completion of the 45-storey Torre Latinoamericana, which remained Mexico's tallest building for over a quarter of a century.

By 2024, the population of the Greater Mexico City area – as shown on the map above – was around 22.5 million, making it one of less than a dozen megalopolises to exceed the 20 million mark. With over a hundred times the number of inhabitants at the time of Tenochtitlán's fall in 1521, the Spanish capture proved to be not the end for the city, but the start of a long transformation in its fortunes.

Res fuerat quondam præstans, & Gloria summa
Orbis subiectus Cæsaris Imperio,
Hic longe præstat, cuius nunc Orbis Eous,
Et Nouus, atq; alter panditur Auspitijs.

Punta de las higueras,
Santi Juton
R:. de Vzalum
Rio, de la palma
Bocas de nauas,
Caribes,
Ganto andres
Rio de totiqualauo
Boca partida
Rio de vanderas
Scivilla de saluados
Almezia
de Sant juan
Sant pedro,
Ysdela treftao
Azchona
prouincia
a michel,
Rio panu
co laoton,
Camacho puicia

yucatam

Puncta de Cuba

La florida,

R:. la palma
Rio de Arboledas
Bo
d Assentos

Rio del spiritusancto

Quilibet punctus magnus continet leucas duode
cim cū dimidia, ita q̃ duo magni puncti continent
viginti quinq̃ leucas, Cotinet autē leuca quatuor
Italica miliaria, ita q̃ omnes puncti qui hic cōspi
ciuntur continent centum leucas.

River City

Paris, 1550

Transport and trade are two of the biggest factors that determine the success or failure of cities. For most of history, travel by land (for people or goods) was slow, expensive and dangerous, and so access to a waterway, in particular a river, has been a boon to urban centres such as London (the Thames), Rome (the Tiber), Cairo (the Nile), St Petersburg (the Neva) and New York (the Hudson). The map overleaf, by Paris-based publishers Olivier Truschet and Germain Hoyau, shows the city bisected by the Seine, the prominence of its waterway accentuated by the map's being oriented with east at the top, so that the river runs from bottom to top.

Although over 1,800 years old by the time the map was published, Paris was something of a backwater for the first two thirds of its life. Traces of human habitation dating to 8000BC have been found in the 15th arrondissement, and elsewhere wooden fishing canoes from about 4500BC. But it was only in the mid-3rd century BC that the Celtic Parisii tribe established an oppidum (an early form of town) by the banks of the Seine, incidentally giving the settlement its future name. In 52BC Julius Caesar captured it, providing the name, Lutetia – probably deriving from *lutum*, the Latin for marsh – by which it would be known for the next 300 years. Lutetia was not an important political centre, though its *cardo maximus*, the main street, still exists in ghostly form as the Rue St Jacques, and a scattering of remains have been preserved. Notable amongst them is the Arènes de Lutèce, the old amphitheatre, which was rediscovered in 1860 on Rue Monge, close to the Panthéon, and saved through a campaign led by the author Victor Hugo.

By the 4th century, the city had reacquired the name of Paris, and though it resisted attacks by Attila the Hun in 451 – it was said through a heroic campaign of prayer vigils and fasts led by its future patron saint, Geneviève – it eventually fell to the Franks, and in 508 became their capital under King Clovis I. By now the city had contracted, making best use of the defensive opportunities of the river to coalesce on the Île de la Cité, which has ever since been the city's spiritual heart, and where the Frankish rulers enlarged the paleo-Christian church of St Étienne, the first version of the future Notre-Dame. Most of the Frankish kings of the Merovingian and Carolingian dynasties and the Capetians who succeeded them in 987 favoured residences outside Paris – the greatest of them, Charlemagne (reigned 768–814) held his court at Aachen. The city weathered a storm of Viking attacks, with the Norsemen, whose navigational skills meant the Seine posed no obstacle, besieging it in 845 and 885, to remerge in the 12th century, when Philippe II Auguste (reigned 1180–1223) restored Paris to its position as royal capital.

The city's location astride trade routes (especially in silver) and on the pilgrimage roads which led south to Rome and Santiago de Compostela also helped. More practically, Philip II built the massive fortress of the Louvre on the right bank of the Seine between 1190 and 1202, and in 1183 enlarged the Les Halles marketplace as an emporium for the merchants who were frequenting the city in increasing numbers. The city's spiritual needs had burgeoned with its population, and between 1135 and 1144 Abbot Suger masterminded the reconstruction of the Basilica of St Denis, which commemorated France's patron, whose martyrology recounts that after his decapitation by the Romans around 250, he had carried his severed head all the way from Montmartre to his future sepulchre, around seven kilometres to the north. The city's intellectual supremacy, too, was assured by the foundation in 1253 of its first university by Robert de Sorbon, which provided support for poor theology students, and where its first printing press would be established in 1469.

By 1328 the city's population had reached 200,000, as it sprawled ever further beyond the Île, creating new social tensions in the crowded streets and leading to a series of uprisings, notably a failed revolt in 1358 by the merchant community led by Étienne Marcel. But the depredations of the plague – which struck the city three dozen times between 1348 and 1480 – and of the English, who took advantage of one of the upswings in their fortunes during the Hundred Years' War to occupy Paris between 1420 and 1436, led to a century-long hiatus in its rise.

In 1528 Francis I began remodelling the Louvre fortress as a palace, complete with new-fangled Renaissance façade by Pierre Lescot, beginning the process by which it became, inexorably, the main royal residence. It was around this time that Truschet and Hoyau published their map, with the Cathedral of Notre-Dame and the Royal Palace clearly visible. The outbreak of a series of vicious religious wars in France after the Reformation again blighted the city, with the St Bartholomew's Day Massacre on August 24, 1572, in which thousands of Huguenots (French Protestants) were butchered in attacks orchestrated by Catherine de' Medici, the Catholic Queen Mother, being the worst incident.

Peace of sorts was restored when the Protestant nobleman Henri de Navarre became king, as Henri IV, in 1589 and converted to Catholicism four years later, memorably declaring, "Paris vaut bien une messe" ("Paris is well worth a Mass").

The decline in the population was reversed and the city acquired a new raft of iconic buildings. Henri IV's widow Marie de' Medici had the Luxembourg Palace constructed in 1615–30 (modelled on the Pitti Palace in her native Florence) and the Seine acquired a new prestige bridge, the Pont Neuf, which was opened to the public after more than 20 years of construction. It was one of the wonders of the city, built with balconies to allow people uninterrupted views along the river, and with its huge length of more than 200 metres (650 feet) and enormous width – at 22 metres (75 feet), wider than any other street in the city – it caused huge crowds to assemble, and entertainers and hawkers to gather, making the structure at times more carnival than thoroughfare.

The population surged to 400,000 in 1643, just in time for the city to experience a last spasm of civil unrest before the French Revolution, as the Fronde – which began with the Day of the Barricades in 1648 as a protest against rising poverty but turned into a series of civil wars that gripped the entire country – only ended in 1653. Soon afterwards, Louis XIV, the Sun King, reached maturity and a golden age began for Paris. In 1677 he moved his residence to the glittering new palace of Versailles, where the aristocracy were kept captive by petty intrigues and compulsory attendance at court. Streetlights first appeared in 1667, along roads which now had cafés, a new innovation serving coffee rather than wine or ale, to invigorate their customers' gossiping and debates.

As the Enlightenment sparked into life in the 18th century, these conversations turned to more practical philosophy and the need for reform, inspired by the works of men such as Voltaire (1694–1778), himself a Parisian, and the more radical ideas of Jean-Jacques Rousseau (1712–78), an occasional Parisian in the 1750s and 1760s, when not exiled or under threat of arrest by an exasperated royal government. Yet, though dissent bubbled dangerously below the surface and social divisions were becoming wider than ever, in 1750 the Seine still ran through a city that was arguably Europe's most beautiful, its second largest (with 600,000 inhabitants, having just lost its crown to London,

which had 50,000 more), and which had, on and off, been the seat of French kings for a millennium and a quarter. Before the century was out, events would be underway to bring this function to an end for good.

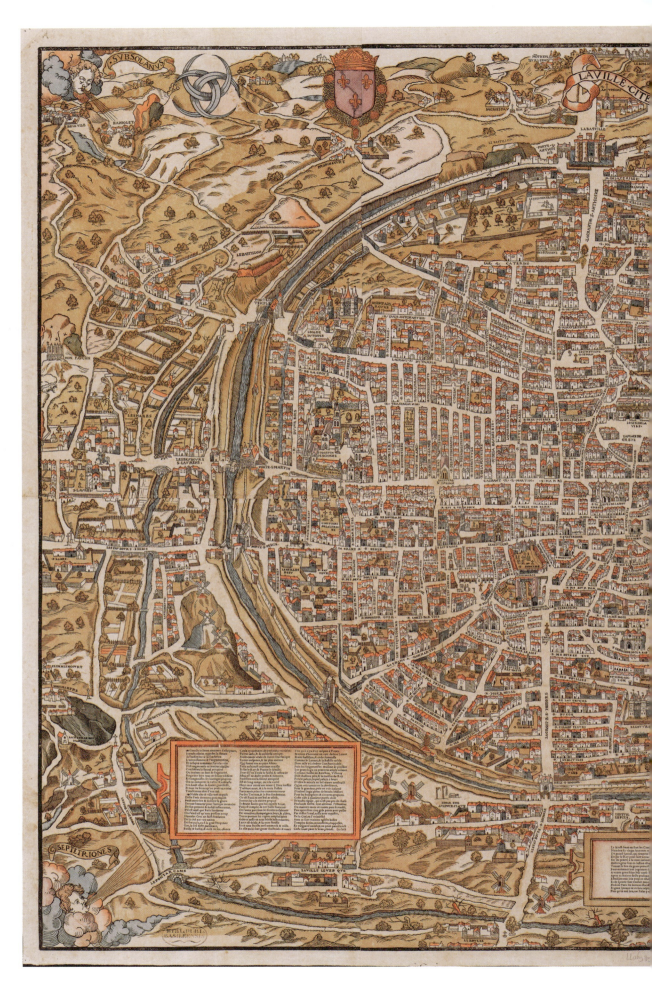

CITE DE PARIS

ORIENS

Icy est le vray pourtraict naturel de la ville, cité, vniuersité
& Faubourgz de Paris, ou sont iustement figurées toutes les Rues & Ruelles correspondantes
l'vne à l'autre, ainsi qui sont de present situées, qui sont en nôbre deux cens quatre vingtz &
sept. Pareillement sont figurées toutes les Eglises, & Monasteres, qui sont en nombre cent
quatre. Aussy sont figurées tous les Colleges, qui sont en nôbre quarante neuf. Et pour con-
gnoistre icelles Rues, Ruelles, Eglises, Monasteres & Colleges, vous trouuerrez leurs noms
escriptz à chûn sur son propre endroict. Côme plus amplement vous poues voir ey dessus.

A Paris, par Oliuier Truschet, & Germain Hoyau, demourans en
la Rue de Montorgueil, au Chef sainct Denys.

FAVONIVS

City of Many Faces

Cairo, 1572

Cairo is a city that has worn many faces and has been refounded perhaps more often than any other major metropolis. Shown overleaf, Braun and Hogenberg's 1572 map from their *Civitates Orbis Terrarum* ("Cities of the World") depicts the city a little past its political apogee, but at a time when its major monuments, clustered in a densely crowded urban landscape of streets, souks and maidans, give it a sense of architectural completeness.

The Cologne-based canon and geographer Georg Braun (1541–1622) and engraver Frans Hogenberg (1535–90) liberally borrowed from a woodcut by the Venetian Matteo Pagano produced just over 20 years before, but that in turn seems based on information from the 1490s. By then, urban life in the Cairo region was already ancient, with the first capital of pharaonic Egypt being established about 3100BC at Memphis, some 25 kilometres to the south of the modern city. Braun and Hogenberg seem fascinated by this epoch in Cairo's history; to the right of the map the pyramids and sphinx are clearly visible – with the latter being interpreted as a monument to Rhodopis, allegedly the wife of an Egyptian ruler. But it is just across the Nile, on its west bank, that the real beginnings of the city are to be found.

Around AD130, the Roman emperor Trajan ordered a canal linking the Nile to the Red Sea to be built; it was to protect this strategic waterway that his successor Diocletian (reigned 285–305) had the fortress of Babylon constructed about 300. Sited opposite to where a fork in the river bends around an island in the Nile, a small town soon grew up around it. But religious dissent in the eastern provinces, a general retraction in imperial reach following the fall of Rome, and a ruinous war with Persia (which occupied Egypt from 619 to 629) meant that by the time the armies of Islam, the new force in the region, arrived there in 640, there was little but the fort itself to put up resistance.

Amr ibn al-As, the Muslim commander, took Babylon after a near year-long siege, but he chose to keep his distance from that version of Cairo, establishing instead a garrison city just to the northwest. This, known as Fustat (or "the camp"), was part of a pattern during the early Islamic conquests of implanting military settlements outside older cities (as also occurred further west with Tunis and Carthage), both to control the indigenous population and to keep the vigour of the conquering army intact. Amr also gave Cairo its first mosque, but Fustat's lifespan, by Cairene standards, was short. When the Abbasid dynasty seized power in 750, they transferred their base in Cairo to a new settlement just northeast of Fustat. Named Al-Askar ("the canton"), this, too lasted only just over a century, as in 870 Ahmad ibn Tulun, sent as governor to restore order following a rebellion, established yet a new version of Cairo, called al-Qata'i ("the wards"), provided with a palace, parade ground, hospital and a mosque (the latter of which still survives and is the city's oldest).

Cairo's refoundations were not yet over. In 969 the Fatimids swept into Egypt from the west, their general Jawhar al-Saqili peremptorily brushing aside both the ruling Ikhshidids and al-Qata'i in favour of a new site, which he called al-Mansuriyyah ("the victorious"), again to the northeast of its predecessor. Legend has it that astrologers were called in to determine the exact hour the first foundations for the city should be dug, to be signalled by bells, but a raven landed, causing them to ring prematurely and forcing the digging to start at an ill-omened hour (and thus explaining the city's later misfortunes). Before long, the new city was renamed al-Qahirat ("the vanquisher"), by which it has been known ever since (save by Cairenes, who called it Misr).

The city began to grow in earnest under the Fatimids, including the foundation in 972 of al-Azhar, its grandest mosque and long the leading seat of scholarship in the

Islamic world. In 1047, the Persian poet Nasir-i Khusraw visited, leaving an awed account of Cairo's wonders, from its souks filled with elephant ivory from Zanzibar and copper vessels from Damascus, to the wondrous seven-storey houses to be found in the old Fustat district. A temporary setback to the city's growth occurred in 1168 when the Fatimid Vizier Shawar ordered it set ablaze to prevent a Crusader force from capturing it. This played no small part in the Fatimids' overthrow three years later by Saladin, founder of the Ayyubid dynasty, who appointed himself as sultan and began the construction of the imposing Citadel – just scarcely distinguishable by its walls at the top left of the map – which remained the seat of government into the 19th century.

The Ayyubids were displaced in turn in 1250 by the Mamluks, former enslaved soldiers who sequestered their predecessors' palaces and built mosques and madrasas there. New wealth came to the city from the spice trade, with European merchants moving their bases there after the collapse of the Crusader states in Palestine in the late 13th century. Yet Cairo was living on borrowed time. A series of plagues in the 14th and 15th centuries reduced its population to about 150,000 and an enfeebled Mamluk army was unable to resist the Ottoman Turkish conquest in 1517.

No longer a capital city, Cairo became a political backwater, though still an important cultural and economic centre, with trade in Yemeni coffee and Indian textiles replacing the spices which, after the Portuguese navigator Vasco da Gama had pioneered a route around Africa in 1498, now bypassed it. The pace of grand monuments slackened, though the city still acquired a large number of Ottoman-era private villas, as it expanded south and west from the Citadel. A brief French occupation from 1798 to 1801, when Napoleon's ambitions to strike east towards British

India brought him to Egypt, broke Ottoman power completely and in 1805 Muhammad Ali, in theory the sultans' governor, declared his independence. Although he sought to modernise Egypt's army and industries, it was his successor Ismail Pasha (reigned 1863–79) who sought to give Cairo yet another new face, using the example of Haussmann's remodelling of Paris (which he visited in 1867 for the Exposition Universelle) to devise a plan which would transform the city into one of great maidan squares and wide boulevards. Little of this came to fruition, though he did bring gas and street lighting to Cairo, and his heroic overspending which incurred unpayable debts to European banks indirectly led to the British invasion of Egypt in 1882 and a new period of colonial occupation. Cairo, though, continued to grow, with the building of a new suburb at Heliopolis ten kilometres to the northeast and the planting of the suburb of Zamalek on Gezira Island in 1906.

This new Cairo had little of the romance of the old shown in Braun and Hogenberg's map. But what it did have was people – the population reached 1.3 million in 1937 and continued to grow as the sprawl spread out ever further and parts of the core were redeveloped to form the massive Tahrir Square. By 2023, the Greater Cairo area encompassed 22 million people, making it one of the world's true megacities. Memphis, Babylon, Fustat, al-Askar, al-Qata'i, al-Mansuriyyah, al-Qahirat – Cairo's 21st-century face is a youthful one, but to find housing, build facilities, provide jobs and hope for such an ever-growing population is a task that any government will find daunting.

Crocodi:

Arena

Dactili

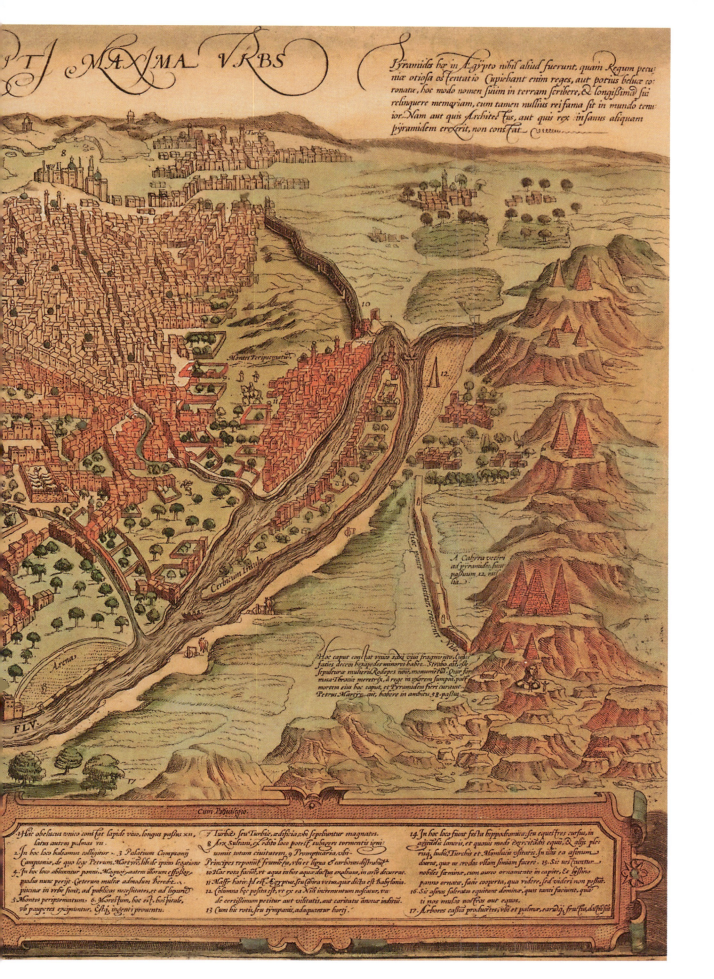

Renaissance City

Florence, 1572

There are cities that are literal works of art, their streets lined with architecturally innovative buildings, their museums crammed with priceless pieces. Florence is one of the few cities that has shaped the very history of art, its merchants' lavish patronage defining artistic sensibility for centuries, its sculptors' hands shaping new visual modes of expression, its artists' canvasses acting as models for generations.

The 1572 view of the city overleaf is by Georg Braun and Frans Hogenberg, the town plans in whose six-volume *Civitates Orbis Terrarum* are some of the most memorable of 16th-century urban landscapes. It shows the city at the end of the Renaissance, the movement that had begun in Italy around 200 years before and at whose very forefront Florence had stood. Two buildings symbolic of Florence's artistic greatness dominate the skyline: the dome of the cathedral of Santa Maria del Fiore, completed in 1436, and the Palazzo Vecchio, begun in 1299 by Arnolfo di Cambio, architect of the main body of the cathedral.

The Palazzo Vecchio overlooked the Piazza della Signoria, which once formed the forum of the Roman town of Florentia, founded in 59BC to house legionary veterans. For the next thousand years, it was a modestly prosperous settlement, though the collapse of the Roman Empire, waves of invasion by Ostrogoths, Lombards, Byzantines and Carolingian Franks, and the chronic fragmentation of the north Italian political landscape meant that by the 9th century, it had scarcely a thousand inhabitants.

Three things saved Florence: wool, banking and a legal framework that emerged after 1115, which allowed popular participation in government, and after the Ordinances of Justice, adopted in 1293, actually barred the nobility from power. Those who rose to the top in this environment were not the poor, but the merchants who were active in the wool trade that served as the engine of Florence's prosperity, and the families who provided them with banking services.

Florence weathered the fratricidal civil wars in the mid-13th century – between the Ghibellines, who broadly supported the Holy Roman Emperors based in Germany, and the Guelphs, who were partisans of the Papacy – during which the Ghibellines demolished 103 Guelph palaces, and the fortified towers which dotted the cityscape were cut down to a maximum of 29 metres in height. Then, it began to rebuild, backed by the city's gold florin coinage, first issued in 1252, that became a universal medium of exchange. The profits from wool and cloth exports and banking poured into the city's coffers, and, more importantly into the hands of patrons such as the Bardi, Peruzzi, Strozzi and Medici.

At the time of the Black Death, which hit the city in 1348, reducing the population from 90,000 to less than half that, Florence had 600 notaries, 100 apothecaries, and, more importantly, 80 banking houses. Tension between the demands of the artisan classes and those of the merchants occasionally boiled over, notably in a great revolt by the *ciompi* (or wool-carders) in 1378, but the city finally found stability and completed its ascent to glory at the hands of one of those merchant dynasties, the Medici. The founder, Cosimo de Medici, never had any formal role in government, but from 1434 he dominated the city as its leading citizen, his lavish patronage responsible for a swathe of grand projects, including the rebuilding of the convent church of San Marco, complete with frescoes by Fra Angelico. For the next century the fount of Florence's artistic achievement seemed inexhaustible, with masters such as Masaccio, Masolino, Paolo Uccello, Piero della Francesca, Filippo Lippi and Ghirlandaio producing works paid for by the city's merchant oligarchs to praise both God and flaunt their own secular wealth.

The most spectacular result was the dome of Florence's cathedral, a building that had been started long before, in 1296. Filippo Brunelleschi, the architect who finally completed it in 1436, solved the problem of how to erect the huge 55-metre- (180-foot-) diameter dome by creating an inner and outer shell and a complex herringbone pattern of bricks, both of which spread the weight and prevented its massive bulk from collapsing.

The Medici family continued to build: churches, libraries and palaces, as well as their own position. By the time of Lorenzo I (known, with good cause, as "the Magnificent"), who ruled over Florence from 1469 to 1492, a new generation of artists enjoyed the Medici patronage, including Leonardo da Vinci, and Michelangelo (whose *David* originally graced the courtyard of the Palazzo Vecchio). The 1478 Pazzi conspiracy, an attempt by disgruntled rival families to overthrow the Medici by assassinating Lorenzo, failed, but French intervention in the perennial squabbles between Italian city states resulted in their expulsion in 1494. In the interim, Florence became a republic, and was temporarily gripped by a kind of remorse for its past excesses, with the firebrand preacher Girolamo Savonarola dominating the city for four years until he was arrested, hanged and burnt in the Piazza della Signoria.

The Medici returned in 1512, and their success in bouncing back was in part the inspiration for Machiavelli's *The Prince*, which lauded the wiles of rulers who preferred to be feared than loved. But Italy's artistic centre of gravity had shifted to Rome, where Michelangelo had gone to paint the frescoes on the Sistine Chapel. The Medici ruled in Florence – as dukes from 1530, and as Grand Dukes of Tuscany from 1569 – until 1737, when the city was subsumed into the Austrian Habsburg Empire, but by then its political power was but a distant memory and its artistic leadership had long passed to others. Symbolic, perhaps, was the conversion of the Uffizi palace, designed by the artist and art historian Giorgio Vasari in 1560, into a gallery for the display of the Medici art treasures just 21 years later. Michelangelo had written that "a noble house in the city brings considerable honour, being more visible than all one's possessions", but the contents of those houses, the architects, painters and sculptors who embellished them, and the Medici, the family whose wealth and patronage made it all possible, continue to bring honour to Florence half a millennium later.

FLORENTIA vrbs est insignis Hetruriæ, olim Fluentia dicta, quod
sita sit ad fluentum Arni fluminis. Et populi ipsi Fluentini, quorum memi:
nit Cato in originib: vt refert Angelus Politianus in quadam Epistola
ad Bartholomæu Scalam. Pulcherrimis tam publicis, quam priuatis orna:
ta ædificijs, et montibus vndiq, septa, ex quibus, dictu mirum, quanta oble:
ctatione visus in hanc vrbem pandatur. Nobilium homiuum sedes est, &
præstantissimorum ingeniorum feracissimus ager

Cum priuilegio

City of the Panther

Cusco, 1574

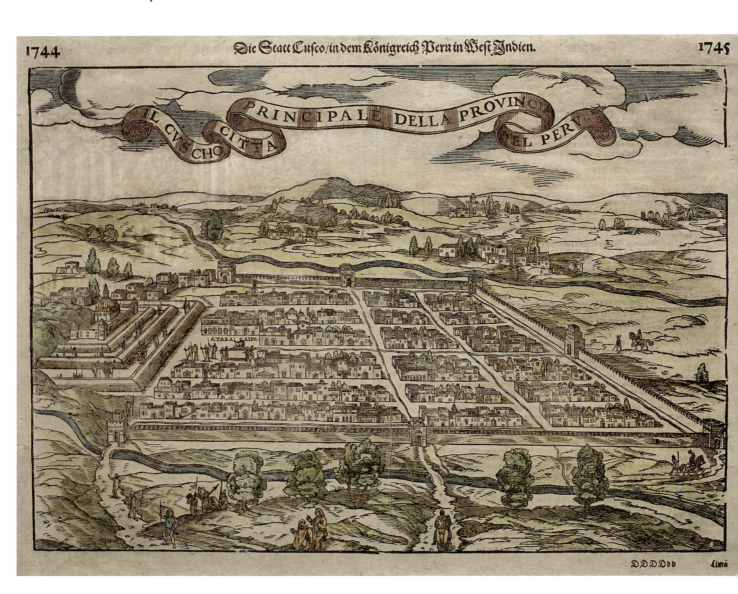

The map, from an edition of the *Cosmographia*, the encyclopaedic compilation by the great German cosmographer Sebastian Münster, shows an idealised vision of the Inca city of Cusco, complete with Inca warriors and their emperor (labelled as "Atabalipa", rather than his real name, Atahuallpa), reclining close to a distinctly Christian-looking temple of the sun. Münster himself adapted his view from one created by the Piedmontese mapmaker Giacomo Gastaldi, who drew it in 1556 without ever having visited the city.

Nonetheless, the Münster-Gastaldi plan became the most widely circulated image, crowding out the real topography of the Inca city, just as the Spanish conquistador Francisco Pizarro reshaped Cusco after its conquest in 1533. The plan does at least give a sense of a sacred city, which the Inca, whose capital it was from the 13th century, believed was founded by Manco Capac, son of the sun god Inti. One story tells that Manco was seeking a place to establish a new settlement, and when his sacred golden staff, the *tupayauri*, sank into the ground, he took it as a sign to found Cusco there (so called because *Qusqu* in the Quechua language of the Inca means navel). The site was riven with ritual connections, surrounded by six sacred mountains, its urban core of around 40 hectares (100 acres) divided into an upper and lower sector, the *urin* and *hanan*, in turn subdivided to mirror the whole Tawantinsuyu, the Inca "empire of four quarters".

It was ruled over by the Sapa Inca, or emperor, the greatest of whom, Pachacuti (reigned 1438–71), defeated the Chanca, inveterate enemies of the Inca, and refounded Cusco, making it a truly imperial city. He tamed the city's two rivers, the Huatanay and Tullumayo, into canals, which met at a point traditionally described as the tail of a panther. The animal's spine was formed by the grand main square, the Huacaypata, where public ceremonies were held and a brazier constantly burnt with the ashes of sacrificial llamas. Its head was the Sacsahuaman fortress to the north of the city, whose huge stones were, as is characteristic of Inca architecture, fitted together without mortar.

Inca Cusco's central district, in which perhaps 20,000 people lived, was dominated by the palaces of the Sapa Inca and his family. These were ringed by the *kancha*, courtyard compounds of the nobility, whose buildings formed a grid pattern. Dominating it all was the Qorikancha, the temple of the sun, set alongside that of Mama Quilla, the moon goddess. The temple was lavish: its walls were decorated with sheets of beaten gold, its courtyard filled with golden models of corn, flowers, llamas and even insects, and its inner sanctuary held the most sacred icon, the Punchao, a solid gold statue of Inti portrayed as a small boy.

Cusco's glory lasted less than a century. In 1533, the Spanish arrived, having already effectively kidnapped Atahuallpa, the Sapa Inca. The empire was already weakened by a civil war between Atahuallpa and his brother Huáscar, and by the smallpox epidemic that preceded the Spanish invasion and killed over a third of the Inca population. Inca resistance was uncoordinated, and though a new emperor, Manco Inca Yupanqui, managed to retake Cusco in 1537 after a 10-month siege, the Spanish recaptured it after just ten days.

Pizarro had already officially refounded Cusco as a Spanish city in 1534 and handed out land grants to his followers. The Spanish systematically dismantled the Inca city, beginning with the establishment of El Triunfo ("the triumph") church on top of the Suntur Huasi, the old Inca armoury. Inca temples became churches, with the site of the Qorikancha itself turned into a Dominican Convent, and the Acllahuasi, the house of the Virgins of the Sun (noble Inca women consecrated to Inti) transformed into the Santa Catalina convent. The old Huacaypata became the Plaza de Armas, the centrepiece of the colonial city.

The process was accelerated by a devastating earthquake in 1650 which damaged most of the city's buildings, allowing much of the remaining Inca stonework to be cleared away and replaced by a transplanted version of the Spanish baroque. For the next 300 years the Inca city slept quietly, largely forgotten, beneath the colonial superstructure imposed upon it by the Spanish.

Then, in 1950, another earthquake shook Cusco, and this time it was the Spanish layer of the city that suffered. As masonry collapsed and villas crumbled, the destruction revealed the Inca foundations and wall-bases beneath, the monumental slabs of stone (and a few trapezoidal doorways) still there, as the City of the Panther, the navel of the Earth, revealed itself after three centuries. It is now possible to visit Cusco, at an altitude of 3,400 metres (11,100 feet) one of the world's highest cities and a literally breathtaking experience for streams of foreign tourists intent on walking the Inca Trail that leads to the even grander remains of Machu Picchu. But now, visitors can get a glimpse of how Inca Cusco really looked, in a way that Sebastian Münster or Giacomo Gastaldi never could.

Templum S. Georgii

Profetti Syriæ domus

Ecclesia Macgna Pauli

Domus Soldani orbis

DAMASCVS, urbs
nobilissima ad Libanum
montem, Totius Syriæ
Metropolis.

The Oldest City in the World?

Damascus, 1575

The map shows the Syrian city of Damascus at the peak of its prosperity, when the wealth brought to it by the great *Hajj* pilgrimage caravans which assembled to the south of the city ensured its place as a jewel in the Ottoman sultans' crown. Yet the map, which comes from a 1575 edition of the *Civitates Orbis Terrarum* ("Cities of the World") by Georg Braun and engraver Frans Hogenberg, still shows a Damascus that has a fair claim to be the oldest continuously inhabited city in the world, bearing the scars of its great age. The cityscape is a palimpsest of layer upon layer of monuments that are witness to a past of troubled greatness.

Although settlement in the region around Damascus may date back to the 10th millennium BC, the city itself, watered by the Barada river, only enters the historical record in the mid-2nd millennium BC. Its name, as Ta-ms-qu, first appears in a context prophetic of its future experiences: a list of 119 cities whose rulers had been captured by the Egyptian pharaoh Thutmose III at the Battle of Megiddo, around 1480BC. Settled just before that date by Aramaean nomads, its position astride key trade routes generated wealth that was perennially coveted by others: over its 3,500-year career, the city has experienced a dizzying succession of different dynasties, dominant ethnic groups, and regimes.

Stories of Damascus's foundation seem somewhat hazy. One legend suggests the founder was Uz, great-grandson of Noah, another that the biblical patriarch Abraham was born there. In reality, the Aramaeans fought long, but ultimately futile campaigns to keep their city independent, vanquishing the mighty Assyrian Empire at Qarqar, to the northwest of Damascus, in 853BC, but falling to them soon thereafter. The new masters were in turn ejected by Babylonians, Persians, Alexander the Great, Antigonids, Ptolemies and Seleucids, before finally coming into the orbit of Rome, when Pompey the Great arrived in 64BC.

The Romans replanned Damascus on a grid pattern, still discernible today amid the irregular accretions of the Old City and its mosaic craze of souks, hammams and madrasas. The decumanus, the main east–west axis of any self-respecting Roman town, was referred to in the New Testament as "the street called Straight", and still survives as Midhat Pasha Street. It was at its eastern end, marked by Braun and Hogenberg with the annotation "Hic D. Paulus baptizatus", that Paul, who had been sent to persecute Christians but instead became one after a vision "on the road to Damascus", received baptism.

Christianity was supplanted by Islam in 634 when the Umayyad army of Khalid ibn al-Walid took Damascus and, after a pause for consolidation, began a programme of mosque building. Its most spectacular result, visible in the centre of the map, is the Umayyad Mosque, completed in 715. It is adorned with beautiful mosaics, rich in glittering gold tesserae and intertwining foliage, which are the survivors of an even more lavish series that perished during a number of fires over the ages (the most recent, in 1893, was caused by a workman carelessly leaving his lit pipe on the roof). The mosque, too, aptly symbolises the city's complex heritage as it was built on the site of the Byzantine Cathedral of St John, which in turn had been constructed on the ruins of the Roman-era temple of Jupiter, which itself replaced a shrine of Hadad, the Aramaean thunder god.

The Umayyads were expelled by the new Abbasid Caliphate in 750 (when 80 Umayyad princelings had their throats cut on the banks of the Barada river), but the city never truly found peace, being contested by Tulunids, Ikshidids, Fatimids, Seljuqs, Zengids and Ayyubids, and attacks by Crusaders, who never quite captured it, and Egyptian Mamluks, whose 260-year reign was interrupted in 1401 by a brutal sacking by the Mongol warlord Tamerlane. The four centuries of Ottoman rule from 1516 to 1918 must have come as a blessed relief, if at the price of political irrelevance, as the imperial court was far away in İstanbul.

Many of Damascus's most notable surviving monuments, such as the 1590 Sinan Pasha Mosque, come from the period, and by the 19th century they were attracting not just pilgrims, but tourists. Many of these were from Europe and North America, whose interventions in the region would soon precipitate momentous and catastrophic changes. Among the visitors, Mark Twain aptly summarised the city's history, commenting that, "To Damascus, years are only moments, decades are only flitting trifles of time."

The Ottoman Empire crumbled in 1918, but Syria, and Damascus with it, found itself sucked into the French colonial empire. Independence came in 1946, but the city's travails were far from over. The outbreak of the Syrian Civil War in 2011 brought fighting that saw the suburb of Ghouta almost destroyed and shelling that hit the heart of the old city itself. Then, in 2023, a fire destroyed the 800-year-old Souk Sarouja. A city as old as Damascus has had its share of triumphs but leavened with deep layers of sorrow.

Trading Leviathan

Venice, 1585

The serpentine coils of a city surrounded by water, the iconic splendour of the Doge's Palace, San Giorgio Maggiore and a dozen other churches, and the majestic sweep of Venice's Grand Canal are all magnificently portrayed in this panoramic fresco, painted under the guidance of Ignazio Danti in the mid-1580s. Danti was a talented mathematician and geographer – progressing from Dominican monk to professor of mathematics at Bologna and pontifical mathematician, with a seat on the commission that crafted the Gregorian calendar reform in 1582 – whose masterwork was the Vatican's Galleria delle Carte Geografiche, of which this portrayal of Venice is perhaps the most striking. It sits at the end of a series depicting other Italian ports, including Genoa, Venice's greatest rival, which is fitting since trade permeated Venice and gave it life. For nearly five centuries, the city achieved the impossible, dominating the eastern Mediterranean in the face of far larger powers – Byzantines, Ayyubids, Ottoman Turks and Austrian Habsburgs – all from the precarious perch of some 118 tiny islands facing an unpromising, marshy hinterland.

Venice's very foundation, too, seemed improbable. In the early 5th century, refugees from the influx of Germanic barbarians into the late Roman Empire built a new settlement on the unstable sands of the lagoon by driving great stakes of alder down until they hit harder clay, which they topped with limestone foundations. By the early 8th century, the city was ruled by doges; the first historically attested one in a line that would stretch to 1797 was Orso Ipato, who took office in 726. The following century, Venice acquired its patron saint by dint of kidnapping the corpse of St Mark from Alexandria, whisked away by Venetian merchants who seemingly secreted it in a barrel of pork to put off the local customs officials (who were Muslim).

By then the nucleus of the city had moved southwards to the Rialto, where the earliest version of the Doge's Palace was constructed about 814, and the first incarnation of the basilica of San Marco consecrated in 1094. Venice's merchants had already begun to make inroads into the eastern Mediterranean, aided by a love-hate relationship with their former (and still de jure until 1187) suzerains in the Byzantine Empire. They outpaced rivals such as Amalfi and Pisa, though it took until 1380, and the definitive defeat of Genoa at the Battle of Chioggia, before their mastery was undisputed.

The city grew impossibly rich on trade in timber and stone from Dalmatia, which by the 12th century had come under Venice's sway, and on silk and spices from the East, aided by the Venetians' lack of scruples by trading with the Muslim states of the Levant. The fractious relationship with the Byzantines had deteriorated by then and in 1204 the army of the Fourth Crusade, though notionally in Constantinople to restore the deposed emperor Alexius IV to the throne, sacked the city and dismembered its empire. Doge Enrico

Dandolo received three-eighths of its territory as a reward for his support, lending the doges the nickname "Lords of a Quarter and half a Quarter".

Venice reached its peak in the 15th century, its merchant fleet exceeding 3,000 vessels, its navy comprising over 100 war galleys. It had also achieved another seeming impossibility: the establishment of a stable republican form of government in a continent largely comprising monarchies. The rather unwieldy Great Council, formed in 1172 from the mercantile aristocracy, was supplemented in 1223 by a Council of 40 to handle judicial matters and a 60-strong Senate which determined legislation and supervised economic affairs. In 1310 a Council of Ten was set up as the ultimate authority beneath the doge, and it was this body, small enough to make decisions rapidly, that ensured Venice's continued prosperity. Wars on the Italian mainland, however, sapped the city's vitality. Despite an artistic golden age which produced masters such as Andrea Mantegna (1431–1506) and Gentile Bellini (c 1429–1507), the city's land forces struggled to deal with growing Italian powers such as Milan, and the increasing interference of France and Austria.

A treaty in 1516 confirmed Venice's possession of much of Lombardy, but this was the city's high-water mark, after which its power ebbed. Caught between growing Ottoman power, which blocked off traditional trade conduits to the East, and the alternative routes around Africa pioneered by the Portuguese from 1498, as well as the impact of plague – which in 1630–31 killed a third of the city's population – Venice's trade withered. The doges still celebrated the traditional ceremony of the Marriage to the Sea, begun in 1177, in which a pontifical ring was hurled into the waters of the lagoon, but the city's maritime reach was contracting. Cyprus was lost to the Turks in 1570, Crete in 1669, and though the Venetians captured the Peloponnese in 1699, it was lost again by 1715. By the time the forces of Napoleon seized the city in 1797, only the ghost of Venice's political might remained.

The city was left to be bartered between France and Austria, until its final absorption into a united Italy in 1866. By then its trade hardly registered, eclipsed by ports such as Trieste and Ancona and the far greater profits from transatlantic and transpacific steamships. It survived as a site of cultural pilgrimage, and then of mass tourism, so much so that the millions who came each year by the 21st century threatened to overwhelm a city that was already sinking 1–2 millimetres each year into the mud from which it had risen in the 6th century. As the prototype of the perfect trading city-state – a model later followed by Hong Kong in the 19th and Singapore in the 20th century – and as a symbol of artistic brilliance, Venice, Most Serene Republic, may be eternal, but the waves now threaten to bring its improbable balancing act to an end.

Trading State

Hamburg, 1585

A successful trading city needs law. Even more, it needs water, the liquid treasure that carries cargo and draws in profit more assuredly than the lumbering land transport of pre-modern times. Water is more evident than the law in Braun and Hogenberg's 1585 view of Hamburg, but the law came from its position as one of the most successful states of the Hanseatic League, a mercantile confederacy that dominated north European trade from the 13th to the 16th centuries.

The city is enfolded by the River Alster, which feeds into the mighty Elbe and is criss-crossed by bridges – around 2,500 of them, more than Venice and Amsterdam combined. Its harbour, established in 1189, is crowded with the ships that took advantage of Hamburg's strategic position on routes leading east to the Baltic, and west into the North Sea.

Hamburg (or Hammaburg) was founded around 800, becoming a conduit for Christianity in northern Germany through the foundation of an archbishopric in 831. But a sack by the Vikings in 845 stemmed its progress, and it was not until this town united with the mercantile settlement around the harbour in the 13th century that Hamburg's rise to prominence began. The key was the 1210 agreement with Lübeck for a common law between them on commercial dealings, which by 1241 had become a formal alliance and the nucleus of the Hanseatic League.

A network of mainly north German towns, secured by similar trading treaties, the Hanse (from a word meaning "troop") used its strength in numbers – over 100 members at its height – to strong-arm its way into becoming a monopoly supplier. In 1253 it secured an agreement with Bruges allowing its merchants a foothold there that developed into one of four *Kontors*, states-within-states where Hanse merchants lived (the others were at Novgorod, London and Bergen in Norway), enjoying legal immunity from their host country.

The Hanse's activities funded lavish building programmes that left almost identikit old towns dotted around the Baltic. Their activities did not go unchallenged; in 1370 King Haakon of Norway issued a formal complaint lamenting "the German tailor of Bergen had assassinated the cousin of the Archbishop of Trondheim. For this we have no redress". The Danes, under Waldemar IV, fought back, although it did him little good, as after a decade-long war and a stinging defeat at Helsingborg in 1368, he was forced to concede free passage through the Öresund.

Gradually, though, the Hanse declined. More centralised states such as France and England and the rise of Muscovy squeezed its ability to intimidate its political rivals, and by the late 16th century the Dutch, too, were eating into its North Sea markets for salt, cloth and herring. Cities broke away, or were absorbed by others, and at the last meeting of the Hanseatic assembly in 1669, there were only six cities present, Hamburg among them.

Unlike other former members of the League, Hamburg did not pause for breath. It weathered the turmoil of the Reformation well. The city accepted Protestantism in 1529 at the same time as a new constitution, the Langer Rezess, which balanced the interests of the city council, merchants and the citizenry in a way that avoided instability. It also accepted useful influxes of refugees, including those from the Spanish capture of Antwerp in 1585 and French Protestants fleeing the removal of religious toleration for their religion exactly a century later. By the 17th century, over half the city's merchants were immigrants, and a 1567 treaty with the English Company of Merchant Adventurers assured Hamburg trading privileges in London, just as previously enjoyed before the Hanse bled away. The city remained financially innovative, in 1558 becoming the first in Germany to establish a stock exchange, and with the Bank of Hamburg, set up in 1619, issuing its own currency.

Officially an Imperial Free City from 1618, Hamburg built on its wealth and privileges, becoming one of the most important trans-shipment ports for goods going to the French colonial possessions in the 18th century. In 1768 it even concluded its long quarrel with Denmark, when the Danish crown finally recognised its independence. As a trading city-state it had long outlived its rivals – Lübeck, Bremen and all the Hanse, even Genoa and Venice in the south – and it survived a devastating fire in 1842 which destroyed much of the city centre, including the church of St Nicholas, whose 153-metre (500-foot) spire looms over

the city in the map. Even though it was finally absorbed within the German Empire in 1871, and its status as a free port was snuffed out in 1888, Hamburg remained a trading leviathan. The near destruction of the docks during the Allied bombing of July 1943 – in which 40,000 people died – was made good following the war, and after a hiatus before Germany was reunified in 1990, the port resumed its dominance in north European trade, now hosting around 10,000 ship visits a year. The model of the trading city-state, pioneered long ago by Carthage and Athens, was perfected by the Hanseatic cities, and, with the success of modern versions such as Singapore, and Hamburg itself, it shows no sign of becoming moribund.

The Perfect City

Palmanova, 1598

Medieval cities were chaotic, unplanned mazes, often squalid, and all decidedly imperfect. The notion of a perfect city was confined to the theological sphere, with the 5th-century Christian writer St Augustine's *The City of God* describing a more moral construct than a worldly aspiration, and illuminated manuscript depictions of the Heavenly Jerusalem, replete with bejewelled pavements, reflected a belief that the virtuous would be rewarded by urban order in the next life, rather than enjoying it in this.

All that changed with the Renaissance. The rediscovery in 1414 of the works of Vitruvius, the 1st-century BC architect, raised hopes of recapturing the elegant lines of Roman buildings and the (at least in theory) planned order of the classical urban grid. The English statesman Thomas More's *Utopia* (1516) described and idealised societies run on egalitarian lines in which a harmonious urban environment contributed to the wellbeing of the citizens. Practical politics mean that much of this remained firmly theoretical. The "Ideal City" represented in the late-15th-century painting – anonymous but associated with the court of Duke Federico da Montefeltro of Urbino – incorporates the contemporary notion that a large public square would bind together the perfect urban centre. In this case, it is flanked by symbolic buildings, a Roman triumphal arch for the greatness of the ruler, a Colosseum-like amphitheatre for public spectacle, and an octagonal building that might be a place of worship, while in the foreground allegorical sculptures represent Justice (with scales), Moderation (with a water jug), Courage (with a column) and Liberality (with a pitcher of water).

The Florentine architect and sculptor Antonio Averlino (1400–69), who recovered from an early career setback when he was expelled from Rome for attempting to steal the head of John the Baptist, designed an ideal city named Sforzinda for his new patron, Francesco Sforza, Duke of Milan. Star-shaped within a circle, it reflected a new interest in symmetry as a guiding principle in art and architecture and the more practical challenge that artillery posed to traditional bastions. Sforzinda was not without its quirks: every second street was to be replaced by a canal, and its "House of Vice and Virtue" featured a brothel at the base, an educational academy on the higher levels, and an institution for the study of astrology at the top.

Sforzinda was never built, but Venice's need for a stronghold to fend off attacks by the Ottoman Turks, who ravaged its hinterland seven times between 1470 and 1500, meant that Palmanova, near Udine in Friuli, became the first Renaissance ideal city to get past the drawing board. It was inaugurated on October 7, 1593, the 22nd anniversary of the Venetian naval victory against the Turks at Lepanto. The city plan by Georg Braun and Franz Hogenberg, one of 546 such views in their monumental *Civitates Orbis Terrarum*, shows a nine-pointed star surrounded by three concentric rings of walls and moat, with a central tower from which nine avenues radiate out. It amply demonstrates Braun's view that "towns should be drawn in such a manner that the viewer can look into all the roads and streets and see also the buildings and open spaces".

The plan for the city – drawn up by the architect Vincenzo Scamozzi (1548–1616) and built by Giulio Savorgnano (1510–95), Venice's most renowned military engineer – seems perfect enough, but it conceals deep-seated tensions and a fatal flaw. The initial proposal, laid before the Venetian Senate in January 1593, called for 11 bastion-studded tips, but already by the autumn cost-cutting had reduced the number to nine. With too many engineers and too little direction, and in June the following year Savorgnano wrote to the Senate, imploring it not to listen to the advice of "idiotic meddlers" and threatening to resign.

Work struggled on with the first circle for nearly 30 years (the final phase would only be completed in 1813), and the result was neither militarily satisfactory – that only six of the bastions on the walls were served by the radial avenues left the other three isolated from their own interior – nor was it appealing to civilians. The sense of supplying civic services so visually present in the Ideal City painting, and so richly described in More's *Utopia*, was nowhere to be found in Palmanova. So reluctant were Venetian citizens to move there that the hoped-for wave of merchants, artisans and farmers failed to populate the city, and in 1622 the Senate had to dole out pardons to criminals to induce them to take up residence there.

Even the ideal city had its imperfections. But this did not stop future generations' efforts to reach the elusive goal of an urban Utopia. They would continue through the Enlightenment in the 18th century, in colonising ventures such as Adelaide, implanted in 1836 in a land that previously had no towns (see page 162) and in the Garden City movement that gave rise to Ebenezer Howard's pioneering Letchworth Garden City in 1903. The search for the perfect city is unending.

Viking Port

Dublin, 1610

Dublin owes its foundation to outsiders: the Scandinavian Vikings who took time out from raiding to establish a *longphort*, a fortified trading outpost on the banks of the River Liffey, in 841. The city, though, took its name, not from their Norse language, but from the Irish *dubh linn*, or black pool, a reference to the dark, tidal pool formed where the River Poddle joins the Liffey. The map, which was compiled by the English cartographer John Speed as part of his *Theatre of the Empire of Great Britain*, published in 1611, first appeared as an inset of a larger map of Leinster. It shows a city on the cusp of bursting its medieval bounds, when it was still a comparatively small settlement of around 10,000 people and before a late-17th-century expansion and a remodelling in Georgian times created the familiar topography and buildings of today's city centre.

Speed includes the walls and gates of the city, a nod to its origins, although he omits the Thingmount, the hillock on Hoggen Green (now College Green), where the Norsemen held their assemblies, and the Long Stone by the port which the Vikings erected to commemorate their first landing. The settlement, a boisterous merchant town of low dwellings facing the river near Wood Quay, survived on trade – in leather, timber, wool and enslaved people – and on the work of artisans such as tanners, brewers and blacksmiths, and it fended off periodic attempts by the surrounding Irish kingdoms to expel the Vikings. Although these finally succeeded in 902, the Norsemen returned again in 917, to remain in possession of the city for the next two centuries, though they concentrated firmly on making money after their political power was neutered following a resounding defeat by the Irish High King Brian Bóruma at Clontarf in 1014.

Dublin's destiny took another turn when a new wave of outsiders arrived in 1169–71. This time they were Anglo-Norman adventurers invited by Dermot MacMurrough, the exiled king of Leinster, who wanted their help in restoring him to his throne. But he fatally underestimated their thirst, and that in particular of their sovereign Henry II, for power. An English occupation followed that would last for 750 years, as Dublin became the main seat of English power in Ireland, solidified by the building in 1204 of Dublin Castle. Although the city obtained limited rights – a charter of liberties in 1192, the right to elect a mayor in 1229 – and became the seat of an Irish parliament in 1297, these were rights for the English and their descendants; the population of around 7,000 crowded into a small wedge of land south of the Liffey did not include the native Irish, who were kept firmly out.

As English power became less certain in much of Ireland, Dublin became the centre of the "Pale", a defended area around the city and its hinterland, which did not stop a Scottish army under Robert the Bruce's brother Edward from threatening the town in 1315. Gradually the English came to rely on local magnates such as the FitzGerald Earls of Kildare to enforce their will. But a series of revolts shook their trust, such as one in 1487 that tried to install the pretender Lambert Simnel – claiming to be the son of Edward IV, and one of the missing "Princes in the Tower", but in truth probably a baker's son – as king, and another in 1534 by "Silken Thomas", the 10th Earl, that came close to taking Dublin Castle. As a result, Henry VIII declared himself King of Ireland and the English crown took more direct control of affairs. The Reformation that followed created a new divide between the Irish (almost universally

Roman Catholic), who were excluded from the city, and English and Scottish incomers (largely Protestant), who came in increasing numbers. The renewed English interest brought new facilities, such as the foundation in 1592 of Trinity College, Ireland's first university, on the site of an old Augustinian friary. Yet it also fostered increasing dissent amongst the old Irish nobility, which broke out in the Nine Years' War in 1593, during which an English garrison was billeted in Dublin, whose gunpowder store near Wood Quay exploded in 1597 – the gap in the houses can be seen on Speed's map – killing 126 people.

Although calm was restored, and the city gained a new customs house in 1621 and its first theatre, on Werburgh Street, by 1637 – set up by John Ogilby, a Scottish-born entrepreneur, who later turned his hand to cartography after he was forced to flee Dublin – a new spasm of violence racked Ireland. The 12,000-strong army of Oliver Cromwell landed in Dublin to exact a terrible revenge for the Irish support of the Royalists in the English Civil War, which included the unintended punishment of a plague in 1650, spread by the soldiers, that wiped out half the city's population.

In its aftermath, and with effective opposition to English rule suppressed for over a century, Dublin began its shift from medieval to modern city. It received an influx of settlers – many of them Huguenots, Protestant refugees from the revocation of religious toleration in France in 1685 – and the population rose from 20,000 in 1640 to 60,000 by the end of the century. New amenities appeared, including Phoenix Park in 1662 and the Royal Hospital (for military veterans) in 1684, and a second bridge was built over the Liffey in 1670. The pace accelerated in the Georgian era, with the construction of new elegant squares such as Merrion Square, built in 1762, and the opening of the Botanic Gardens in 1795.

This era of muted tolerance and gracious cultural life – which saw luminaries such as Oliver Goldsmith and William Congreve active in Dublin's literary scene – came to a grinding halt in 1801 when the Act of Union absorbed Ireland into the United Kingdom, abolishing its parliament and rendering Dublin (from the Westminster government's point of view) a political backwater. Agitation for political rights grew – Catholics had been excluded from owning property and also from the professions since 1695. In 1841, Daniel O'Connell became the first Roman Catholic mayor since the 17th century.

During his tenure, Dublin stood on the brink of a new transformation: the railways arrived in 1834, with an 11-kilometre link to the port at Dún Laoghaire, and the centre had been provided with its first gas lights in 1825 (with electricity to follow in 1881). The population continued to grow, as many left destitute by the Potato Famine in 1845–52 flooded into Dublin, creating enormous social and health problems in the overcrowded tenements that sprang up. By 1900 the population had begun to grow again after a period of stagnation, and had reached 400,000. It was only 21 years later, after an uprising in the city at Easter 1916 and an effective insurgent campaign against the British, that Dublin was able to take the final step and become the capital of an independent nation. Seven hundred and fifty years after the Irish – and the Viking founders of Dublin – had lost it, the city could determine its fate once more.

DUBLINE
1610

OSTMAN or *ORMUNTOWNE*

St. M.rchants Church

St. Marys Lane

Church

St. Marys Lane

Pill Lane

The Inns

The Bridge

The Bridge Gat

Merchants Key

Wood Key

Bridge Street

Cocke Street

Rame Lane

School House Lane

St. Mich.

St. Johns ch.

Christ

St. Michaels Lane

aels ch.

Christ Church

The Mills

Ormonds Gate

New Rowe

St. Owens ch.

High Street

Skinners

The Toll

St. James's Gate

St. Iamess Street

Johns House

Tennis Court Lane

New Gate

Back Lane

St. Nicholas street

St. Nicholas church

St. Thomas Street

St. Cathrens ch.

St. Nicholas G.

St. Thom. Court

St. Francis Street

St. Patricks Street

Brid

Chur

St. Patr

New street

The Come

church

The Ancient Seal of the City of Dublin
1459

+ SIGILLVM : PRÆPOSITVRÆ : DVBLINIE +

The Hospital

The Colledge

S.t Augustines

Dames Street

S.t Andrews Church

Brid ewell

Georges Lane

ames Gate

The Castle

chal Pole

eepe Stre

St. Stevens Street

St. Peters Church

St. Stevens Church

rosse Lane

White Friers

Kevan Str

An Imperial City Finds its Way

Kyoto, c 1626

The map shown in full overleaf seems starkly utilitarian, the city blocks arrayed in a grid broken up only by the imperial palace to the north, and varied by the street names included and the diagrammatic sketches of important buildings arrayed along its border. Yet the plan marks a new beginning, both for Kyoto, which had been deprived of its position as imperial capital of Japan just a few decades before, and for mapping, as it marks the first city map in Japanese history intended for use by ordinary people, as opposed to bureaucrats.

Although a little unwieldy to carry around at 116 by 54 cm (45 by 21 inches), the Kyoto plan was a pioneer, certainly for Asia, and it predated "pocket maps" that appeared in Europe, such as Robert Sayer's 1765 map, by a century and a half. It probably dates from around 1626 – the "licensed quarter", Kyoto's red-light district, where geishas and less refined company could be found, was moved to Shimabara, off the area of the map, in 1641.

Kyoto has been Japan's cultural heart for over 1,200 years, for the first eight centuries also acting as its capital city. Its retention of its status marks it out as one of only a very few cities – including Luang Prabang in Laos, Mandalay in Myanmar and Kraków in Poland – that have retained their aura as the cultural soul of a country long after losing their political role.

The city was established as the royal residence in 794 by Emperor Kanmu, who was keen to escape the increasingly suffocating influence of the Buddhist hierarchy in the former capital of Nara. As a consequence, it at first had relatively few Buddhist temples, though the grand 90-metre- (98-yard-) wide boulevard of Suzaku-oji, which led from the imperial palace, was flanked at its southern exit from the city – the imposing two-storey Rashomon gate – by the To-ji ("East Temple") and Sai-ji ("West Temple"). Known as Heian-kyo, or simply Kyo-to ("the capital city"), the next four centuries saw a largely peaceful cultural flourishing, which produced the refined poetry of the *Kokinshu* ("Collection of Poems Ancient and Modern"),

one of twenty-one imperially sponsored anthologies, and, in the reign of Emperor Ichijo (986–1011), the works of two towering female writers: Sei Shonagon, author of *The Pillow Book*, a lovingly detailed account of court life; and Murasaki Shikibu, who produced *The Tale of Genji*, Japan's first novel (and one of the world's earliest).

The good times could not last forever, and the Hogen revolt of 1156 destabilised imperial rule, leading to the establishment of rule by the shoguns, warlords from the samurai class. In 1192 the shogun Minamoto no Yoritomo transferred his court to Kamakura, to the east, leaving the emperors stranded, and politically neutered, in Kyoto's imperial palace. This Kamakura period ended in 1333 when Shogun Ashikaga Takauji returned to Kyoto, inaugurating an era in which the city was adorned with some of its most renowned temples, including the Kinkaku-ji ("Golden Pavilion"), built in 1397, and the Gainkaku-ji ("Silver Pavilion"), erected in 1482, becoming at the same time the headquarters of many of sects of the Zen form of esoteric Buddhism.

Kyoto's tranquillity was periodically interrupted by fires which tore through the wooden buildings of the capital, one of which, the Angen Fire in May 1177, destroyed much of the palace, and by earthquakes, the largest of which in August 1185 devastated large parts of the city. Perhaps the worst disaster, though, was political, when the shogunate, and with it Japan's unity, dissolved in the 15th century, culminating in the Onin War (1467–77) in which much of the city was reduced to ruins amid street fighting between rival samurai factions.

Japan, and Kyoto, would not be knit back together for a century, until a series of warlords with grander vision – Oda Nobunaga, Toyotomi Hideyoshi and Tokugawa Ieyasu – defeated their rivals and restored central control. Yet that control was not to be exercised from Kyoto. In 1603, the victorious Tokugawa Ieyasu inaugurated the Tokugawa shogunate which would rule Japan for the next 265 years, but he chose as his capital, not Kyoto, but the parvenu city of Edo (which then became known as Tokyo, "eastern capital").

The emperors, though, remained immured and powerless within the walls of the imperial palace in Kyoto. Partly as a result, and partly because the Tokugawa shoguns, despite abandoning it as a capital, still invested in its reconstruction, Kyoto experienced a renaissance. The next century saw the emergence of the refined culture of the tea ceremony, of Noh theatre and of flower arranging. Where bureaucrats abandoned the city, merchants moved in, increasing its prosperity as compensation for its lack of political power. Despite setbacks such as the Great Tenmei Fire that once again destroyed the imperial palace in 1788, its experience, during Japan's period of isolation from the 1630s when the Tokugawa excluded almost all foreigners and sought to limit foreign influence, gave its original name of Heian-kyo ("city of peace and tranquillity") a real resonance once more.

The last shogun was deposed and imperial power restored in 1868, but the young Emperor Meiji chose to move his residence to Tokyo. For the first time in over a thousand years, the palace at Kyoto had no emperor. But once again Kyoto survived the transition, becoming in the 20th century the heart of Japan's burgeoning film industry, one of whose masterpieces, by the director Kurosawa Akira (1910–98) takes its title *Rashomon* from Kyoto's iconic gateway. Surviving the Second World War relatively unscathed – the US Secretary of War Henry Stimson ordered that it not be targeted in mass air raids – it recovered rapidly after 1945, becoming a major industrial centre, including hi-tech businesses such as the game and software manufacturer Nintendo. It also gained a reputation as Japan's culinary capital, with Kyoryori ("Kyoto cuisine"), based on soybean products, attracting connoisseurs from Japan and overseas. And Kyoto's rich history has given it a sense of the importance of preserving the future: known as the "soul of the nation" in Japan, it sought, as the venue of the conference which agreed the Kyoto Protocol on limiting greenhouse gases in 1997, to be the world's conscience.

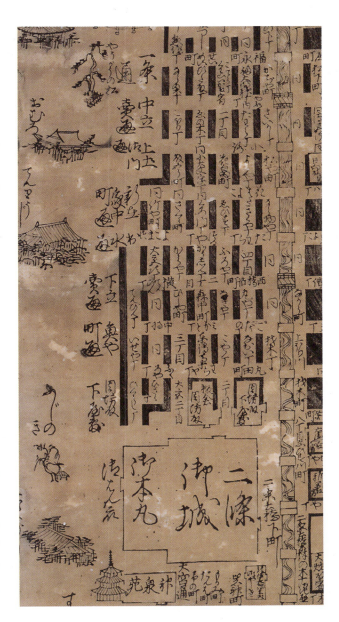

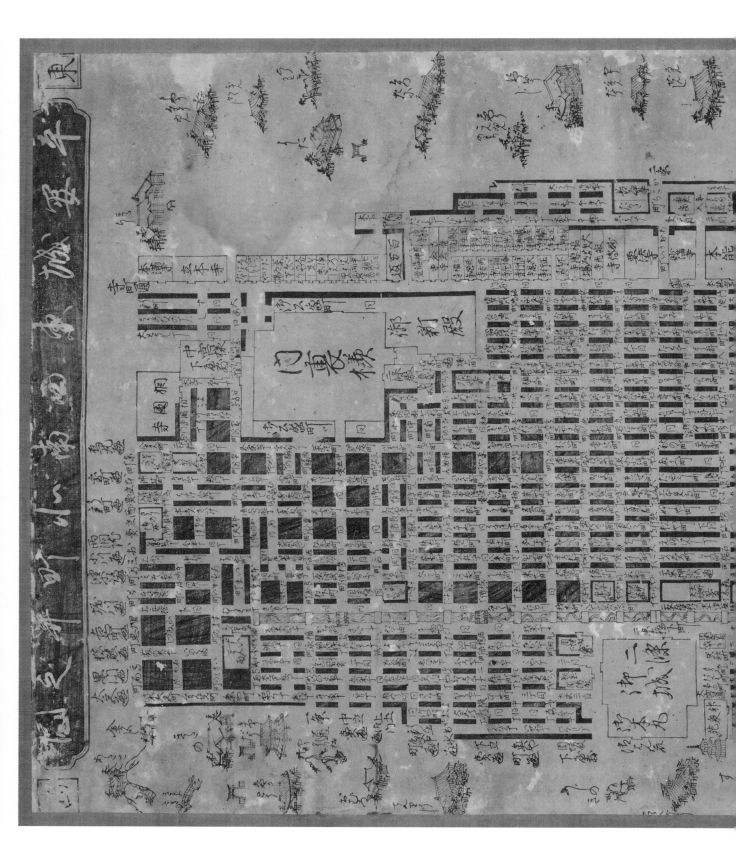

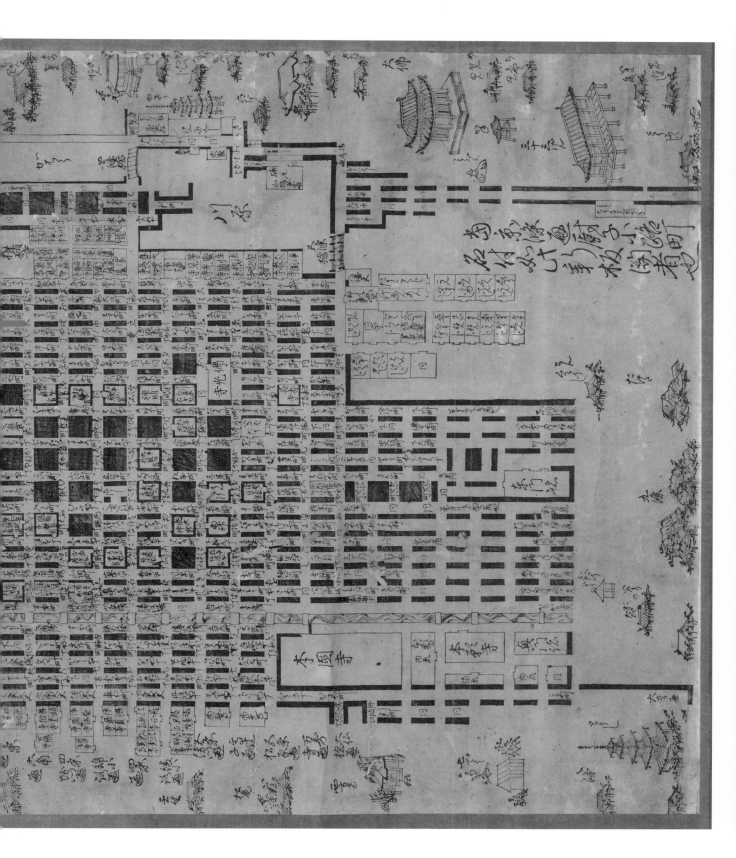

Northern Powerhouse

Stockholm, 1640

The map (shown in full overleaf) was produced in Denmark and shows Stockholm in the mid-17th century, a time when it sat at the heart of an unlikely European and global empire which gave Swedes a taste for internationalism and its monarchs the funds to create a city of gracefully assured architecture that made the most of its island archipelago setting.

The city was founded in 1252 by Birger Jarl, a Swedish noble who sought to establish a stronghold that would dominate trading routes through Lake Mälaren and overshadow the far older Viking-founded town of Birka nearby. He did his work well: two sons, Valdemar and Magnus became kings of Sweden and a cluster of buildings grew up in a maze of streets in the Gamla Stan (Old Town), dominated by what would become Stockholm Cathedral, a Franciscan monastery (now the Riddarholmen Church) – both begun in the 1270s – and the royal castle on the northeast corner of the island. Its prosperity was fuelled by German merchants and an early development of a civic consciousness (which thoughtfully decreed that those murdering a person in a public square before midday be fined 80 marks, but reduced the fine for afternoon homicides to half that level). With a population of a mere 5,000 in the 15th century, and ambitiously described as the "capital of the realm" in a 1436 charter, Stockholm's ascent to Scandinavian powerhouse only really began when Gustav Vasa threw off Danish rule in 1523 (which had become fatally unpopular after the massacre of 80 noble opponents of the Danes in 1520).

Enriched by trade in salt and iron, Stockholm's wealth grew sufficiently for it to outlaw new wooden buildings in 1552, while the coming of the Reformation and the secularisation of church property released new areas for development. But it was in the reign of Gustavus Adolphus, who ascended the throne in 1611, aged 16, that it became the capital of an empire. Sweden's greatest general, his intervention on the Protestant side in the multi-layered Thirty Years' War (1618–48) brought stunning victories and control of large parts of northern Germany, Estonia and northern Latvia, until his premature death in the latter stages of the Battle of Lützen against the Habsburgs in 1632. A global dimension was added by the acquisition of "New Sweden", a lodgement in previously Dutch-controlled Delaware that lasted 17 years (1638–55), control of a string of forts on the Gold Coast (modern Ghana) that was even more short-lived (between 1650 and 1663) and a vanishingly ephemeral presence at a fort at Parangipettai in Tamil Nadu in India that survived a mere month in 1733.

Gustavus's reign saw the earliest signs of formal city-planning, as the city's first governor Admiral Clas Larsson Fleming laid out Norrmalm, the northern section of Stockholm, with an elegant grid-pattern contrasting with the labyrinthine Gamla Stan. In 1642 the first *slussen* (lock), connecting arteries between the city's islands and linking those to the mainland, was built between Gamla Stan and the island of Södermalm, and long elegant boulevards such as the Drottninggatan appeared. Even more ambitious plans were devised by the French architect Nicodemus Tessin the Elder, appointed city architect in 1661, but the sheer expense led to numerous delays until a disastrous fire in 1697 razed the old fort, forcing the beginning of its redevelopment into Stockholm Palace. Even then, the disastrous defeat of King Karl XII against the Russian Tsar Peter the Great at Poltava in 1709, which led to a five-year period of enforced exile in Ottoman Moldavia, halted further development, and a bout of bubonic plague in 1710 which killed 18,000 Stockholmers subdued the appetite for expensive projects.

Largely shorn of its empire, Stockholm recovered as the 18th century progressed. The royal palace was finally completed in 1754, its more than 600 rooms mercifully untouched by the Great Stockholm Fire five years later which destroyed 300 buildings in Södermalm. Under Gustav III (reigned 1771–92), the city acquired its first theatres and a new grand set-piece square, the Gustav Adolfs torg, though his taste for absolutist rule led to his assassination in 1792 at a masquerade ball in the Opera House he had commissioned.

The 19th century brought industrialisation. Stockholm acquired its first gaslighting in 1853, and its first proper sewerage system in 1861 (helping to allay the threat of cholera, which killed 3,500 Stockholm residents in 1834), while trains reached the city in 1860 (although its central station did not open until 1871). Sweden remained resolutely neutral during the two World Wars (though food shortages caused hunger riots in Stockholm in 1917) and stood aloof from Nato until fears arising from the Russian invasion of Ukraine caused it to join in 2024. Its social and economic model, guided by the Social Democratic Party which governed the country with few breaks for a century from 1917, was widely admired, and Stockholm Concert Hall's role as the venue for the annual Nobel Prize giving ceremony brought the city further international attention. Though no longer a first-rank political or military power, culturally and diplomatically Stockholm remains a northern powerhouse.

Half the World in a Square

Isfahan, 1657

The view of the Iranian city of Isfahan comes from the *Theatrum Urbium* ("Town Atlas"), a compilation of 500 town plans published by the Dutch cartographer Johannes Janssonius as part of his mammoth 11-volume *Novus Atlas Absolutissimus*. Originally engraved by the Swiss master Matthäus Merian, it depicts an orderly, yet crowded cityscape of green tile domes and ochre brickwork, dominated by the vast open space of the Maydan-e Naqsh-e Jahan, the "Image of the World Square".

It is this, and in particular the architectural assemblage which encircles it, that gives the city its proverbial nickname in Farsi, *"Esfahan nesf-e Jahan"* ("Isfahan is half the world"). At 560 by 160 metres (1,837 by 525 feet) it is one of the world's largest squares, though dwarfed by others such as Beijing's Tiananmen Square (at about 880 by 500 metres, or 2,890 by 1,640 feet) and, largest of all, Xinghai Square in Dalian (also in China) which covers a massive 1.1 million square metres (nearly half a square mile). Such public spaces, like Mexico City's Zócalo or London's Trafalgar Square, have always been the symbolic heart of the city and the epicentre of public discontent, in riots and demonstrations against the government in power: Paris's Place de la Concorde was a key gathering place during the French Revolution and Cairo's huge Tahrir Square saw large-scale occupations during the Arab Spring protests of 2010–11.

Isfahan, though, is special. Its splendour springs from the vision of one man: Shah Abbas (reigned 1587–1629), greatest of the Safavid rulers of Iran, who took a settlement that was already at least 2,000 years old and thoroughly remodelled it as an imperial capital. High on the central Iranian plateau, Isfahan (whose name may come from *aspadana*, "place of the army gathering") coalesced from two smaller towns: Jay to the east, which existed by Achaemenid times around 600BC, and the smaller Yahudiyah, which originally had a significant Jewish population. Under Toghril Beg (reigned 1037–63) it had become capital of the Seljuk Empire, which stretched from Central Asia to the Aegean, and, according to the Persian poet Nasir i-Khusraw, was adorned with "fine tall buildings and a beautiful Friday mosque".

Almost all of this, save the Friday mosque, was destroyed during two centuries in which Isfahan suffered a series of devastating sacks, beginning with several by the Mongols between 1226–1241. Then, in 1387 the Mongol warlord Tamerlane retook it after a revolt in which his garrison had been slaughtered and, in revenge, ordered "the carpet of pity be folded up". Among the 70,000 killed were 7,000 children taken outside the city and trampled to death by the Mongol cavalry. In the aftermath of the massacre, the historian Hafiz-i Abru came across 28 towers, each containing 1,500 skulls of the decapitated victims. In the 1460s, Isfahan was destroyed yet again by the Qara Qoyunlu, a tribe of Turkoman nomads, who slaughtered 50,000 of its inhabitants.

So, when Shah Abbas I was in search of a new base far enough east of the then capital of Tabriz to be safe from the predatory designs of the Ottoman Turks, the Safavids' perennial regional rivals, Isfahan was an obvious choice. The city was partly in ruins, and badly in need of reconstruction. The shah appointed the poet, philosopher and astronomer Sheikh Baha al-Din as chief architect, and in 1590 work began.

Baha al-Din's implementation of Shah Abbas's vision was a triumph. The open space of the maydan was bordered by a perimeter of arcaded shops, a water channel in black marble and a line of plane trees. The frantic pace of commerce that was conducted on the square's edges was matched by the carnival atmosphere of the dancing, poetry recitals and equestrian archery competitions (with golden quivers of arrows given by the shah as prizes) which took place in its centre.

Most stunning of all was the trio of formal buildings he erected. On the west was the square bulk of the Ali Qapu palace, part pavilion and part gateway to the private royal quarter of Bagh-e Naqsh e-Jahan which lay behind it. Opposite, on the eastern side (and accessible by a private tunnel from the royal palace) was the Sheikh Lotfollah Mosque, begun in 1602, with cappuccino-coloured domes and an interior of *haft-rangi*, seven-coloured tiles that became a Safavid hallmark. The climax of the building programme was the Masjid-e Shah, the Royal Mosque, built at the end of Shah Abbas's reign, entered by a grandiose 30-metre- (98-foot-) high portal, and with a dome of resplendent turquoise tiles that soared to 52 metres (170 feet) high.

Even the Maydan did not exhaust Abbas's ambitions. In 1596 he ordered the building of the Chahar Bagh ("the four gardens"), an imposing 50-metre- (164-foot) wide, 2.5-kilometre (1.5-mile) avenue lined with gardens (including the enticingly named Gardens of the Nightingale and Mulberry Gardens) which were open to the people, and with a central marble water channel and trees to provide respite during the searingly hot summer months. The Chahar Bagh crossed the Zayanderud river, which divided Isfahan in two, at the imposing Si-os-se Pol (the 33-span bridge, which extended 300 metres or 328 yards across the river).

The European travellers who came to the Iranian court were impressed, most notably the Frenchman Jean Chardin, author of a 10-volume work on Iran, who spent four years there in the 1670s and counted 162 mosques in the city.

To them, much of the information which then appeared on Janssonius's map is owed, though it lacks the new suburbs that sprang up as Shah Abbas's reign progressed, such as Abbasabad to the west, populated by refugees from Tabriz who fled during the Ottoman–Safavid war of 1610, and Julfa, the Armenian quarter south of the Zayanderud, which had 30 churches by 1722.

In 1629 Shah Abbas died, moving his biographer to remark the "radiant sun, in the shadow of whose justice men lived in tranquillity had set". For the Safavids, it heralded a slow dusk. Although Shah Abbas II built the Chihil Sutun ("40 Columns") palace in 1647 and the Hasht Behesht ("Eight Heavens Palace") to the southwest in the 1660s, the final generations of Safavids were political ciphers and in 1722 the last, Soltan Hosayn, was deposed by an invading Afghan army led by Mahmud Ghilzai. Reduced to eating shoe leather during the Afghan siege of their city, the people of Isfahan saw their former shah beheaded four years later and his head sent to the Ottoman general who was attacking the city.

Although it had become an urban giant of 600,000 people, Isfahan's days as the centre of political power were over: the capital moved, first in 1736 to Mashhad, then to Shiraz, before finally settling on Tehran in 1786. For Iranians, though, and especially Esfahanis, Isfahan and the Maydan-e Naqsh-e Jahan would forever remain "half the world".

ISP

A . *Maidan* .
B . *Alla capi* .
C . *Ædes Regis* .
D . *Mestzid Mehedi* .
E . *Tzil mestzil* .

F . *Baſ*
G . *Kele*
H . *Kala*
I . *Cæn*
K . *Cænd*

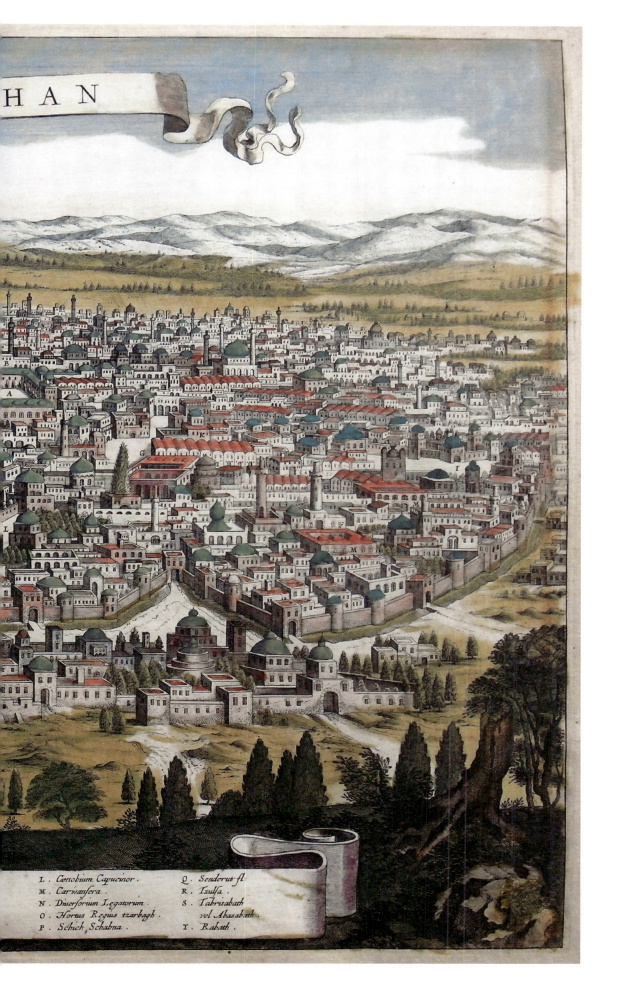

HAN

L . *Coenobium Capucinor.*   Q . *Senderut fl.*
M . *Carwansera.*   R . *Tzulfa.*
N . *Diverforium Legatorum.*   S . *Tabrisabath*
O . *Hortus Regius tzarbagh.*   *vel Abasabath.*
P . *Schich Schabna.*   T . *Rabath.*

War and Disorder

New York, 1660

The faint hint of what would become New York's famous grid pattern can be seen in the mid-17th-century map, overleaf, of New Amsterdam, the Dutch-founded forerunner of today's global financial capital. Named the Castello plan for the prominent star-shaped outline of Fort Amsterdam, established by the Dutch in 1625 to defend their tiny toehold on the southern tip of Manhattan Island, it shows some of the streets whose fame would become international in the centuries to come. Leading out of the fort is the wide strip of Broadway (or Heeren Straat, "Gentlemen's Street", in the original Dutch), which would receive its first large venue in 1798, with the opening of the Park Theatre.

At the right-hand edge of the settlement, the jagged line marks the stockade that would eventually form the line of Wall Street. Built under Governor Stuyvesant in 1653, it was set up to strengthen the defences against the local indigenous groups with whom violence had flared ever since the realisation that the bargain by which the Dutch bought Manhattan for 60 guilders' worth of trade goods from local Lenape people in 1624 had been interpreted by the Europeans as a right to drive them from their land. Almost at once it was called on, as in 1655 the Peach Tree War broke out, after a Dutch farmer shot an Indigenous American woman who was gathering peaches in his orchard, sparking a conflict in which 100 colonists and dozens of indigenous people were killed.

Cities are often scenes of violence, whether those associated with their foundation, or inflicted by invaders – such as the Mongols who devastatingly sacked Baghdad in 1258, or the German mercenaries who ransacked Rome in 1527. As tempting targets, economically or because of their strategic position, military force is frequently deployed to seize them. In this way New Amsterdam became New York when a British squadron under Colonel Richard Nicolls sailed into New York Bay in September 1664, threatening to pound the houses of the 2,000 inhabitants into dust. After a brief Dutch recapture in 1673, and a year under its most ephemeral name, New Orange, the city reverted to a century of British rule.

The crowded conditions and often disappointed hopes of city-dwellers have often sparked protests, or violent riots. Few have been as large-scale as the Nika Riot in Constantinople in 532, when partisans of the Green and Blue chariot-racing teams united to try to topple Emperor Justinian, leading to, by some estimates, 30,000 dead. As New Yorkers, along with residents of the Thirteen Colonies more generally, grew ever more discontent at their perceived under-representation and over-taxation by the British, the city experienced bouts of political turbulence. The first riot was by protesters against the imposition in 1765 of the Stamp Act – which levied a tax on all printed documents – who paraded through the streets with a coffin labelled "Liberty" and burnt an effigy of the British governor.

Although the Act was repealed the following year, violence flared again during the War of Independence as revolutionary and loyalist mobs clashed and the city was reduced to a state of anarchy. With order restored after the American colonists' victory, New York became the capital of the new United States between 1785 and 1790 – with what was intended to be the presidential mansion built on the site of the demolished fort. Yet it did not enjoy freedom from disorder. Its ever-growing population, which surged from 33,000 in 1790 to 270,000 in 1835, when it overtook

Philadelphia to become the United States' largest city, meant seemingly minor incidents could rapidly spiral into violence, and tensions between New York's complex mosaic of communities frequently provoked rioting. In 1788 the Doctors' Riot broke out after protests against the practice of grave-robbing by medical students, leading to a two-day orgy of violence against doctors around Columbia College (the city's oldest higher education institution, founded in 1754).

The Dog Riots of 1811 were sparked when the city authorities tried to levy a tax on dogs and round up those whose owners would not pay, and an even more violent eruption occurred after they banned pigs from the city altogether in 1821. 1834 became known as the "Year of the Riots" as violence associated with a highly contested presidential election, riots against abolitionists and protests by stonemasons against the city's use of prison labour on new buildings led to anarchy on the streets. Most abstruse of all was the Astor Place Riot of 1849, caused when partisans of the American actor Edwin Forrest stormed the theatre where his long-time English rival William Macready was playing Macbeth, and in the ensuing mayhem, armed state militia shot 22 people dead.

The mid-19th century saw increasing clashes between the growing Irish Catholic population and Protestant evangelical groups, and during a riot in 1857 prompted by the levying of an excise duty on alcohol, gangs such as the Dead Rabbits clashed with New York City Police (a service only established in 1845). Perhaps the most serious of all were the 1863 Draft Riots, when protests by poorer German and Irish communities against the ability of the rich to avoid conscription into the army during the American Civil War, turned violent, leading to attacks on businesses and, as the mood turned uglier, onto African Americans, leading to a number of lynchings and acts of arson against their houses.

Against the seething cauldron of hope, despair and occasional anger that boiled over into violence, New York continued to grow. Its grid system was extended by the Commissioners' Plan of 1811, effective city government was made easier by the consolidation of the Five Boroughs of Brooklyn, Queens, Manhattan, the Bronx and Staten Island under one administrative umbrella in 1898. And the city acquired its iconic skyline of skyscrapers with the honing of cast-iron architecture which gave it leviathans such as the Singer Building, the tallest in the world in 1908, before it was surpassed in turn by the Metropolitan Life Tower, Woolworth, Chrysler and Empire State Buildings, and the World Trade Center (built in 1971), all of them in New York.

Down on the streets, conditions deteriorated, with violent crime becoming endemic in several districts, before a turn-around in the 1990s cut its homicide rate by three quarters. Then, in one of the most traumatic acts of violence ever inflicted on it, planes piloted by the al-Qaeda terrorist group smashed into the World Trade Center on September 11, 2001, killing nearly 3,000 people. The atrocity occurred barely half a kilometre from the old line of Wall Street, just outside the boundaries of the Castello Plan settlement. But just like the greatest cities through history, New York, which had seen a fair share of war, disorder and violence in the previous 377 years of its history, took stock, mourned and rose again.

Palace as Power

Moscow, 1662

Sometimes, buildings become the embodiment of a nation's power, an architectural epitome of its history, written in stone and domes and pillars. The Kremlin in Moscow, for centuries the centre of Russian power, of tsars and commissars, is one such, shown nestled in an arm of the city's Moskva river in the 1662 map by the Dutch cartographer Johannes Blaeu, from his *Atlas Maior*, which is shown overleaf.

Moscow, and Russia, are not the only example of former palaces becoming synonymous with the nation's rulers. In Britain, Whitehall, the nerve centre of government, is named for an episcopal residence that stood in various forms on the site from the 13th century, until sequestered by King Henry VIII in 1530 and burnt to the ground in 1698. France has its Élysée Palace, named optimistically for the Greco-Roman vision of heaven, but originally built in 1722 for the French nobleman Louis Henri de la Tour d'Auvergne, while the United States has the White House – not named, as is often supposed, for a paint job necessitated after British troops burnt it in 1814, but for the whitewash used since the late 18th century to protect its façade from cracking during the bitter Washington winters.

The Kremlin has always been the heart of Moscow. Surrounded by high walls and spread over 28 hectares (69 acres) the fortress, church and palace complex has its origins in a wooden stockade built by Prince Yuri Dolgoruky in 1156 atop the strategic Borovitsky Hill. Although it became a prosperous trading settlement, Moscow remained a minnow in the competition between early Russian principalities, dominated by nearby Vladimir-Suzdal and almost snuffed out by the invasion of the Mongols in 1236–40, during which it was comprehensively sacked.

The destruction of its nearest rival Tver, by the Mongols in 1327, coincided with the rise of Moscow as an important ecclesiastical centre, after Ivan I built the stone cathedral of the Assumption in 1326, which became the centre of the Orthodox patriarchate. Prince Dmitry Donskoy added stone walls in 1367 to create the first version resembling today's Kremlin (though they did not keep out the Mongols who sacked it in 1382). It took a century for Moscow and the Duchy of Muscovy (by now virtually the last man standing among the former Russian states) to recover. Under Ivan III (reigned 1462–1505) it did so with a vengeance, as Muscovy self-consciously took up the mantle of leader of the Orthodox Church left vacant by the fall of Constantinople to the Ottomans in 1453. He finally threw off the yoke of Mongol suzerainty, refusing to pay taxes to the Khanate of the Golden Horde (which, usefully for Ivan, then disintegrated in 1466). He imported a series of Italian architects to remodel the Kremlin on Renaissance lines, with Ridolfo Fioravanti (1415–86) rebuilding the fortress buildings in brick and creating masterpieces such as the Dormition Cathedral, consecrated in 1479, and Marco Ruffo, who in 1487–91 created the Palace of Facets, the city's oldest surviving secular building, named for the reflective quality of its sharp-edged limestone façade.

A fire that destroyed much of the centre in 1547 allowed a new wave of rebuilding under Ivan IV ("the Terrible"), which included the iconic nine domes of St Basil's Cathedral (consecrated in 1561), a new set of defences (on the site of what is now the Garden Ring ring road) and, perhaps surprisingly considering his reputation for tyranny, the city's first printing press in 1553. The "Time of Troubles" the political turbulence of the late 16th and early 17th century left the Kremlin dilapidated and choked with rubble, but the early Romanovs, beginning with Mikhail I from 1613, restored it. The city's population reached 200,000 and it expanded well beyond the Kremlin's confines into districts such as Meshchanskygorod ("peasants' town") north of the Garden Ring, settled in the late 17th century with deportees from what is now Ukraine and Belarus.

The triumphant horseback entry of Peter the Great into the city in 1710, after his comprehensive defeat of Sweden the previous year, proved to be a distinctly false dawn for Moscow, as within two years the capital had been transferred to the tsar's new foundation of St Petersburg. There was still building – the Great Kremlin Palace was constructed from 1838 to 1849 – and the location for the tsars' coronations remained the Assumption Cathedral, but the city relapsed into political irrelevance; by 1750 the population had fallen by a half.

Culturally, Moscow fared better, with the establishment of the Moscow State University in 1755, and the foundation of the Moscow Conservatoire in 1866, which ensured that musical giants such as Tchaikovsky (who headed it), Rachmaninov (who studied there from 1885), Prokofiev and Shostakovich, spent much time there, even if writers from the golden age of Russian literature, such as Dostoyevsky and Tolstoy, did not.

Moscow's period of political exile ended in 1917 with the Russian Revolution, the overthrow of the tsars leading to the transfer of the national capital away from St Petersburg. As the centre of government of the Soviet Union from 1922, the Kremlin became synonymous with international communism, the repression of dissidents and the epicentre of the Cold War. Although churches were closed, and some in the Kremlin itself demolished, the city opened a Metro system in 1935 with its stations acting as a gigantic gallery for Soviet realist art. It also received a wave of brutalist architecture, notably the "Seven Sisters" skyscrapers, among them the Moscow State University building, and thousands of soulless high-rise apartment blocks to resolve an overcrowding crisis, which saw the population reach 4 million by 1939.

Moscow had faced trial by war in 1812, when it was burnt during Napoleon's occupation of the city, and, though the advance of the Germans in the Second World War did not quite reach the centre, the disruption to the city (and wholesale destruction of the regions to its west) was considerable. Nonetheless, it recovered, weathered the collapse of the Soviet Union in 1991, a coup attempting to restore it in 1993, and the vicissitudes of the post-Soviet Russian regimes of Boris Yeltsin and Vladimir Putin. Over eight centuries since its foundation, the Kremlin remains the face of Russian power.

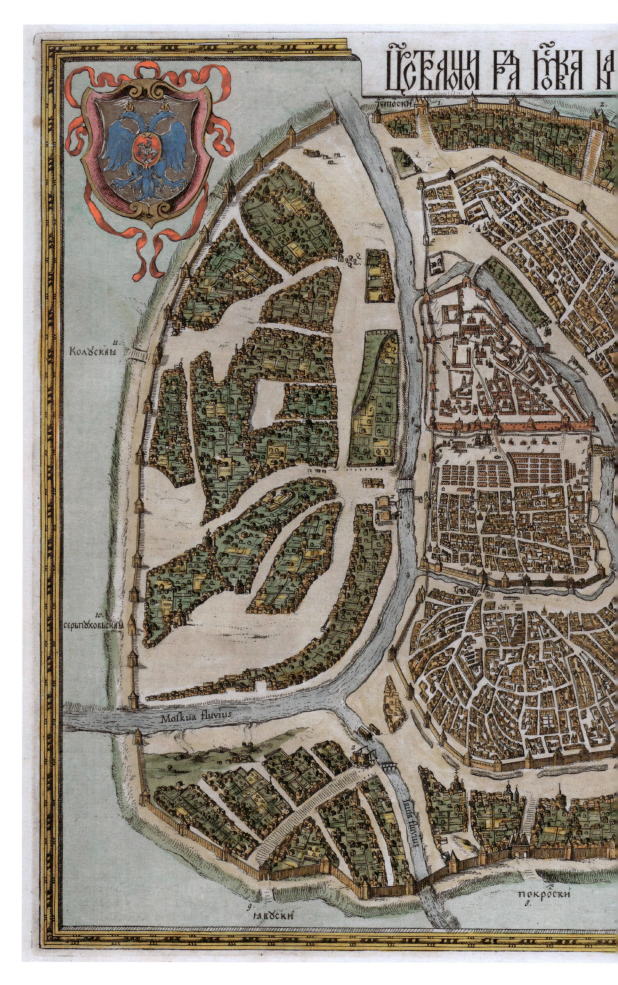

ЦСВЛЮЮ ГА ПЖА ІА

ТЕПОСКИ 1.

КОЛУСКАН 11.

серпуховьскан 10.

М오skua fluuius

Tautla fluuius

покроски 8.

навоски 9.

3. НИКНЦКН

4. ТВЕСКН

5. ДМИТРОСКН

6. ПЕТРОСКН

Neglina fluvius

остреместкн
7.

Benevole Lector, in hac tabulâ *VRBIS MOSKVÆ*
quadripartitam sectionem, aut murorum quatuor munitiones vides:
quarum intima *KITAYGOROD* dicitur, ipsaque est *VRBS*.
Huic proximè adiacet Castellum, aut Regia, muris seclusa, appellaturꝗ
KREMLENAGRAD, quæ duæ muro cinguntur Lapideo, nonnul-
lâ materiâ adiectâ. Civitas, quæ ab Oriente, Septentrione, et Occidente has
cingit *TZARGOROD* dicitur, Cæsarea civitas: muro ex albo
lapide cingitur, sed materiâ terreâ aggestâ. Extrà circumcingens has
SKORODVM nominatur, murum habet ligneum, sine ullâ terrâ;
pars huius Meridionalis, ultra flumen Moskua sita, etiam *STRELZ:*
KA SLABODA dicitur, quod domos istas milites inhabitent, et custodia
Magni Domini Cæsaris, et Magni Ducis, alijque alumni Martis.

In *KITAYGRAD*, id est, in intimâ Vrbe,
numeris suis hæc notata loca designantur.

1. Troyts; Templum Sᵗᵉ Trinitatis, etiam Hierusalem dicitur; ad quod Palmarum festo Patriarcha asino insidens, à Cæsare introducitur.
2. Turris cymbalaria templi prædicti.
3. Nalobnemeest ꝗ Conclave, seu cœna: culum è latere extructum, in quo Patriarcha diebus supplicationum nonnullos canit cantus, etiam ser: vit publicis promulgationibus.
4. Plosset, planities supplicijs dicata.
5. Porta Negline, quæ et Porta leonū nomina: tur.
6. Porta ad flumen Moskua.
7. Officinæ ocreas vendentium.
8. Tamosene. Telonium quo omnes mer: ces quæ importantur vectigal pendunt.
9. Mercatorum tabernæ, ubi omnes mer: ces venduntur.
10. Tabernæ pictorum.
11. Hospitium, quo Russi ex circumiacē: tibus urbibus hospitio excipiuntur, ut merces suas vendant.
12. Officina monetaria.
13. Aula Anglorum Moskuæ negotiantium.
14. Vosnesenie. Templum Ascensionis Christi cuius turris tegumentum deauratum est

15. Aula Mikiti Romanovits, qui Avus fuit hodiè regnantis Cesaris Michaelis Fœdorovits.
16. Aula Bulgakoviorum.
17. Aula Legatorum.
18. Aula Metropolis Novogradensis.
19. Aula Stephani Vaciliovits Godonoff.
20. Turmen, Carceres sunt.
21. Varvarsche vorod, Porta est.
22. Porta Elinschie.
23. Porta Nicolai.
24. Typographia. *de Vogelaer*
25. Aula Ioannis de Wal, postea Adriani Faes, nunc
26. Aula Michaelis Mikitovits Romanoffschi.
27. Aula Knees Petri Bonoffschio.
28. Aula Knees Andreæ Teleterske.
29. Aula Petri Mikitovits Selemetgffschi.
30. Aula Knees Boris Tzerkaske.
31. Armamentarium, quo tormenta bellica adservantur.
32. Aula tribunalis, ubi quæstiones Civiles de cernuntur et de levioribus criminibus ut furto, similibꝗ alijs suppliciū sumitur.
33. S. Nicola; Monasterium, quo crucis basiationes, formâ iuramenti fiunt, ut dubia omnia solvantur.

In *TZARGRAD*, notata sunt hæc.

1. Cæsaris equile.
2. Porta ad aquas ducens, ut inservi: at stabulis.
3. Hortus herbifer Pharmacopei Cæsarei.
4. Nova civium Curia.
5. Nosocomium.

6. Domus quâ tormenta bellica côflantur.
7. Forum equarium.
8. Aula Mercatorum Polonorum, cui con: tigua Mercatorum Armenianorū Aula.
9. Nosocomium, ubi sal et Pisces venduntur.
10. Brasnik turmen, Carcer ebriosorum.

Nomina portarum in exterioribus
Vrbibus.

1. Tzortoffskie.	5. Dmitroffskie.	9. Iauskie.
2. Orbaetskie.	6. Petroffskie.	10. Xerepagoffskie.
3. Nikitskie.	7. Oustretenskie.	11. Koluskie.
4. Tverskie.	8. Pokroffskie.	12. Froloffskie.

Duodecima porta est in muro lapideo; decima et undecima sunt tantum in ligneo muro;
nona in ligneo muro Bolbansche vorod dicitur, cui proximè adiacent sepulturæ Germano

SKORODVM has notas habet.

1. Magni Ducis hortus.
2. Aquæ calidæ seu Thermæ.
3. Forum lignarium.

A City Forged in Fire

London, 1680

London's destiny was shaped right from the start by the periodic blazes which forced its people to rebuild their hometown. The map shown in full overleaf was produced by the glazier and cartographer John Oliver (c 1616–1701). It depicts London less than 15 years after the greatest fire of them all, which swept through and destroyed four fifths of its core after sparks from a baker's shop on Pudding Lane turned into an uncontrollable conflagration one fateful September night in 1666.

London is not unique in suffering this fate: most premodern cities were built largely of wood and so were especially vulnerable to the outbreak and rapid spread of fire. Ancient Rome was chronically prone to bursting into flames; in AD64 it experienced its own "Great Fire" when most of the centre was destroyed, leading to rumours Emperor Nero had orchestrated the whole thing to make way for a new palace. More recently, Tokyo (then Edo) saw three quarters of the city razed and around 100,000 people killed in its Meireki fire in 1657 (allegedly begun when a priest tried to incinerate a cursed kimono), while the İstanbul fire of 1660 devastated two thirds of that city.

London, which was founded (as Londinium) in AD47, around four years after the Roman invasion of Britain, suffered its first major tryst with fire just 13 years later. Its strategic position athwart the best fordable (or bridgeable) position over the River Thames made it an enticing target for Boudica and her Iceni rebels, intent on chasing the Romans out of Britain. So, up in flames London went in AD60, only to be rebuilt on much the same spot. This version of London was far grander, boasting stone buildings such as a large fort, an amphitheatre and a 150-metre-long basilica (or law court) built to honour the visit of Emperor Hadrian in AD122.

Rome's control over its northernmost province grew uncertain, necessitating the building of defensive walls around AD200, which for the next millennium marked the broad bounds of the settlement. By the early 5th century the Romans had left, replaced by Anglo-Saxon invaders who initially abandoned Londinium before establishing a smaller settlement, named Lundenwic, to its west, along the modern Strand. With about 10,000 inhabitants, this was around a fifth the size of its Roman predecessor, and it seesawed between the control of the kingdoms of Essex, Mercia and, ultimately, Wessex. Surviving as a trading emporium, it became subject to the predatory designs of Danish Viking raiders, leading Alfred the Great of Wessex to move it back for safety inside the Roman walls in the 880s.

Now named Lundenburh, the city struggled on, but was again sacked by Vikings, this time led by Olaf, king of Norway, in 1014, whose attack is said to have given rise to the traditional nursery rhyme *London Bridge is Falling Down*. Before long, William of Normandy's invasion and seizure of the throne in 1066 gave London new masters. It experienced a fire then, too, during his coronation, when William's Norman guards mistook a commotion outside Westminster Abbey for an attack by an Anglo-Saxon mob and, in the ensuing chaos, neighbouring buildings were set alight.

With Norman control solidified, the city drifted a little west as the centre of government came to be in Westminster, although to the east the Normans also built the imposing White Tower, the first stage of the Tower of London, in the 1070s. They gave the city its first stone bridge, when London Bridge was rebuilt in 1209, but the structure found itself at the epicentre of another blaze, which broke out in Southwark (south of the river) in 1212. Crowds fleeing the fire became trapped on the bridge, and it is said that over 3,000 perished.

The city grew steadily over the following centuries, reaching a population of 80,000 by 1300, crammed into the winding streets inside the Roman walls. It saw the turmoil of the Peasants' Revolt in 1381, when the rebels also set the centre ablaze, burning the palace of the hated Lord Chancellor Archbishop Simon Sudbury before being dispersed by a set of faithless promises made to them by the young King Richard II. In Tudor times London burgeoned, as aristocratic residences replaced the monastic houses dissolved by Henry VIII in the 1530s (the old leper hospital of St James became St James's Palace). Theatres appeared, beginning with the imaginatively named "The Theatre" in Shoreditch in 1576, and grand new developments mushroomed, such as the Piazza of Covent Garden in 1632.

Disaster struck in 1665, with the outbreak of plague in the city's unsanitary streets, killing around 70,000 people (about a fifth of the population) by the following year. Scarcely had the city drawn breath than high winds turned the minor fire in Thomas Faryner's bakery into an all-consuming inferno. The Great Fire blazed for three full days from September 2, and in its aftermath around 80 per cent of the city had been turned to ashes. The diarist John

Evelyn recorded the terror of those nights and the "noise and cracking and thunder of the impetuous flames, the shrieking of women and children ... like a hideous storm".

Fortunately, there were few human casualties, but more than 13,000 buildings had been destroyed, among them St Paul's Cathedral, its destruction accelerated by the large number of books stored within it for safekeeping. The rebuilding began almost at once. A first plan was presented just six days after the fire by Christopher Wren, which involved the carving of broad highways and boulevards through the old labyrinth of the city. This was dismissed, and in any case, Londoners had already begun clearing away the ruins and returning to their old homes. By October 10, surveyors were appointed, whose ranks John Oliver joined in 1670, and by

1671 the foundations of 8,394 restored buildings had been laid out. In June 1675 the first stone of the new St Paul's was laid, by which time Oliver was also part of the team of its principal architect Christopher Wren.

Oliver's map shows a city rebuilt largely on the footings of the old. The urge to restore, rather than to revolutionise, the cityscape was just too strong, and the practical need for speed rather than lengthy contemplation, too compelling. London's Great Fire, though, would remain seared in the popular imagination as one of the defining moments in its arc of development, alongside the Blitz of 1940–41 which wrought similar destruction, and, for those who remembered its Roman history, of the Boudican fire which came at the city's very beginning.

A Mapp of the Cityes of LONDON & WESTMINSTER & Burrough of SOUTHWARK

Names of Places contain'd in this Mapp

1 Westminster Abby
2 Westminster Hall
3 Palace Yard
4 Privy Trance
5 Old Palace yard
6 Privy Garden
7 Banqueting house
8 Whitehall Court
9 St James House
10 Spring Garden
11 Clarendon house
12 St Iames's Market
13 May Market
14 The Mewes
15 Leicester house
16 Newport House
17 Charing Crosse
18 Suffolk house
19 Covent garden Church
20 Bedford House
21 St Giles's

22 Long Acre
23 Drury Lane
24 The Strand
25 The Maypole
26 St Clements
27 Essex House
28 Arundell house
29 Somerset house
30 The Savoy
31 Worcester house
32 Clare Market
33 Bassett Court
34 Arrillery yard
35 The Temple
36 Lincolns Inn
37 Grays Inn
38 Furnivall Inn
39 Staton Garden
40 Chancery Lane
41 St Dunstans
42 Flert Street

Places in Southwark
1 St Mary Overs
2 St Olaves
3 St Thomas's
4 St George's
5 St Magdalen's
6 The Old Abby
7 Winchester house
8 The Kings Bench
9 The Marshallsea
10 The Bare garden

The Road to Uxbridge

St James's

Parke

St James's Feilds

THE RIVER THAMES

Westminster bridge

Parliament stairs

Bare of Tuth feilds

Lambeth marsh

St George's

LAMBETH

Lambeth bridge
Lambeth Ferrey

SOUTHWARK

Fields

Kensington

Kensington

Ibhn Oliver fecit

Two Hundred Years of Solitude

Nagasaki, 1680

The *Nagasaki ezu* ("Illustrated Nagasaki Map") shown overleaf was produced in Japan around 1680 and was collected by the German physician and naturalist Engelbert Kaempfer (1651–1716) during his two-year sojourn from 1690 to 1692 in Nagasaki. Kaempfer (who also travelled widely in Iran and Russia) served as chief physician to the Dutch merchants, the sole foreigners permitted to reside there, and amassed a huge collection of Japanese manuscripts and paintings, although his *History of Japan* was only published posthumously in 1727.

Although by Kaempfer's time, the Japanese authorities kept outsiders penned in Dejima, the fan-shaped artificial island in the centre of the map, the city owed its very origins to the gradual penetration of Japan by Europeans in the 16th century. They came first in the form of Fernão Mendes Pinto (c 1509–83), a serial adventurer whose tales of his epic travels across Asia, during which he claimed to have been enslaved 17 times and had his thumbs severed for plundering the Ming imperial tombs in China, were so fabulous that they became a byword for outrageous lies.

In 1543, one of Pinto's many shipwrecks saw him cast ashore on Tanegashima, an island around 300 kilometres (185 miles) southeast of Nagasaki. His reports of the rich country he had stumbled upon brought more Portuguese: Jesuit missionaries led the way in 1549, followed by merchant ships which arrived in Hirado, north of Nagasaki, the following year. At first the burgeoning trade suited both parties, with the Portuguese exchanging Chinese silks and other textiles for silver, but the trade brought two more problematic imports. The first were Portuguese firearms, arquebuses that were soon copied and manufactured by the Japanese, and which threatened to further destabilise a Japan already racked by civil war between its *daimyo* warlords. The second was Christianity, with the Jesuits evangelising large numbers of ordinary Japanese, but also succeeding in converting several daimyo, most notably Omura Sumitada, who was baptised in 1563.

Sumitada took his new religion seriously, ordering the destruction of Shinto shrines and Buddhist temples, and in 1571 granting the Portuguese a small fishing village and harbour at Nagasaki. Under the stewardship of the Captain-Major Tristão Vaz da Veiga, the new trading settlement grew rapidly: eight years later it already had 400 houses, its prosperity ensured by the profits from the "Great Ship" that came annually from the Portuguese trading station at Macao. In 1580 Sumitada handed over control of the infant town to the Jesuits, who then ran Nagasaki as an extra-territorial enclave for the next seven years.

The Portuguese, though, had over-reached themselves, the growing number of Christian converts causing grave concern to Toyotomi Hideyoshi, the warlord who was then in the process of bringing an end to Japan's nearly 150 years of disunity. In 1587 he seized back control of the town and ordered the Christian missionaries expelled. His order was only partially obeyed, and so to reinforce his point, in 1597 Hideyoshi ordered the crucifixion of 26 Japanese Christians in Nagasaki.

The reunification of Japan was completed by Tokugawa Ieyasu in 1603, and under his rule, and the line of Tokugawa shoguns that followed, the eradication of foreign influences was conducted with increasing ruthlessness. To dilute the power of the Portuguese, the shogun allowed the Dutch East India Company to establish a trading factory at Hirado in 1609, joined by their English counterparts in 1613. In 1614, Catholicism was outlawed, beginning a wave of persecutions in which thousands of Japanese converts were executed, and most of the Christian daimyo renounced their new religion.

In 1637, thousands of Japanese Christian peasants rose up around Shimabara, to the east of Nagasaki, in opposition to heavy taxation melding with resentment at the persecutions to produce a last, potent, spasm of rebellion. The uprising was only put down with the assistance of a Dutch gunboat, and in its aftermath the last Portuguese merchants were expelled. The shogunate had already begun the building of the artificial island of Dejima in Nagasaki harbour, as a post in which to confine foreign traders. The Dutch, now the only European merchants allowed to reside in Japan – Chinese traders continued to operate relatively freely – moved into Dejima in 1641 and for the next two hundred years were virtually the only foreigners who visited Japan under its strict policy of *sakoku*, or isolation. Nagasaki, whose population had reached 15,000 by 1690, once again became something of a backwater, although its role as Japan's only window to the outside world is reflected in the care with which the foreign boats are drawn on the *Nagasaki ezu* map.

Much of the city was destroyed in a serious fire in 1663, necessitating a programme of rebuilding which included the construction of a new Chinese quarter in 1689. Kaempfer arrived the following year, penning a portrait of a city already half a century into its period of isolation. A partial easing in 1720 came when a ban on the import of Dutch books was lifted, causing many Japanese scholars to move to Nagasaki to study *rangaku* ("Dutch learning"), which began the slow infiltration of European scientific ideas into Japan.

Kaempfer was able to visit Edo (now Tokyo), the shogunal capital, twice, as part of the annual Dutch tribute journeys there. One of the few non-Dutch foreigners to obtain this privilege was the German physician and naturalist Franz von Siebold, who established Japan's first European-style medical school in Nagasaki in 1824, but was expelled from the country five years later, when a search of a Dutch vessel that had run aground revealed a cache of maps of Japan which he had illegally copied. Change finally came in 1853, when a United States expedition under Commodore Matthew Perry forced its way into Tokyo Harbour, extracting treaties from the shogun, which opened Nagasaki to American traders, followed by the British in 1854.

A formal treaty in 1858 gave European and American merchants significant commercial privileges, which were partially revoked in 1899 when the city became a free port, in which all could trade on equal terms. Among those who took advantage of the new-found freedoms were the *kakure kirisitan*, a community of around 30,000 crypto-Catholics who had remained hidden around Nagasaki for three centuries, concealing their prayers as Buddhist chants, and modifying statues of the Virgin Mary and saints to conform to Buddhist iconography.

Nagasaki's efflorescence as an international trading post was short, with commerce drying up after the Russo–Japanese War of 1904–05. Instead, the city became a centre for heavy industry, particularly the shipbuilding and steel enterprises established by Mitsubishi and the Mitsubishi-Urakami Ordnance works. As a result, it became a prime target for US strategic bombers during the Second World War, and on August 9, 1945, suffered the second (and to date the last) use of a nuclear weapon in combat, dropped by a US Boeing B-29 Superfortress. Nagasaki had only been the back-up target, but heavy cloud over the primary target of Kokura, 150 kilometres (93 miles) to the northeast, meant that the "Fat Man" bomb killed 35,000 people almost instantly, condemned tens of thousands more to radiation-induced diseases, and destroyed around 40 per cent of the city's buildings.

Once again, Nagasaki had to be rebuilt, producing today's ultramodern city of around 400,000 inhabitants. Only a few of its ancient buildings survived, among them the Sofokuji Chinese temple, built in 1629, which stands as a melancholy reminder of Nagasaki's two centuries of solitude and the forces from the outside world that have brought it successively prosperity, turbulence and destruction.

From Company Town to Regional Powerhouse

Jakarta, 1681

Batavia (as Jakarta was known until 1942) has an air of orderly trade – signalled by the eleven ships outside its harbour – and well-regulated governance, which is indicated by the regular grid pattern of streets and canals, on the map and accompanying panorama shown overleaf. It was published by the Italian historian Gregorio Leti (1630–1701), who possessed a unique capacity for upsetting his patrons, having to move from Italy after writing a scurrilous biography of Pope Sixtus V, then later transferring to England where a promising start with a commission from Charles II to write a history of England turned sour when he also published a book of anecdotes which mortally offended the king.

The Amsterdam where Leti ended up was the headquarters of the *Verenigde Oost-Indische Compagnie* (VOC), the Dutch East India Company. Founded in 1602, it acted as an umbrella for merchants from the Netherlands participating in the lucrative trade in spices such as nutmeg and cloves from the islands of the Indonesian archipelago. The VOC needed an eastern headquarters to co-ordinate its operations, and the most obvious ports, such as Malacca, were already occupied by the Portuguese who had entered the area around a century earlier.

Instead, the Dutch chose a site at the mouth of the Ciliwung river in northern Java, where the Portuguese had tried to secure a lodgement in the 1520s, but had been driven out by the Sultan of Banten. By 1610 they had secured an agreement to build a warehouse, but the local prince granted the English a similar privilege in 1615. A trade war ensued, and in 1618 an English fleet besieged the small fort at Jayakarta which Jan Pieterszoon Coen, the company's governor-general in the east, had built.

Coen's response was decisive. Having driven off the English, he attacked Jayakarta and razed it to the ground. On its ruins he built an entirely new Dutch colonial city, whose design self-consciously echoed the canals of those back home in Amsterdam. Even the architecture, with steep roofs and stepped gables, resembled those of the Dutch capital, and its overall layout was influenced by the work of the Dutch mathematician and engineer Simon Stevin, whose "Plan for an Ideal City", published posthumously in

1650, had a canal bisecting his vision of urban utopia. The city, named Batavia after the pre-Roman group of people who lived in the area of the Netherlands, existed for trade. Its harbour, protected by an enlarged fort (and walls which were completed by 1645) was lined with warehouses stacked with spices, and later with tea, coffee and silks. It generated fabulous wealth, above all for the Dutch merchants, but also for their Chinese counterparts, who in 1673 made up around a tenth of the population of 27,000.

Batavia was a city with rigid hierarchies. The Europeans tended to live along the Tijgergracht ("tiger canal") in the southeast of the city (at the top right of the urban area on the map, which is oriented with east at the top), together with their richer Chinese counterparts, while the local Sundanese lived in the north, together with the Mardijkers, a sixth of the population, who were Portuguese-speaking Christians – a legacy of the brief Portuguese engagement in the area. Outside the city walls lived 13,000 enslaved people who worked on the 131 sugar mills and plantations that dotted the surrounding rural area.

Sultan Agung of Mataram, the strongest local ruler, tried to expel the Dutch, but two sieges in 1628 and 1629 failed, in part through the disease which afflicted his army (and also killed Coen during the second siege). Instead, an uneasy co-existence was patched up, with VOC troops occasionally acting as enforcers for the Mataram sultans during the 17th and 18th centuries in exchange for their tolerance of the company's trading activities.

Coen had hoped that large-scale Dutch migration would transform Batavia from the mixed population that emerged into a mainly Dutch town. But its reputation for unhealthiness – malaria outbreaks were rife and 85,000 people died of the disease between 1733 and 1795 – meant few came to settle permanently. Tensions between the Europeans and other ethnic groups also festered: in 1740 the VOC suspected the Chinese community of planning a rebellion, and repressive measures spiralled into a general massacre of the Chinese, in which around 10,000 were killed.

By then, the VOC's grip on the eastern trade was waning, as the British and French muscled in on its colonial

empire, and profits from the spice trade dried up. In 1799, bankrupt and its charter expired, the VOC dissolved, and the Netherlands government took direct control of its possessions. A brief period of British control during the Napoleonic Wars during which Sir Stamford Raffles toyed with the idea of making Batavia, and not Singapore, the main British base in the east ended after five years in 1816.

Batavia reverted to being a neglected colonial backwater, although the building of a new port at Tanjung Priok in 1886 would reap dividends in the future. The city's population expanded as Europeans moved out of the centre, where the canals had become stagnant breeding grounds for malarial mosquitoes, and, as an 18th-century visitor commented, did "exhale an intolerable stench". By 1900, there were around 115,000 inhabitants strung out on a 12-kilometre (7.5-mile) arch of land running north to south through the old settlement.

Increasingly, that population aspired for freedom from Dutch colonial control, while the Japanese occupation between 1942 and 1945 (during which the city reverted to

a version of its old name as Jakarta) destabilised European rule. Independence, declared in 1945, was recognised by the Netherlands government in 1949, with Jakarta as the capital. The modernisation of the city was slow at first: under the regime of Sukarno, Indonesia's first president to 1967, focusing on prestige monumental projects, such as the new parliament building, stadium and national monument, but under the governorship of Ali Sadikin, from 1966 to 1977, with his policy of *pembangunan* (development) beginning the construction of the infrastructure the city would need to keep up with rapidly developing Asian competitors.

Growth in trade and population was rapid in the late 20th and early 21st centuries, providing wealth for the middle classes and opportunity, leavened with poverty, for the large numbers who migrated from rural areas and outlying islands. By 2021, Jakarta's port of Tanjung Priok was the twenty-third busiest in the world, and the city's population had reached 11 million. What was once a company town built on the ashes of defeat was now able to reach out to the world as a major trading power.

Waere affbeeldinge Wegens het Casteel en̄e
gelegen op't groot Eylant J A

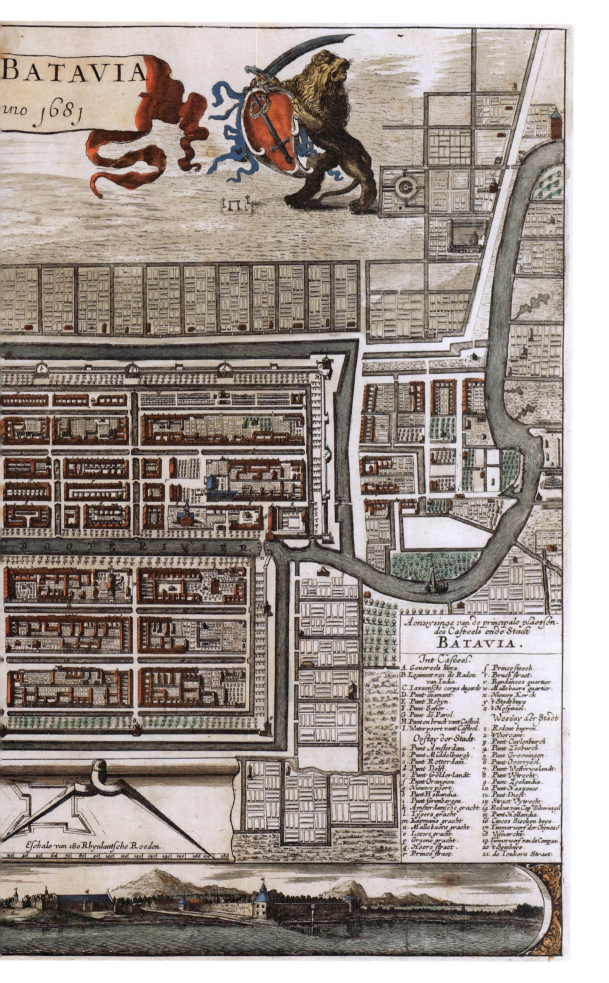

Global Island

Mumbai, 1685

The list of small island settlements that have grown to become trading powerhouses and first-rank global cities is select. Hong Kong and Singapore, both acquired by the British in the 19th century, feature prominently, but Mumbai seems the most unlikely of all. Shown here in a map by John Thornton, official hydrographer of the British East India Company, it was a series of seven marshy islands when the British acquired the area in 1662, and even then, it took almost two centuries for the city to begin its ascent to economic titan and India's most populous urban agglomeration.

Its first known inhabitants were the Koli, a group of fisherfolk, and the area had been involved in maritime trade with Babylon, Persia and Egypt from the 8th century BC. A small trading outpost, known to the Greco-Roman geographer Ptolemy as "Heptanesia", continued in a modest way through rule by the Mauryan emperor Ashoka, and a succession of south Indian dynasties such as the Chalukyas and Rashtrakutas, until its conquest by the Delhi Sultanate in 1348, and absorption by the Sultanate of Gujarat in 1391.

The arrival of the Portuguese, who forced Bahadur Shah of Gujarat to cede the islands in 1534, at first changed little. Overshadowed by Goa to the south, Mumbai (which the Portuguese called Bombay, possibly from a confusion between the Portuguese *bom baim* or "good bay" and Mumba, a local form of Parvati, the consort of Shiva), received little investment. Only eleven Portuguese families came to settle, and the isolated colony's main exports were coconut fibre matting and mangos.

Increasing English concern that the Dutch might trump them in acquiring portions of the rapidly dissolving Portuguese Empire led King Charles II to demand Bombay as part of the dowry for his marriage to Catherine of Braganza, daughter of John IV of Portugal. The dowry proved as disappointing as the marriage. When Captain Brown of the *Dunkirk* – which transported Abraham Shipman, the first British governor – caught sight of the 47 square kilometres (18 square miles) of swamp his sovereign had just acquired, he remarked that it had been "most strangely represented to His Majesty". Worse still, the Portuguese governor refused to hand it over, and Shipman

died of a fever in October 1664, before his successor Humphrey Cooke took possession.

A disappointed British Crown palmed off Bombay onto the East India Company just as soon as it could in September 1668, for the cut-price rental of £10 a year. It would be the making of the city. The company built quays, a customs house, began constructing Bombay Castle, and established a mint and printing press, all within two years. The population, just 10,000 in 1661, rose six-fold by 1675. And in 1687 the company moved its main base of operations in western India from Surat – by now vulnerable to predations from the rising power of the Marathas – to Bombay. It encouraged migration to its new Indian base, which notably included the Parsis – descendants of Zoroastrians who fled the Islamic conquest of Persia in the 7th century – who would become one of the main engines of its economic growth.

That growth was stuttering at first, reliant on exports of salt, rice, ivory, lead and sword blades, and hemmed in by pressure from the Marathas. The reclamation of land by Governor William Hornby, who ordered the construction of the Hornby Vellard embankment in 1782, united the seven islands into a single landmass, allowing the population to grow still further, to 113,000 by 1806.

The defeat of Bajirao II, the Maratha Peshwa, in 1818 removed the main security threat, and from then Bombay was unstoppable. Steamers began to call in 1838, linking it into a burgeoning global network, and the establishment of the first cotton mill in 1854 (by Cowasjee Nanabhai Davar, a Parsi), began an industry that by 1925 employed over 148,000 workers in 82 mills.

The site of India's first higher education institute in 1857, Bombay also became the midwife of its nationalist movement, with the inaugural session of the Indian National Congress held there in 1885, and as the epicentre of the Rowlatt Satyagraha non-violent protest movement initiated by Mahatma Gandhi in 1919. The heady growth of its population was temporarily halted by an epidemic of bubonic plague in 1896–97, which killed around 20,000 people and caused half the population (by then about 800,000) to flee the city.

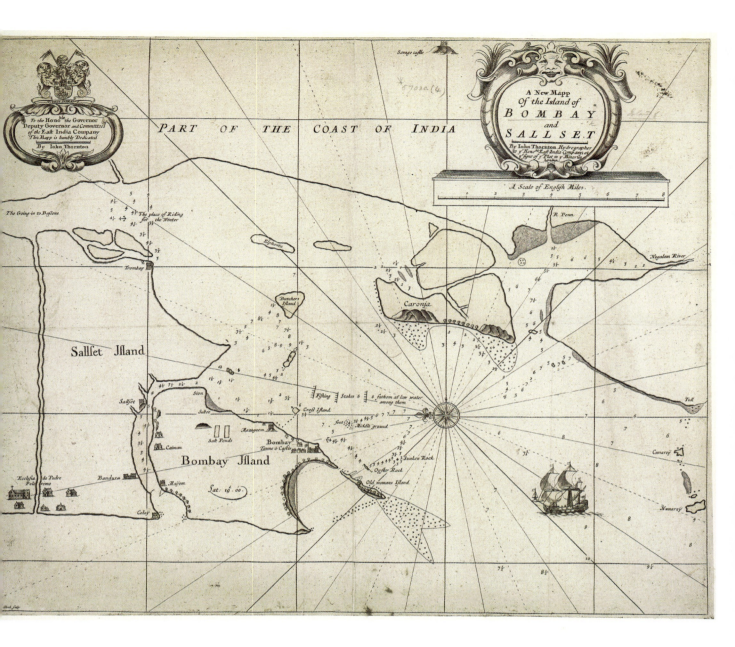

The city drew them back, to its factories, its growing slums and its promise that somehow things would get better. One promise was fulfilled in 1947 when India became independent, though Bombay's resentment at being lumped together with Gujarat led to violent protests and its excision as the capital of the Marathi-speaking Maharashtra state in 1960.

Since then, the city – officially renamed Mumbai once more in 1995 – has grown even larger, reaching around 12 million inhabitants by the 21st century. It has seen its share of troubles, in its massive informal settlements such as Dharavi (see page 213), in periodic intercommunal riots – in one of which, in 1992, over 1,000 people died – and in flooding, an almost inevitable consequence of its marshy heritage. Yet as a centre of India's new wave of hi-tech industries and the headquarters of Bollywood – the Indian film industry which produced its first film in 1913 and now generates around $3 billion in revenue annually – Mumbai lives up to its nickname of the City of Dreams.

Moderation and Power

Amsterdam, 1701

The plan overleaf, from French cartographer Nicolas de Fer's *Atlas Curieux* ("Curious Atlas"), shows a city at the summit of its wealth and power, just before a century-long fall from grace. De Fer, who achieved the heights in his mapping career of official geographer to the Dauphin (in 1690) and then to both Louis XIV of France and Philip V of Spain, depicts an orderly city, defined by its canals, the sources of its wealth suggested by the ships clustered in its harbour and by key sites such as the *Magazin des Indes d'Orient* (the stores of the East Indies).

Amsterdam was an unlikely candidate for the global trading giant and centre of European finance it became in the 17th century. It achieved this trick by being a piece of real estate which nobody else wanted, in unpromising marshy territory along the Amstel river. It was a city that took moderation to excess, developing a society in which neither kings nor clerics had the ultimate say, but, again like Venice, a mercantile middle class, that allowed just enough freedom and stability for commerce to prosper, and exercised just enough control to ensure that no revolutionary fervour took hold. In Amsterdam, the bourgeois was king.

Like Venice, it was a city of canals and bridges, the Grachtengordel, the concentric girdle of canals and the more than 1,200 bridges outshining the Venetians' mere 400 crossings (though remaining in the shade of Hamburg's 2,500 and far short of modern Chongqing's colossal 10,000 bridges). And like Venice, it was reclaimed from the marshes, by driving great wooden piles into the soft waterlogged soil beside the Amstel and then, around 1270, draining away the excess by building the dam from which the city derives name.

In 1275, Amsterdam first appeared in the historical record when Count Floris V of Holland granted it a charter. Already its merchants were making tentative forays into the Baltic, gradually acquiring a portion of the lucrative trades in timber, grain, salt and herring. The profits financed the building of the first large church, the *Oude Kerk* (Old Church), completed in 1306, and the construction of a new line of walls – reinforced by the driving of 12,000 stakes into the mud – in 1425 along the line of the Geldersekade, just after a catastrophic fire accelerated the evolution of the city into a metropolis made of stone.

Even so, by 1538 the population was just 12,000. For all the early Amsterdammers' entrepreneurial spirit, it was external events that gave their city its great opportunity. The Reformation came to the Netherlands in the 1530s, at first in a small way, with the arrest of nine radical Anabaptists in Amsterdam in 1534, and the decapitation of two more moderate Lutherans on the Dam four years later. But the new Protestant creed took hold and sparked an uprising by the Seventeen Provinces of the Netherlands against Spain in 1568. Amsterdam was at first reticent, only defecting to the rebel cause in 1578, but the Spanish capture of its main commercial rival Antwerp in 1585, and an influx of ambitious and industrious refugees (as well as many Jewish people expelled from Portugal after the Spanish crown took over there in 1580), marked the beginning of the city's Golden Age.

The population of the city tripled between 1565 and 1619, but what Amsterdam did above all was trade. The city fathers managed to poach a Venetian glassblower, Anthony Obisy, to set up a rival industry there, and in 1604 paid the Portuguese merchant Manuel Rodrigues de Vega a hefty subsidy to set up two silk mills in the city. It was trade to the spice islands of the Indonesian archipelago, though, that provided the real profit. A first tentative voyage went out in 1595, returning with a modest and unprofitable small cargo of pepper (and with barely a third of its original crew surviving), but it showed the way. In 1602 the *Verenigde Oost-Indische Compagnie* (VOC), the Dutch East India Company, was set up to co-ordinate the trade in cloves, nutmeg and pepper that the pioneering voyage had identified. The Heren XVII, the seventeen directors of the company, established themselves as the leaders of a bourgeois elite of families such as the Huydecopers and de Graeffs, who delivered fabulous profits and an eastern empire based on Batavia (Jakarta).

By the time the Dutch finally won Spanish recognition of their independence in 1648, Amsterdam had added the world's first stock market (in 1602) to the fiscal innovations that enriched the city. Amsterdam's streetscape was remodelled in 1613, with the adoption of the Three Canals plan, which first expanded it westward beyond the Singel, and then from 1663 to the east, creating the city's characteristic shape with the building of the Herengracht, Keizersgracht and Prinsengracht (oddly named "lord", "emperor" and "prince", for a hierarchy the inhabitants had long rejected). In pragmatic fashion, everything that could be profited from was monetised: land around the new canals was sold to developers, though in a typical show of moderation, anyone who bid without having funds to pay was labelled a "schaap" (sheep) and could be bleated at in public (and whipped for a third offence). In a sign, though, that the trend for public participation in finance had gone too far, the craze for buying tulips (introduced from Turkey around 1550) reached such heights in 1637 that the price of the rarest Switzer variety spiralled from 125 guilders a pound on December 31, 1636, to 12 times that level a month later, and when the inevitable crash came after few weeks it ruined thousands of ordinary Amsterdammers.

With a population now of 200,000, the city's future seemed secure. But other more populous nations – Britain and France – had entered the imperial game, using their advantage in manpower to squeeze the VOC out of the trade routes and from its colonial lodgements. The 18th century saw a retrenchment, as London and Hamburg overtook Amsterdam as trading centres, and the French occupation of the Netherlands in 1795, together with Napoleon's trade embargoes on Britain, brought on a further decline. The restoration of independence as a monarchy under King William I preceded a revival of growth, helped by the completion in 1876 of a canal providing direct access for seagoing vessels from the North Sea to Amsterdam. The population doubled in 50 years, to 500,000 by 1900 and the city's footprint spread to the areas beyond the Singelgracht. The Netherlands avoided involvement in the First World War, but the Second brought immense destruction, including the loss of most of the city's 70,000 Jewish population, murdered in the Holocaust. Yet, with typical moderation, the Dutch rebuilt, and from the 1960s reinvented the city as the capital of one of the most liberal societies in Europe, with a tolerance for lifestyles that were criminalised elsewhere. The British historian Thomas Macaulay had commented in his *History of England*, published in 1861, that Amsterdam was "a desolate march overhung by fogs and exhaling diseases" that even so possessed enough wealth to have bought the whole of Scotland. By not demanding greatness, Amsterdam has always, somehow, managed to achieve it.

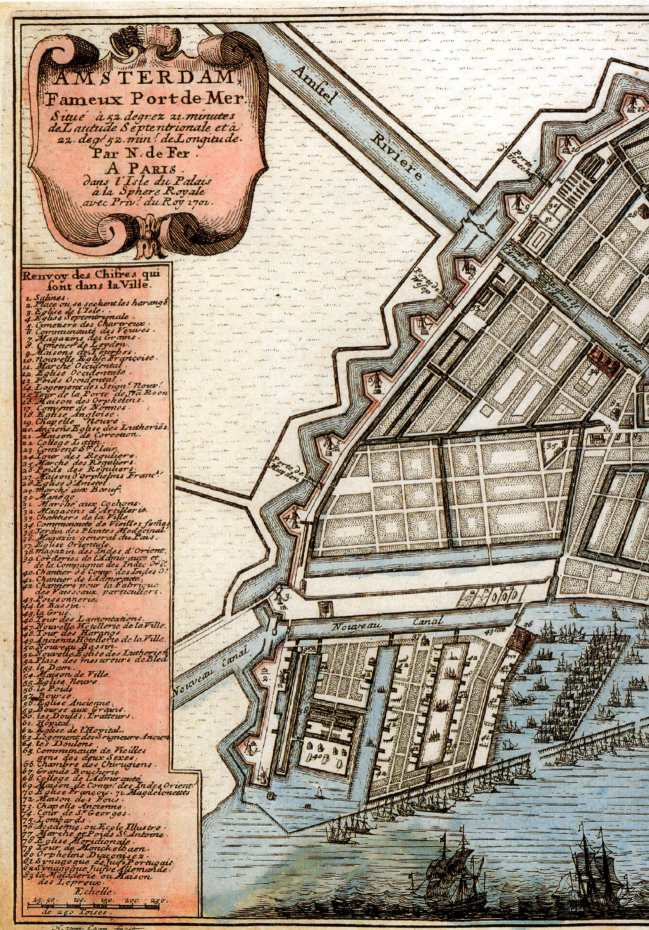

AMSTERDAM,
Fameux Port de Mer.

Situé à 52. degrez 21. minutes
de Latitude Septentrionale et à
22. degt 52. mint de Longitude.

Par N. de Fer.
A PARIS.
dans l'Isle du Palais
à la Sphere Royale
avec Privt du Roy 1701.

**Renvoy des Chifres qui
sont dans la Ville.**

1. Salines
2. Place ou se seçhent les harangs
3. Eglise de l'Isle
4. Eglise Septentrionale
5. Cimetière des Chartreux
6. Communauté des Veuves
7. Magazins des Grains
8. Lanier de Leyden
9. Maisons des Tourbes
10. Nouvelle Eglise Françoise
11. Marché Occidental
12. Eglise Occidentale
13. Poids Occidental
14. Logemens des Seignrs Nouvt
15. Tour de la Porte de Haerlem
16. Maison des Orphelins
17. Convent de Nonnes
18. Eglise Angloise
19. Chapelle Neuve
20. Ancienne Eglise des Lutheriens
21. Maison de Corection
22. College Latin
23. Convent St Clair
24. Lozer des Reguliers
25. Marché des Reguliers
26. Pont des Reguliers
27. Maison d'Orphelins Francs
28. Eglise d'Amstel
29. Marché aux Boeuf
30. Manége
31. Marché aux Cochons
32. Magasins d'Artillerie
33. Chantiers de la Ville
34. Communauté de Vieilles femes
35. Jardin des Plantes Medecinal
36. Magazin general du Pais
37. Eglise Orientale
38. Magazin des Indes d'Orient
39. Corderies de l'Admirauté et
    de la Compagnie des Indes Orie
40. Chantier de Comp. des Indes O
41. Chantier de l'Admirauté
42. Chantiers pour la Fabrique
    des Vaisseaux particuliers
43. Poissonnerie
44. le Bassin
45. la Grue
46. Tour des Lamentations
47. Nouvelle Hôtellerie de la Ville
48. Tour des Harangs
49. Ancienne Hôtellerie de la Ville
50. Nouveau Bassin
51. Nouvelle Eglise des Lutheriens
52. Place des mesureurs de Bled
53. le Dam
54. Maison de Ville
55. Eglise Neuve
56. le Poids
57. Bourse
58. Eglise Ancienne
59. Bourse aux Grains
60. les Doulés Traiteurs
61. Hôpital
62. Eglise de l'Hôpital
63. Logement des Seigneurs Anciens
64. les Doulens
65. Communauté de Vieilles
    gens des deux Sexes
66. Chambre des Chirurgiens
    Grande Boucherie
67. College de l'Admirauté
68. Maison de Comp. des Indes Orient
69. Eglise Françoise. 71. Magdelonettes
72. Maison des Fous
73. Chapelle Ancienne
74. Cour de St Georges
75. Lombards
76. Academie, ou Ecole Illustre
77. Marché et Poids St Antoine
78. Eglise Meridionale
79. Tour du Marché Saen
80. Orphelins Diaconées
81. Synagogue des Juifs Portugais
82. Synagogue Juive Alemande
83. la Maladerie ou Maison
    des Lepreux

Echelle.
25. 50.   100.   150.   200.   250.
de 250 Toises.

H. van Loon fecit.

Amstel Riviere

Porte d'Utrecht

Porte de Weep

Porte de Magden

Nouveau Canal

Nouveau Canal

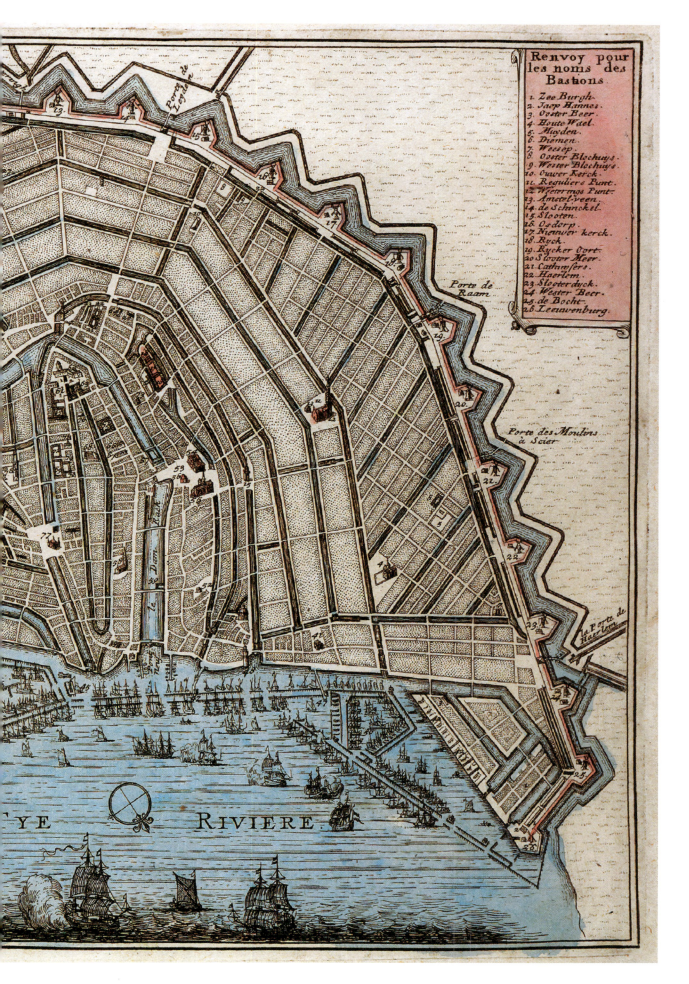

Porte de
Leyden.

Porte de
Raam.

Porte des Moulins
à Scier

la Porte de
Harlem

YE RIVIERE.

Heart of the Habsburgs

Vienna, 1710

Vienna stood at the heart of an enormous European empire when the military architect Werner Arnold Steinhausen drew his map of the city in 1710. It had already been in the Habsburg domains for over 400 years by then, but with the threat of the Ottoman Turks greatly diminished in the early 18th century, it was entering a period as the European imperial city par excellence, far outstripping later rivals such as Paris and Berlin, or the Habsburg cousins in Madrid with their unwieldy transatlantic empire.

Steinhausen's map is neat, precise and orderly, qualities that the Viennese have valued over time, giving detail even down to the placement of altars in churches. The colour-coding of buildings in ten categories creates a visual mosaic that is a mirror of the multi-ethnic empire which Austria – and its satellite possessions in Italy, Hungary, Romania, Poland and the Czech lands of Bohemia – was creating.

It was not always so, though Vienna's parallel role as a border city dated back to its 1st century AD foundation as Vindobona, the fortress of the Roman Legio X Gemina. With the collapse of the western Empire in the 5th century, a small settlement clung on, re-emerging in the 9th century, and by 1155 becoming the capital of Margrave Henry II of Austria. Its defences were bolstered around 1200 by the building of a new set of walls, paid for by the ransom Duke Leopold V extorted for releasing Richard I of England, whom he detained while returning from the Third Crusade.

Rudolf I was the first Habsburg to gain control of the city, which would remain in their hands, barring brief interludes of Hungarian occupation in the 1480s, and two stints as part of Napoleon's empire in 1805 and 1809, until the end of the First World War. These early Habsburgs remodelled the Stephansdom, Vienna's cathedral, work which had begun after a huge fire in 1258, and proceeded at a snail's pace until it halted with one tower incomplete in 1511. The city acquired all the paraphernalia of imperial pretensions, including one of Europe's oldest universities, established in 1365, though its rulers did not quite achieve imperial dignity – as Albert II, who was elected King of the Romans in 1438, a kind of waiting-room status before being crowned as Holy Roman Emperor, died before a coronation could be arranged.

By the early 16th century, the Ottoman Turks were pressing hard against Austria's outer ramparts, and in 1529 Suleiman the Magnificent's army came crashing against the walls of Vienna, only to be frustrated by a premature winter and an outbreak of disease. The Protestant Reformation, which gained large numbers of adherents in the Habsburg lands (and particularly in Bohemia) shook their control, but by the time Ferdinand I made it his imperial capital in 1558, the Counter-Reformation was in full swing, winning back adherents to the Catholic faith. A second Ottoman siege in 1683 failed, in part thwarted by new fortifications built in the 1540s. Now finally no longer a frontier outpost, Vienna acquired a string of orange baroque palaces in the 18th century – such as the Schönbrunn and Belvedere – and by 1724 its population had reached 150,000 people, all still largely crammed within the old medieval walls. The city also acquired the reputation for cultural refinement, in particular for musical excellence, which it has never lost: Mozart conducted the first performance of his *The Magic Flute* at the Theater auf der Wieden.

A devastating flood in 1830 led to the rerouting of the Danube, and the straightjacketing of its central urban section into the Danube Canal, while the city limits were expanded in 1850 to include the area within the Linienwall (or outer fortifications). Even this was not enough to contain its growth and in 1858 the old fortifications were demolished, to be replaced by a new outer ring road, the Ringstrasse, lined with prestige buildings such as the Vienna Opera house, built in 1861–69.

Industrialisation fuelled an influx into the city from rural areas, bringing Czechs, Hungarians, Slovaks, Poles, Greeks and Jewish people (the latter numbered almost 200,000 by the Second World War, crammed into the Leopoldstadt district). In the aftermath of the First World War, sparked by the assassination of one of its own Archdukes, the Habsburg dream dissolved, as the empire broke up into its constituent parts and the last emperor (by now of Austria, since Napoleon had abolished the Holy Roman Empire in 1806) abdicated. Riven by social and economic tensions, in the 1930s Vienna generated the intolerant Austrofascism of Engelbert Dollfuss, and then fell into the orbit of Nazi Germany with the Anschluss (annexation) in 1938. After the war it became a frontier region once more, divided between the four victorious Allied powers until it escaped their tutelage and regained independence by the State Treaty in 1955. Shorn of imperial pretensions, Vienna was able to rebuild itself, though still trading on a Habsburg past that has left it a legacy of beautiful neoclassical and

baroque buildings, an unequalled musical reputation, with a touch of artistic flair added by the Jugendstil Art Nouveau movement in the 1920s, and grand coffee houses such as the Café Central, frequented by Leon Trotsky and Sigmund Freud. Twenty-first century Vienna remains Habsburg to its core.

Imperial Centre

Madrid, c 1715

The early 18th century was a particularly tricky time for Madrid, shown overleaf in the map by Johann Baptist Homann. He mapped an imperial city of surprisingly humble origins, whose rise to greatness came largely through not being at the centre of the rivalry between Spain's historical kingdoms, while sitting firmly in the country's geographical centre. Homann, whose Nuremberg cartographic company, founded in 1702, became one of Europe's leading map publishers, may have exchanged a wry smile with his patron, the Holy Roman Emperor Charles VI (who appointed him imperial cartographer in 1715). Just six years before, Charles had entered the Spanish capital during his attempt to assert his claim to be king of Spain during the War of the Spanish Succession, and was then just as swiftly deposed.

Charles was the candidate of the pro-Habsburg camp contending with Philippe of Anjou, grandson of Louis XIV, for the Spanish throne. Charles's expulsion – foreshadowed by the ominous shuttered shops and deserted streets which greeted him when he arrived three months before, and hastened by his own troops' ransacking of Madrid's churches – was only the latest in a series of trials by war which the city had endured. From the very start, Madrid had a martial past, beginning as Mayrit, a walled outpost on the Manzanares river established by Emir Muhammad I of Cordoba as a bulwark against Christian expansion. Ultimately this failed, and Alfonso VI of León took it in the mid-1080s, meaning the now Christian fortress suffered similar depredations when the Almoravid general Yusuf bin Ali subjected it to a siege in 1109 during a period of Muslim resurgence.

Madrid remained tiny, a 500-by-800-metre (547-by-875-yard) enclave clinging to the east of what is now the Calle Major,

with a few thousand inhabitants dependent on agriculture. Its status as a member of the Cortes (assembly) of Castile, to which it sent a member, brought Madrid some prestige but little real importance, and though Isabella of Castile and Ferdinand II of Aragon – the patrons of Columbus's 1492 expedition, which brought Spain its New World empire – spent many months in the city, it was still firmly in the shadow of Toledo to its south.

The first Habsburg ruler, Carlos I (or, as he was known in his other domains, Emperor Charles V) experienced a spasm of Madrileño anger in 1520, when the city joined the Revolt of the Comuneros, provoked by the high taxation levied to fight his wars elsewhere. During the chaos that ensued, Madrid's citizens constructed a fort in the east of the city, its entrance topped with a rising sun emblem, that would later become the Puerta del Sol, the point from which all Spain's distances are marked. Peace restored in 1523, Carlos delighted Madrid by trailing the captive French king François I through its streets and granting the city the right to a royal crown on its coat of arms. But it was his son Felipe II, who moved the court to Madrid in 1561 and transformed the city's fortunes. Though he based himself in the brooding bulk of the Escorial Monastery, some 40 kilometres (25 miles) to the northwest, Felipe brought with him thousands of officials, so that by the end of the century the population had quintupled to around 100,000.

Still hemmed inside its old medieval walls, by 1600 Madrid boasted 391 taverns, whose clientele's behaviour grew so rowdy that the municipal *concejo* (council) banned innkeepers from providing them with chairs and tables. The city survived a brief scare when Felipe III moved the court to Valladolid in 1601, provoking the exodus of half the population of the city – which was top-heavy with nobles, bureaucrats and hangers-on – but recovered by dint of offering the king a 250,000-ducat bribe to return. Felipe committed himself to Madrid with a will, commissioning the building of the Plaza Mayor as the symbolic heart of the city; a venue for bullfighting (shown in one of the illustrations at the base of the plan), it also saw the canonisation of the Jesuit founder Ignatius Loyola and public garrotings until these were halted in 1765.

Weighed down by the costs of maintaining Spain's transoceanic empire and by the disastrous inflation South American silver caused in the mother country, Madrid's growth paused in the late 17th century. As the Habsburg dynasty's vigour waned, the rising power of Louis XIV's France eyed Spain greedily, and his attempt to put his grandson Philippe of Anjou on the throne sparked a continent-wide war. As Felipe V (reigned 1700–46), the first Bourbon king, he initiated a new phase of architectural growth for Madrid, in 1737 beginning the building of the Royal Palace, after a disastrous fire destroyed the Alcazar fortress, the previous royal home. Felipe also gifted the city the Royal Spanish Academy, the National Library and a son, Carlos III (reigned 1759–88), whose dedication to the architectural adornment of his capital was even more heroic. As well as more practical measures, including the banning of disposing of rubbish on the city streets, he employed a cohort of talented architects such as the Sicilian Francisco Sabatini to give Madrid a neoclassical makeover, with buildings such as the Puerta de Alcalá (1778) and the Prado (1785) making it one of Europe's most splendid cities.

Disaster struck the Bourbons in 1808, when Madrid found itself under foreign occupation by the troops of the French emperor Napoleon, who installed his brother Joseph as king. Although the Bourbon monarchy was restored in 1813, it was to a changed world in which Spain's American colonies broke away over the next two decades. In Madrid itself, ecclesiastical properties were sequestered, and the old churches and convents demolished to make new, wide squares. In the 1860s, the plan for the *ensanche* (enlargement) of Madrid saw the city's size expand threefold, and a constant state of near warfare between constitutionalists and monarchists resulted in the brief deposition of Queen Isabella II in 1868.

By 1871, Madrid had its first tram service, and electric power arrived in the 1890s. Reconstruction of the centre continued apace with the building of the Gran Via, which bisected the city north to south, at the start of the 20th century. The Madrid Metro opened in 1919 to facilitate the movement of a population that had by then exceeded 600,000. The city also received its first cathedral, eight centuries after the Spanish Christian kings had captured it. Or it nearly did so, since the church was only finally completed in 1993. By then Madrid had experienced further turmoil, as a battleground in the Spanish Civil War from 1936 to 1939, when it suffered aerial bombardment, starting with bombs tossed from a German Luftwaffe bomber in August 1936, and street fighting between rival left-wing factions when the nationalist government collapsed in March 1939. The deadening hand of General Francisco Franco's fascist regime which then took the city was only released on his death in 1975, allowing Madrid to become the vibrant, sleep-deprived, decidedly post-imperial city that it is today.

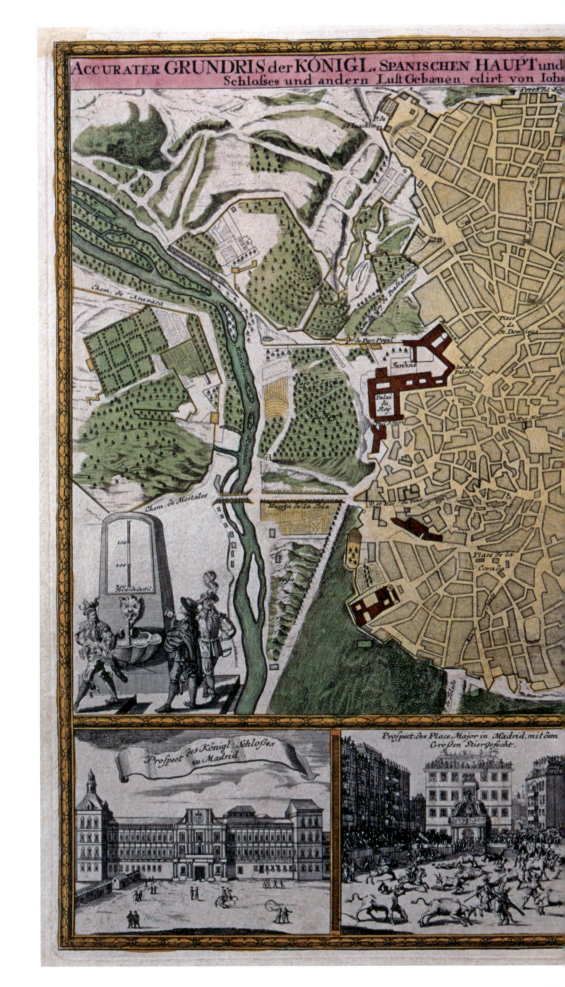

Prospect des Königl. Schlosses zu Madrid

Prospect des Place Major in Madrid, mit dem Großen Stiergefecht.

ENTZ STADT MADRIT mit denen Prospecten des KÖNIGE

Homanns Kayſerlichen Geographi ſeeligen Erben in Nürnberg. Cum Priv. Sac.Caeſ.Majeſtt.

Heremitage St.Antonio.

R. et Paes de la Reine

R. et Conuent St. Barb

Augustines

St Monoy.

P. Alcala

Ri. Chi co

Prado Alto

Place Major

St Isi.

Chartreux

Canal

Palais Jar.
Royal

Palais Jar.
et Parc del
Jin
Petiro

R. et Conuent St. Barb.

Pa. lais

R. d. Alcala

Capucines

Camp St. Blaiſe

Rio h. Atocha Valleca.

Porte
Valleca.

St Jabele

Rosemaria

Hospital
General

Peremitage St. Hiroſime.

Camp St. Blaiſe

Notre D. de Atocha.

Der Königl. Spanische Luſt Palaſt
Buen Retiro bey Madrid.

Aranjuez meil von Madrid

The Politics of Language

Québec City, 1744

The plan of Québec shown overleaf, by Jacques-Nicolas Bellin (1703–72), official hydrographer to the French crown (and member of both the prestigious Académie de Marine and the Royal Society of London), shows a jewel of the French empire. Situated on strategic heights overlooking the confluence of the St Lawrence and Charles Rivers, it entered the French orbit after Jacques Cartier encountered the Iroquoian village of Stadacona in September 1535, and, under the command of Samuel de Champlain, in 1608 became the site of the first permanent settlement in the French colony of "Nouvelle France" (New France).

The walls and redoubts which play such a prominent role in Bellin's map are a sign that French control was not uncontested. The British Thirteen Colonies to the south and a British fur-trading concern around Hudson Bay to the north created a linguistic frontier that would shape the destiny of Québec, caught in a perpetual struggle between Anglophone and Francophone worlds.

Québec's situation is not unique. Cities have ever been urban babels, with merchants and migrants creating a complex mosaic of tongues. Modern London is said to be home to speakers of 300 languages, and ancient Rome hosted a linguistic soup of Latin, Oscan, Etruscan, Greek, Aramaic, Coptic, Gaulish and Brythonic to name but a few. Yet language can become a source of bitter tensions, particularly where a minority feels itself under threat from a dominant or ruling linguistic community. Sometimes this gives birth to a new nation – the granting of equal status to Finnish in 1863 played a key role in the eventual emergence of an independent Finland in 1918, while in the former Austro-Hungarian empire, the Czech, Hungarian and Serb languages were at the forefront of nationalist campaigns for separate states. In Spain, the opposition to the suppression of Basque identity under the Franco regime, was centred on the Basque language (and now around half of the population of Bilbao speak it), while in Wales, where speaking Welsh in court was illegal from 1535, the persistence of the language helped preserve a sense of distinctiveness rewarded in 1993 by its being placed on an equal legal footing with English.

In 1744, Québec was resolutely French and Roman Catholic; the presence of the Hôtel-Dieu, a church-run hospital founded in 1637, of the cathedral and properties owned by the Jesuits and Ursulines are an indication of the strength of clerical influence. French control had less than two decades to run. True, a band of Scottish Huguenot privateers in English employ had taken it in 1629, transporting Champlain and a few hundred French colonists back to England before being forced to return them, and control of Québec, three years later, but a series of wars since then had only nibbled at New France's margins. Then, in 1759 General James Wolfe, with a fleet of 49 ships and around 4,500 soldiers, landed on the river's south shore. The Marquis de Montcalm, the French commander, thought he was safe high above the British landing point, but Wolfe had his men scale the Heights of Abraham undetected and then, on the plain outside the city, the French were defeated in one of history's shortest battles: a mere quarter of an hour that saw both generals dead and Québec in British hands.

Britain's control confirmed by the Treaty of Paris, the question arose of how to deal with the city's 8,000 or so French speaking "canadiens". At first, fears that they might support the growing tide of revolution in the Thirteen

Colonies to the south led the British to tread cautiously, passing the Québec Act to allow the use of French civil law and to guarantee the right to Catholic worship. The Revolutionaries tried, and failed, to take Québec in 1775, but the flight of 75,000 mainly English-speaking Loyalists from the United States to Canada after the end of the Revolutionary War in 1783 began to tip the balance between what became in 1791 Upper Canada (later Ontario) and Lower Canada (Québec).

Resentment by the traditional Francophone professional elite spilled over into demands to guarantee their rights and the establishment of the Parti canadien, the first proto-nationalist party, which in 1834 presented its "92 Resolutions" demanding reform, including greater autonomy for Québec. When this was rebuffed, the party's leader Louis-Joseph Papineau led the Rebellion of the Patriotes in 1837–38, which, though defeated, shook the Anglophone establishment to the core and led Lord Durham, commissioned to write a report on how to resolve the issue, to comment that he had found "two nations warring in the bosom of a single state".

The eventual federation of the Canadian provinces into a single entity in 1867 did nothing to assuage the fears of the Québécois. The traditional cultural conservatism of the Church generated a kind of Catholic nationalism, and opposition to the conscription of French Canadians in the First World War (leading to serious rioting in 1917). But it offered little to secular-minded Francophones and the long years of premiership of Maurice Duplessis from 1936 to 1939 and 1944 to 1959, with ever closer church–state relations, became known as *La Grande Noirceur* ("the great darkness").

A loosening came in 1960 with the beginning of the Quiet Revolution, in which church influence was diminished and a modern secular Québec began to emerge. But it also saw the growth of modern nationalism, with the foundation of the Parti Québécois and calls for protection for the French language which were answered in the 1977 Charter that made it the official language of the province (and the city). For the next 20 years the language issue almost tore Canada apart. René Lévesque's PQ government held a first referendum on independence in 1980, in which 60 per cent of Québécois voted no, but, after successive attempts to find a satisfactory place for French Canadians within the overall constitutional framework failed, another referendum was held in 1995 (under the auspices of the even more radical Bloc Québécois), that fell just short of success, with 49.4 per cent voting for independence.

Since then, the tide of independence has ebbed. The Canadian House of Commons mollified matters slightly by recognising the Québécois as a nation within Canada, but the increase in 2022 of the number of legislative, administrative and educational settings in which French is mandatory suggests that the capacity of language politics to inflame tensions remains undiminished. Legislation may build a wall behind which a language can shelter, just as Montcalm sought protection within the walls of Québec, but ultimately it is the commitment of its users to their culture and heritage, and the sheer facts of demography, that determine its fate. In this for the moment, Québec, and its Old City, with buildings dating back to the era of Bellin's plan, seems secure.

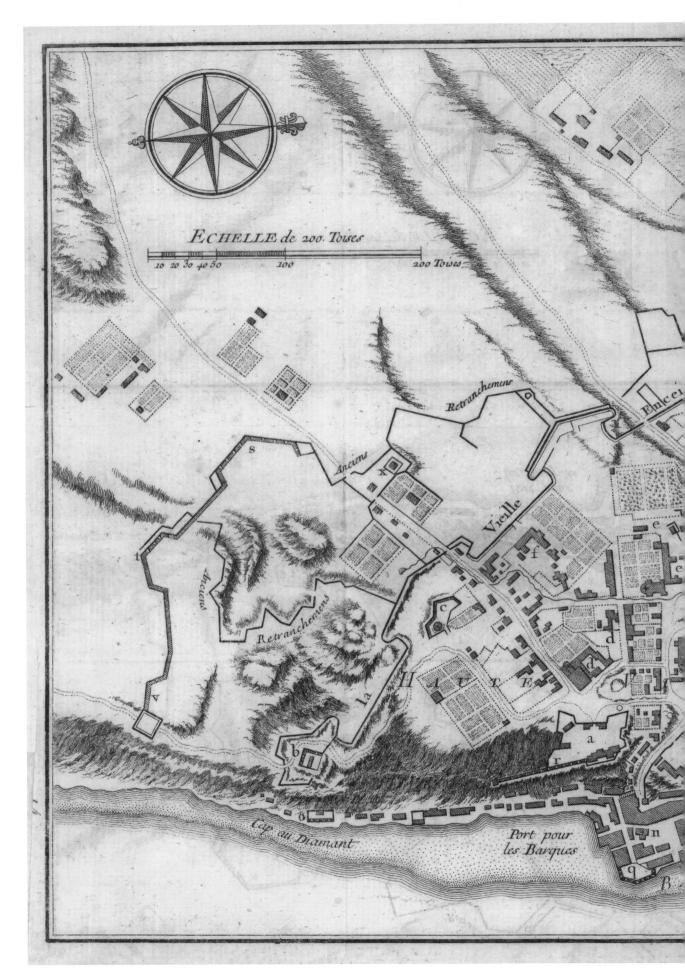

ECHELLE de 200 Toises

10 20 30 40 50   100   200 Toises

Retranchemens

Anciens

Vieille

s

Anciens

t

Retranchemens

la   HAUTE

f

c

d

d

V

b

a

r

o

Cap au Diamant

Port pour
les Barques

n

q

B

Passage à gué
de la petite Rivière

Chénal de la Rivière Saint Charles

VILLE

Plan de la Ville de
QUEBEC

a. Fort St Louis.

b. Redoute du Cap au Diamant.

c. Cavalier du Moulin.

d. Les Récolets.

e. Les Jesuites et dépendances.

f. Les Urselines.

g. La Paroisse avec le Séminaire

et dépendances.

h. L'Evêché.

i. L'Hôtel-Dieu.

k. St Roch.

l. Le Sault au Matelot.

m. L'Intendance.

n. Eglise de la basse Ville.

o. Batterie de Vaudreuil.

p. Batterie Dauphine.

q. Batterie Royale.

r. Batterie du Château.

s. Bastion St Louis.

t. Bastion de la Glacière.

v. Demi Bastion de Joubert.

x. Redoute Ste Ursule.

y. Redoute au Boureau.

z. Redoute St Roch.

&. Coteau de la Potasse.

Dheulland Sculp.

A Capital Deposed

St Petersburg, 1753

The map shown overleaf honoured St Petersburg's 50th birthday. It was created by Ivan Fomich Truscott (1719–86), the son of a Scottish merchant settled in Russia, who became head of the cartographic department of the St Petersburg Academy of Sciences in 1746. Nine years after its foundation, the new city had toppled Moscow from its centuries-long reign as Russian capital. That it would in turn be deposed by Moscow in 1728, and again in 1918, marks St Petersburg as one of a very few cities (İstanbul prominent among them) that have experienced the trauma of such a change and managed to retain their status as one of their nation's major cities.

The city was the dream of Tsar Peter the Great (reigned 1682–1725). He was a man of grandiose plans – declaring himself emperor in 1721 – and his vision of moving Russia's capital away from the stifling grip of the boyars, the traditional Russian aristocracy, and the Orthodox hierarchy, was perhaps the greatest of all. Although providing a "window on the west", which was Peter's ambition, fuelled by several years' travelling in Europe, the site was an unpromising swamp. But, just as a marshy background did not hold back Venice's (see page 60), nor that of Aztec Tenochtitlán (see page 40), so the great tree trunks driven into the marsh eventually provided a stable base for Peter's new capital.

Legend has it that, as the tsar himself cut the first two turf foundation strips on May 27, 1703, an eagle hovered over the scene to foretell the city's greatness. More solidly based is the story of the city's very first dwelling house, a wooden cabin built for the tsar on the north banks of the Neva river, which was preserved and can still be seen today. Peter's plans, though, were very much for a city of stone with straight streets (unlike the chaotic curves of older Russian towns), and he dragooned around 40,000

serfs to work in appalling conditions to create it. The most important structures were the Peter and Paul Fortress, whose 300 cannons jutted out from bastions over the river, and the Cathedral of St Peter and Paul, finished in 1733, which would become the final resting place of Peter and all but two of his successors. The Neva and its tributaries created a water-world not unlike Venice, though at first Peter, bafflingly, was against the idea of bridges, and so the city had no permanent crossing over the Neva, with a temporary pontoon, St Isaac's Bridge, being erected each summer between 1732 and 1916.

In 1712, Peter decreed the capital's move to St Petersburg (not named for him, but for his patron saint). Not everyone was happy, and the British Ambassador Charles Whitworth acidly remarked that it had "the most disagreeable situation and climate I ever met with". The city slowly acquired the stately buildings, such as the Monplaisir and Great Peterhof palaces (completed by 1725), needed to allow it to compete with rival European royal capitals. He commissioned the Kunstkammer on Vasilievsky island as the world's first museum the general public could access, with free refreshments (including vodka) to pull in the crowds who gawped at wonders including the 4-metre- (13-foot-) diameter Great Globe of Gottorp, with its map of the world on the outside and into which visitors so-minded could clamber to get a view of its interior. Less successful was the public library he founded in 1719, which ultimately had over 12,000 volumes, but which in 1724 had only five readers take out books.

Peter's wife Catherine survived his death in January 1725 just long enough to open the Academy of Sciences, but Peter's vision suffered a setback when the capital was moved back to Moscow by their grandson, Peter II, in a bid to escape the grasp of his grandfather's former courtiers. The interlude was short-lived, as St Petersburg regained its crown in 1732, and under the Empresses Elizabeth (1741–62) and Catherine II (1762–96) entered its glory years. A serious fire in 1737 necessitated considerable reconstruction, allowing grand buildings to cluster along the Nevsky Prospect, which became the city's main street. Elizabeth's talented Italian architect Francesco Rastrelli designed the Winter Palace, while Catherine gave the city the Smolny Institute, the first educational institute in Russia for girls. She also built the Tauride Palace in 1783-89 for her lover Count Potemkin, which became notorious for its lavish balls, one of which in April 1791 featured musicians concealed in giant chandeliers.

St Petersburg in the 19th century was the city of Gogol, of Pushkin, whose poem *The Bronze Horseman* remembers the city's worst flood in November 1824, when the Neva rose 4 metres (13 feet) above its normal level, drowning thousands of people. It was also the home of Dostoyevsky, who studied at the city's Engineering Institute and who had one character remark that "there's nothing you can't find in St Petersburg". Yet it was also a city of increasing poverty. Better communication links, with the railway to Moscow opening in 1851, and the abolition of serfdom in 1861 brought hundreds of thousands of rural peasants into the city, so that by 1869, houses in the Haymarket district were home to an average 247 people.

Such conditions bred discontent. There had been elite protests against the tsars such as the failed Decembrist uprising in 1825, but the squalor and hopelessness helped fire the growing industrial proletariat to join the two revolutions of 1917, in the second of which (in October) the Winter Palace was stormed and the tsar deposed.

In 1918, the new communist regime moved the capital from Petrograd (as St Petersburg had been known since 1914) back to Moscow. Then in 1924, after the death of Vladimir Lenin, the Revolution's leader, it was rechristened Leningrad. For all its former association with the Tsarist regime, the city was neglected as investment flowed towards Moscow. Far worse, though, was to come, as in September 1941 the advancing German armies reached Leningrad's outskirts and then subjected it to a 29-month siege in which a million civilians died, many of them from cold and starvation; rations were reduced in late 1941 to just 125 grams (4.5 ounces) of bread daily for women and children, barely sufficient to sustain life. Leningrad, though, did not buckle, surviving due to the tenuous Road of Life, which brought a meagre trickle of supplies across the frozen Lake Ladoga.

By the end of the war the population had fallen by over two thirds to just 800,000, and it took decades to rebuild its infrastructure and remove unexploded mines and bombs. In consolation, it received the title "Hero City" in 1945, and the St Petersburg metro opened in 1955. Yet the city was still not allowed to breathe, as thousands of writers, artists and other intellectuals were executed in the 1940s and 1950s during the "Leningrad Affair", a clampdown on intellectual dissent. It was only in 1991, when a referendum confirmed its name change back to St Petersburg, that the city recovered its pride. Yet whether, as Moscow continues to assert its authority both within and outside Russia, St Petersburg can once again be a "window to the west" and not just a deposed capital living off the shadow of Peter the Great's glorious dream, has yet to be seen.

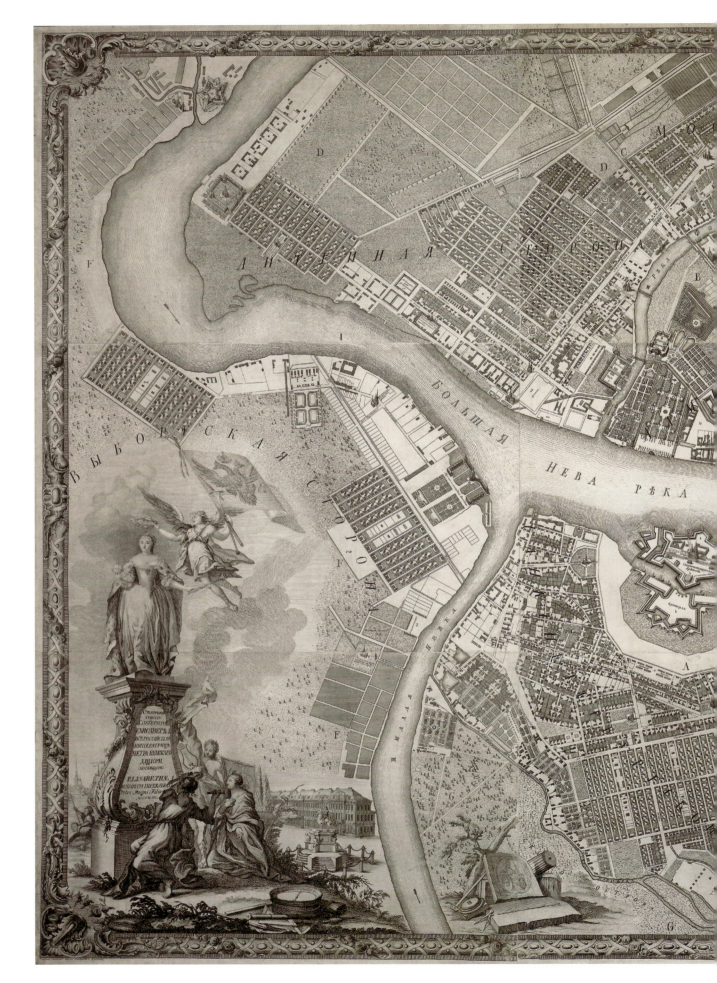

Д   C   М О

D

F

D

B

А Д Т И Н Н А Я   С Т О Р О Н А

I

Б О Л Ь Ш А Я

В Ы Б О Р Г С К А Я   С Т О Р О Н А

Н Е В А   Р Ѣ К А

F

II   М А Л А Я   Н Е В К А

Столичной
городъ С.ПЕТЕРБУРГЪ
ЕЛИСАВЕТЪ I
ВСЕРОССІЙСКОЙ
ИМПЕРАТРИЦЕ
ПЕТРА ВЕЛИКАГО
ДЩЕРИ
посвященно.

ELISABETHÆ I.
RUSSORUM IMPERATRICI
Petri Magni Filiæ
sacrum.

А

G

F

G

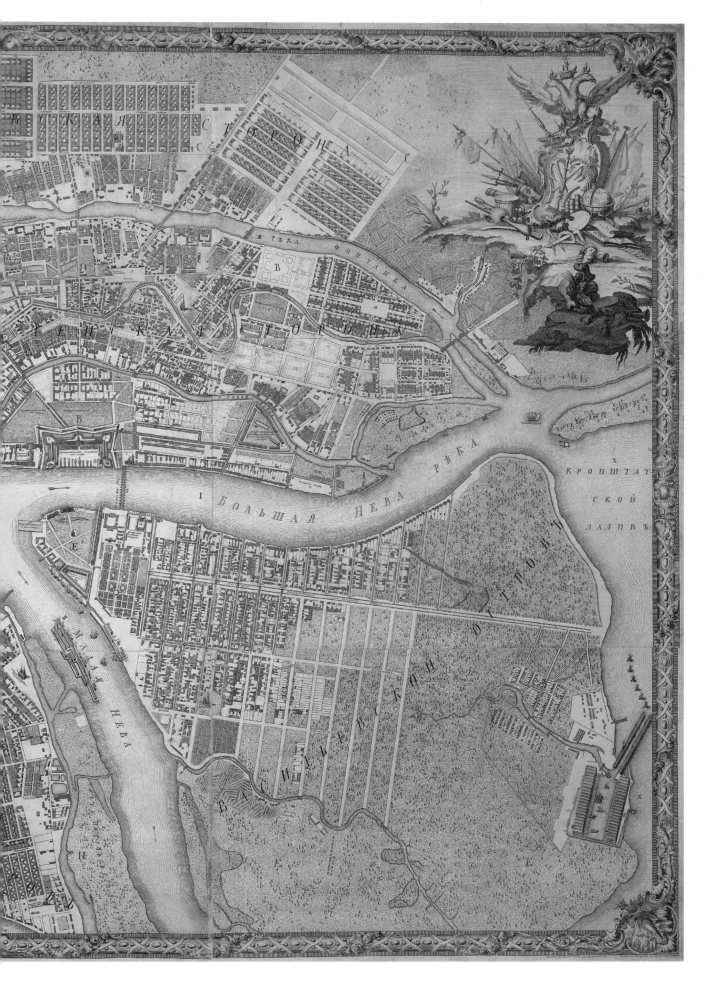

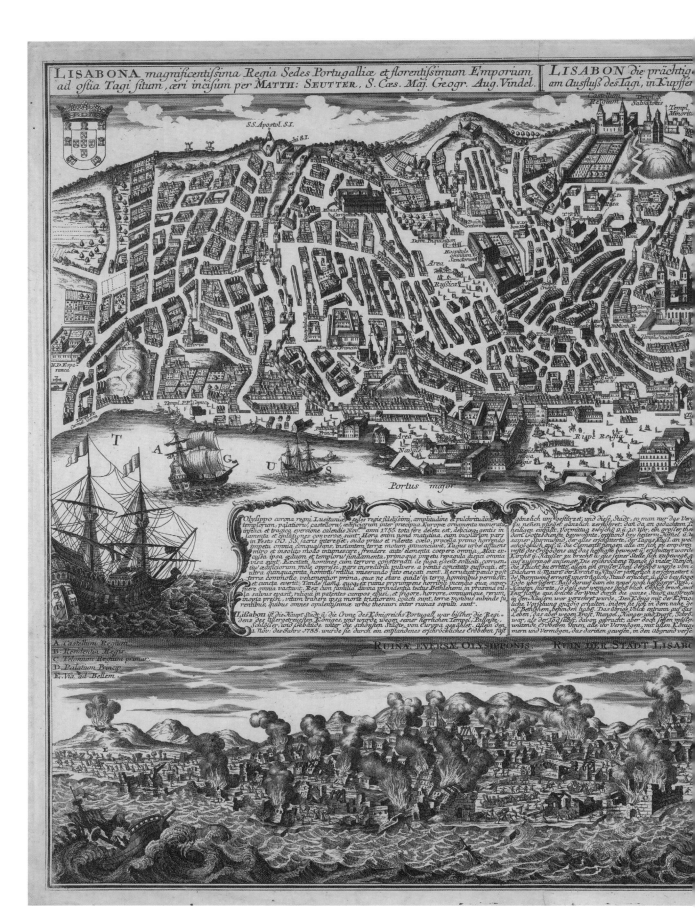

Benigna de Franca

Monast S Maria de gratia

S. Drequez

S. Vincenti

Maria storio

Spirit

Monast S. Clare

Monast Oratorion

S. D. de Paraiso

S Petr

S. P. Francifcanori

Umagria

V I U S

A Daß Königl Schloß
B Die Königl Residentz
C Die Königl Haupt. Mauth
D Printzen Pallast
E Weg Nach Bellem

Earthquake City

Lisbon, 1755 & 1833

In one map nature seems at war with the city, in the other at peace. The tranquillity of the Lisbon shown overleaf in English architect and cartographer William Barnard Clarke's 1833 view and map of the city belies the 80 years of reconstruction necessary to resurrect it from the devastating 1755 earthquake and tsunami mapped in 1756 by Matthäus Seutter, who turned from brewing to set up a hugely successful cartographic company in Augsburg.

Although legend has it that it was the Homeric hero Odysseus who founded the city on the north bank of the Tagus river, it was probably established by the Phoenicians around 1000BC. Its name in their language, *Alis Ubbo*, or "delightful little port", refers to the maritime economy which would always be at the heart of the city's prosperity. But its location on a series of terraces at the very edge of the Sintra Mountains concealed an awful secret: its inhabitants, by 1755 over 160,000 of them, were living close to a series of seismic fault lines, cracks in the Earth's crust that are formed when its tectonic plates collide.

Earthquakes have been a perennial source of dread among populations, even more so than other inevitable urban scourges such as fire and flood. The Aztecs believed that they were caused by a jaguar leaping at the sun, and in Japanese mythology the culprit is a *namazu*, a monstrous catfish wallowing in the mud beneath the surface of the Earth. They can be utterly devastating: one in Shaanxi province in China in 1556 destroyed the town of Huaxian, with a loss of life estimated at 830,000, the worst ever recorded. Yet those living in earthquake zones have a perplexing urge to rebuild in the self-same spot. Antioch (now Antakya in Turkey) suffered multiple earthquakes in classical times. One, in December of AD115, almost killed the future emperor Hadrian, and resulted in the loss of 260,000 other lives. Yet the Antiochenes were undeterred, restoring their neighbourhoods, doing so again in 458 after another quake flattened half the city, and once more in 526 when 240,000 died. Even when another struck just two years later, the survivors still returned to their homes.

Lisbon, too, had suffered prior warning, with damaging earthquakes striking in 1344 and 1531. But the city was too well established to abandon. The Phoenicians had been succeeded by Romans in 205BC, then by Visigoths and Arabs, before finally falling to the Portuguese Christian king Afonso Henriques in 1147. Each added a jumble of buildings, but a new level of sophistication was reached under Manuel I (reigned 1495–1521), fuelled by Portugal's share of the spice trade in the East Indies and its infant empire in Brazil. He gifted the city the Tower of Belém, a landmark for all those Portuguese navigators, and the imposing Jerónimos Monastery, as well as remodelling the Rossio (the area beside the harbour) with a new palace, the Paço da Ribeira – complete with a 70,000-volume library – and left Lisbon in much the state that Seutter shows it.

Manuel was not the retiring type: in 1514 he sent a white Indian elephant to Rome as a gift for the Pope, and topped it the following year with a 20-tonne rhino named Ganda. But the death of his great-grandson Sebastian in battle against the Moors in 1578 led to a dynastic crisis, during which Lisbon stagnated. The restoration of independence

in 1640 began a recovery, and the discovery of gold in Brazil in 1693 swelled the royal coffers through the *quinto del rey*, a one-fifth tax on all production, which by the 1750s was yielding around £2 million a year. João V (reigned 1706–50) used this to engage in an orgy of construction, expending huge sums on a massive palace-church complex at Mafra, northwest of Lisbon, and a grand Patriarchal church attached to the royal palace.

Around 9.30am on November 1, 1755, much of this came crashing down. Residents, including the visiting English merchant Thomas Chase, heard the "most dreadful jumbling noise" and then houses in the crowded alleys began collapsing like a pack of stone cards, while 5-metre-wide chasms opened up in the streets. People fled towards what they thought was the safety of the harbour, finding there the astonishing sight that the water had receded, leaving boats marooned in the mud. Half an hour later it returned with vengeful force, as a six-metre-high tsunami slammed into the lower city. Candles laid in all

the churches for All Saints' Day toppled over, setting off a series of fires that blazed for six days. The Paço da Ribeiro with its precious manuscripts and books was incinerated, as well as around 85 per cent of the city's other buildings.

King José was almost unhinged at the loss, refusing ever after to live in a building, preferring the tent city that housed the myriad of refugees. Estimates of the death toll range from 12,000 to 40,000, and the city's complete downfall was only prevented by the forceful hand of the prime minister Sebastião de Carvalho. Re-establishing law and order – including by judicious executions of looters – within a month he had a reconstruction plan in place that utterly reshaped the destroyed harbourside area, replacing the maze of streets and alleys with an orderly grid of 48 streets behind a large new square, the Praça do Comercio, all lined with elegant neo-classical buildings. This "Pombaline" style (named after he was elevated by a grateful king to be marquis of Pombal) even had an early form of earthquake proofing, with cages of protective wooden frames around the interior structures. By 1833, when the second map was produced, the transformation was almost complete.

The city underwent new phases of change, with electric lighting being introduced in 1878, and electric trams, long one of the hallmarks of its transportation system, arriving in 1901. A new central axis for the city, the Avenida da Liberdade, was cut through in 1886, and the autocratic Estado Novo regime of prime minister António de Oliveira Salazar bequeathed it brutalist buildings such as the National Library and Royal Mint. Yet the 1755 earthquake, the "Wrath of God", was never forgotten. Modern seismologists estimate it as a one in two- or three-thousand-year event, but caution that a smaller earthquake closer to the city could cause even worse destruction. It is perhaps appropriate therefore that Lisbon (and Portugal) gave the world the concept of *saudade*, a constant sense of nostalgia for something lost, tempered with a sense of fatalist resignation, which informs its haunting signature musical genre of *fado*.

The Cost of Prosperity

Liverpool, 1765

Sometimes, the prosperity of a city is founded on the suffering of others. This may be through war or, as in the case of Liverpool, from the profits of enslavement.

John Tarleton, the mayor of Liverpool – to whom John Eyes, the city's surveyor, dedicated the 1765 map shown overleaf – together with the "merchants and tradesmen" of the city, was deeply involved in the transatlantic trade in enslaved people. His interests included a sugar refinery, the rum trade and a tea warehouse that swelled his fortune to over £53,000 in 1763. Only 20 years before, his home city had overtaken Bristol to become Britain's principal centre in the trade, which for Liverpool began in October 1699 when the merchant William Clayton began a voyage during which he purchased over 200 enslaved people in Africa and shipped them to the Americas on board the *Liverpool Merchant.*

Liverpool, of course, was not unique in this regard. London and, in particular, Bristol had pioneered the trade before it. And many other cities in history had built their fortunes – or, in many cases, literally built their monuments – on the backs of those in involuntary servitude. It is estimated that the enslaved population of Athens may have been as high as a third of its total in the late 6th century BC, many working in appalling conditions in the silver mines at Laurion, while the agricultural estates, state mines and aristocratic households of ancient Rome relied on the labour of enslaved people, who made up 10 to 20 per cent of the population. The entire plantation system in the southern states of the United States, the Caribbean and South America depended on enslaved labour in the 18th and 19th centuries, and large numbers were transported north across the Sahara to Islamic countries, or sold in markets in east Africa, such as Zanzibar, whose merchants, and rulers, grew rich at their expense.

The scale of the trade in Liverpool was immense. By the time of abolition, in 1807, Liverpool-registered vessels are estimated to have transported around half the three million enslaved people trafficked across the Atlantic by Britain. It was a future that would have been hard to predict when Liverpool was first mentioned, as "Liuerpul", in a charter of the 1190s. It received its own charter as a borough from King John in 1207 and began as a tiny market town on a grid of seven streets, with the building of a castle in 1232 the only sign of its strategic importance. By 1346, its population was scarcely 1,000, then the Black Death, which killed over half its people, led to a further century of stagnation. Noble families such as the Stanleys and Molyneux still tussled over it – one riot in 1424 involved more than 3,000 of their partisans – but it was only after the Civil War of 1642–51, during which the city changed hands five times, that Liverpool really started to grow.

The gradual silting up of Chester's port pushed trade towards the city. New streets were laid out to the north of the old grid, merchants began to dominate the town council, and a first voyage to Barbados brought back a load of sugar in 1666. The influx of wealth gradually percolated into public monuments with the building of a new town hall in 1673, and into philanthropic ventures such as the Bluecoat School for poor children, founded in 1708, and the opening of the Liverpool Infirmary in 1749.

As the levels of trade – including that in enslaved people – increased, the old port arrangements became wholly inadequate and in 1715 a new enclosed wet dock, Europe's first, was completed. Although the cost, at £15,000, caused years of wrangling in the city council about who would foot the bill, the port tolls soon paid it off. Known as the "Old Dock" even from its early days, it was soon joined by three others: Canning, Salthouse and Canning Graving Docks. These developments allowed the city to accommodate the growing trade in salt – which rose from 26,000 bushels a year in the 1670s to 428,000 bushels in the 1720s – and a 30-fold increase in the tobacco trade between 1670 and 1750.

The Zong massacre in 1781, in which the crew of a ship part-owned by William Gregson, the mayor of Liverpool, murdered 122 enslaved Africans by throwing them overboard to claim insurance money, fuelled calls for abolition of the trade, and in July 1807 the last slaving vessel, the *Kitty's Amelia*, left the port on its final voyage. Liverpool fell back on its other trades, in tea, salt, coal, tobacco and cotton, though the latter two continued to rely on enslaved labour for their production until the 1830s. Cotton imports rose from 40,000 tons in 1810 to 360,000 by 1850. Shipping lines such as the Bibby and White Star (founded in 1845) criss-crossed first the Irish Sea and then the Atlantic, with White Star's *Titanic* being both the most famous and tragic of the Liverpool-registered vessels. This new stream of mercantile wealth allowed the city to fund grand civic buildings such as the Philharmonic Hall (1849) and the Walker Art Gallery (1877), and the laying out of public spaces such as Stanley Park (opened in 1870). Topping them all were the Cunard Building and the Liver Building, which opened in 1911, with its two clock towers bearing statues of the city's iconic liver birds, an imagined form of cormorant.

The opening of the Liverpool and Manchester Railway in 1830, the world's first passenger line, made the city more accessible by land, but it was by sea that the largest new influx came, as the Great Famine in Ireland sent streams of refugees – over 300,000 of them in 1847–48 alone – through the city. Many made their way to the Americas, but thousands stayed, giving the city one of the largest Roman Catholic populations in Britain. The increase in population, to 375,000 in 1851 and 685,000 half a century later, created a true metropolis, but also severe social problems as "court houses" of four storeys became slums, with dozens of families dependent on a single standpipe for water. It was no accident that Europe's first municipal medical officer was appointed in Liverpool, in 1847, or that the city was one of the first in Britain to establish a police force, in 1836 (Charles Dickens became an honorary constable for a night in 1860).

The docks remained the lifeblood of the city. They began to struggle after 1914 as passenger liners moved to Southampton, and received a pounding in the Second World War, during a blitz that killed 2,500 Liverpudlians. Poor industrial relations also blighted the docks, and despite the reputation of its football teams and the publicity brought to the city by the Beatles, Liverpool's population fell by almost half from its peak in the 1930s, to 450,000 in 2000. But regeneration had already begun, again centred on the docks, where Royal Albert Dock was revived as a tourist, cultural and entertainment hub from the 1980s. And as a sign that a city can acknowledge the darker aspects of its past, in 2007 Liverpool chose the dock as the site of the new International Slavery Museum.

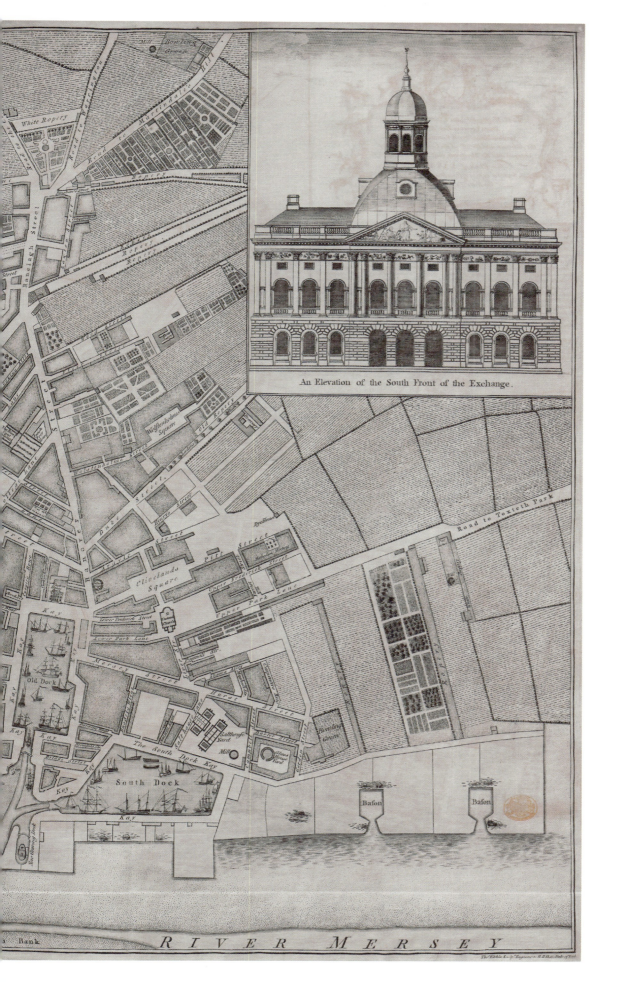

An Elevation of the South Front of the Exchange.

White Ropery

Ranelagh Street

Wolstenholme Square

Cleveland Square

Pitt Street

Upper Frederick Street

Lower Frederick Street

Lower Park Lane

Upper Park Lane

Mersey Street

Old Dock

Kay

Kay

Kay

Kay

Kay

Kay

Kay

Kay

Salthouse Yard

Mill

The South Dock Kay

South Dock

Kay

Bowling Green

Mill

Road to Toxteth Park

Bason

Bason

Bank

R I V E R   M E R S E Y

Athens of the North

Edinburgh, 1765

William Edgar's plan captures Edinburgh on the cusp of a transformation from a medieval warren of wynds, closes and vennels into a more orderly neoclassical affair and centre of intellectual refinement. Shown in full overleaf, this is a second edition of Berwickshire-born Edgar's map, the original, created in 1742, having the distinction of being the first plan of Edinburgh "from above" (as opposed to a panorama). It shows the initial moves to clean up a city with a reputation as one of the most unhealthy in Europe, but which would soon become known as the "Athens of the North".

Whilst the accolade of Venice of the North is fairly widespread in cities with a heritage of urban waterways (such as Bruges, Amsterdam, Birmingham and Hamburg), only a select few, such as 17th-century Stockholm, can claim that of an alternative Athens. Edinburgh won it for the extraordinary intellectual renaissance that took hold in the 1740s, further fuelled by the establishment of the Royal Society of Edinburgh in 1783. Its leading lights included the empiricist philosopher David Hume (1711–76), author of *A Treatise on Human Nature*, the pioneer of political economy Adam Smith (1723–90), who wrote *The Wealth of Nations*, James Hutton (1726–97), whose theories of rock formation revolutionised geology, and the historian William Robertson (1721–93) who wrote important histories of Scotland and America. With figures such as these, the city well merited its status as epicentre of the Scottish Enlightenment.

Edinburgh by then was over a thousand years old, having been founded in the 6th century as Din Eidyn, a hillfort of the Celtic Gododdin. By the 7th century it had fallen to the English kingdom of Northumbria, who rechristened it Edin Burgh, and only came into the Scottish control in 1018 when it was captured by King Malcolm II. By the 12th century a small settlement had begun to flourish, clustered around the castle that Malcolm had built on Castle Rock and Holyrood Abbey, established by David I in 1128 as a house for Augustinian canons. The latter is remembered by Canongate, one of the most prominent features of Edgar's map and part of the "Royal Mile", which also includes the "Land Market" (now Lawnmarket), where cloth and linen, to become a signature produce of the city, were sold.

By 1329 Edinburgh was officially a town, with a charter, but its growth was held back by the almost perpetual state of war between Scotland and its southern neighbour. The English captured it in 1296, holding on until evicted by Thomas Randolph, Earl of Moray, in 1314. They came back in 1334, laying siege to the castle, once more in 1385 when they burnt much of Edinburgh, which by then only had around 400 houses, and yet again in 1482 when they took the town during a bid to place their candidate, the Duke of Albany, on the Scottish throne. Edinburgh suffered further sackings by the English in 1544 and 1548, the former during the "Rough Wooing", an attempt by Henry VIII to force the marriage of his son Edward to Mary Queen of Scots.

Despite all of this turbulence, building continued apace in the increasingly crowded centre, including the Old Tollbooth, planted squarely in the middle of the High Street in the 1390s, which served as the site of most Scottish parliaments in the mid-15th century (and which was finally demolished in 1817, when Sir Walter Scott made off with its medieval doorway and keys).

The Scottish Reformation, spearheaded by preachers such as John Knox – whose preaching in St Giles Kirk in the 1550s did much to establish it – further frayed ties with England, where a less radical form of Protestantism held sway. The longer-term result of this was yet another English invasion in 1650 under Oliver Cromwell, when in the complex shifting of alliances during the British Civil Wars, Scotland found itself supporting the Stuart king Charles II against the English parliament. Edinburgh, predictably, was sacked yet again.

With peace, for the moment, restored, Edinburgh began a modest expansion, amid efforts to resolve the problem of the Nor' Loch ("North Loch" on the map), formerly a stretch of fresh water north of the Old Town, but by the 18th century a stinking repository for the much of the city's waste. It is this phase of Edinburgh's life that Edgar's maps chronicles. New squares such as Argyle Square were laid out in the 1730s, and a workhouse, in the neoclassical style that became the hallmark of Edinburgh's architecture, was constructed in 1739 (with accommodation for 484 adults and 180 children), while in 1729 the city received its first modern hospital, the Edinburgh Infirmary, which moved into a new building designed by William Adam in 1741.

By the time the second version of Edgar's map was published, the cartographer had sadly passed away, of exhaustion at Fort Augustus in July 1746, while accompanying pro-government troops during the suppression of the Jacobite

Uprising. He missed, therefore, the construction of the Royal Exchange in 1761, to another neoclassical design by Robert and John Adam, and the building of the North Bridge – a long mooted project for a crossing of the Nor' Loch – whose foundation stone was laid in 1763. Edinburgh was also about to acquire a wholly new aspect, with the finalisation of the plan for the New Town to the north of the loch, with its elegant design by James Craig, who was awarded a silver box and the freedom of Edinburgh for his prize-winning design. By then, the Nor' Loch had finally been drained (in 1759). Fashionable squares such as Charlotte Square (laid out by Robert Adam in 1791) and new thoroughfares such as Princes Street, completed in 1805 – and which King George III had demanded be renamed, since the original, St Giles Street, reminded him of a London slum district – drew more prosperous residents north out of the Old Town.

The older parts of Edinburgh suffered as a result, again becoming warrens of poor quality tenement housing, ravaged by the cholera epidemics that hit the city in 1832 and 1848–49, though the City Improvement Act of 1867 swept away many of the narrow alleyways, which had formed the grizzly backdrop to the West Port murders, a spate of serial killings by William Burke and William Hare who went one step further than grave-robbing in their quest to supply corpses for medical schools to dissect.

Further sections of the Old Town were demolished in the 20th century, but by 1999 Edinburgh had rediscovered its way as the headquarters of the Scottish parliament, Scotland's first autonomous legislature since 1707. In emulating the ancient Greek city's constitutional reforms, Edinburgh had become another form of "Athens of the North".

▶

The PLAN
of the City and Castle
of EDINBURGH by
Willm Edgar Architect
anno 1765

DIEU ET MON DROIT

NISI DOMINUS FRUSTRA

N.B. All the New Buildings &c. are Expressed in this Plan
to the Present Year by an Eminent Engineer.

The NORTH LOCH
now drained

A Bog or Marsh at the Head of the Loch

Lions Gate
Multers Hill

Flesh
Market
upper Market

Green
Market

The CASTLE

Castle Hill Walk

Castle Hill Street

Land Market

James Court

Parliament Close
Parliament
House

Tron
Church

The Way to St Cuthberts

Grass Market   Corn Market

Head of The Conegate

Canegate

Gray Friars
Church Yard

Bowling
Green

Mr Adams
Close Build

Portsburgh   West Port

Portsburgh

Mr Ramsays

Gardens
Property

Herriots
Hospital

Argylls Square

College

Mr Adams
Property

Bowling
Green

The Road to Portsburgh

Lauriston   Lauriston

Avenue to
Watson's
Hospital

Lady Nicholson
Park

CALTOUN CRAIGS.

The Author of this Plan, having inserted the Names of the Principal Streets and Buildings, and referred to the Names of the most noted Wynds, Courts and Closes within the City Wall by proper numbers in the Plan and Table following, amounting to 97. besides which, he shews us that there are 121. others within the Town Wall which together with 76. in the Canongate make the number 294. exclusive of those in the other Suburbs. which joined to the former, make the number of all the Streets Squares Wynds Courts Closes &c. within the City and Suburbs of Edinburgh amount to 320. the additional Names of which shall be set forth in the Body of the History for the information of the Reader.

The Names of the Principal Wynds Courts Closes &c. within the City referred to in the Plan and the Places following the Table not inserted therein are referred to by Letters in the Plan as followeth

1 Lady Stair's Close	26 Hutcheson's Close	51 Grants Close	76 Peebles Wynd	To distinguish the Places whose Names are inserted in the original Plan that cannot for want of Room be put in this Reduced Plan from those in the above Table, they are here referred to by Letters is followeth
2 Upper Baxter's Close	27 Fowler's Close	52 Currys Close	77 Martins Wynd	A Reservoir
3 Wardrope's Court	28 Newbank Close	53 Riddels Close	78 Nidries Wynd	B Tolbooth
4 Patersons Court	29 Lyons Close	54 Fishers Close	79 Kinloch's Close	C Haddon's hold Church
5 Middle Baxter's Court	30 Jacksons Close	55 Lord Cullens Close	80 Dicksons Close	D Tolbooth Church
6 Lower Baxter's Court	31 Fleshmarket Close	56 Walter Willes's Close	81 Cants Close	E Fishmarket
7 Morocco Close	32 Middle Fleshmarket Close	57 Old Bank Close	82 Lord Streighan's Close	F Marys Chappel
8 Galloways Close	33 Bulls Close	58 Goffords Close	83 Black-friers Wynd	G Chandler
9 Dunbars Close	34 Mills Square	59 Libertons Wynd	84 Todricks Wynd	H Magdalen Chappel
10 Cellers Close	35 Riding School	60 Carthraes Close	85 Murdochs Close	I Lord Mintos
11 Browns Close	36 Stables	61 Forresters Wynd	86 Skinners Close	K Lady Yesters Church
12 Byres Close	37 Hathertons Wynd	62 Back of Bests Wynd	87 Grays on Mint Close	L The Market Cross
13 Advocats Close	38 Kinlochs Close	63 Bests Wynd	88 Hyndfords Close	M The Town Guard House
14 Roxburghs Close	39 Carrubbers Close	64 Steils Close	89 Fowlers Close	N The Girth Cross
15 Dons Close	40 Grays Close	65 Fishmarket Close	90 Fountain Close	O Aikins Square
16 Waristons Close	41 Morrisons Close	66 Back of Borthwicks Close	91 Marquess of Tweedales Close	P Canongate Charity Work House
17 Writers Court	42 Bailey Fifes Close	67 Borthwicks Close	92 Worlds end Close	
18 The Royal Bank	43 Smiths Close	68 Assembly Close	93 Craigs Close	
19 St. Cecilias Hall	44 Barringers Close	69 Cons Close	94 Scots Close	
20 Monro's New Flatt	45 Chalmers Close	70 Covenant Close	95 Hastics Close	
21 Allans Close	46 Sandilands Close	71 Burnets Close	96 Robertsons Close	
22 Craigs Close	47 Menteeths Close	72 Bells Wynd	97 High School Wynd	
23 Old Posthouse Close	48 Trunks Close	73 New Assembly Close		
24 Anchor Close	49 Penmures Close	74 Stanelaws Close	Q Sugar Work House	
25 Swan Close	50 Dr. Sinclair's Close	75 Kennedys Close	R The dotted lines Shews Road along ye intended Bridge	

S Pier of ye Bridge Founded

The End of Enlightenment

Berlin, 1773

Berlin in 1648 was a ruin, ravaged by the Thirty Years' War, its population starving and desperate. The map overleaf shows the city's transformation by 1773, effected by a line of four great rulers, who constructed the buildings shown by the cartographer Johann David Schleuen (1711–71) in vignettes on the borders of his plan, and lifted Berlin to the ranks of a great European capital.

The rulers' magic trick, apart from longevity – the Elector Frederick William reigned for 48 years from his accession in 1640 – was a judicious mix of absolutism, that royal authority should not be challenged, with enlightenment (or in German, *Aufklärung*), that rationalism, and not superstition, and education, not dogma, would create a strong, efficient nation. Schleuen, a carter's son who became well known for his city maps and views of Berlin, hints at this in the poem he includes at the top of his map, which lauds "an established throne which power and prudence sustain" (while not resisting jibes at other cities such as "the proud splendour of the Tiber must now fade before the Spree").

It was near the confluence of the Spree and the Havel rivers that Berlin had its 12th-century beginnings as a tide of German expansion lapped eastwards into territories settled by Slavs around half a millennium before. Albert the Bear, first Margrave of Brandenburg, seized the area in a series of campaigns against the Wends from 1137 to 1157 – ultimately bequeathing Berlin its symbol of two bears – and by 1244 there were two settlements: Berlin on the northeast bank of the Spree, and Cölln to the southwest (the two merged in 1432). A prosperous little trading settlement soon emerged, equipped with imposing churches such as the Marienkirche (c 1270). A member of the Hanseatic League trading alliance – which it joined around 1359 – Berlin-Cölln, with only around 8,000 inhabitants, was a decidedly unenlightened place, from 1411 ruled by the first of the Hohenzollerns who would be its sovereigns for over 500 years. The city's *Stadtbuch*, which chronicles its medieval laws, has women being buried alive for stealing from churches, and liars being boiled to death.

The Reformation came to Berlin in 1539 as Duke Albert accepted Lutheranism, but a century later the Thirty Years' War (1618–48), fought by competing religious factions – largely across German territory – devastated Berlin. Starvation, disease – in 1630–31, plague, its path made easier by troops movements, killed 2,000 Berliners – and fighting halved the city's population to just 6,000. In 1640 Frederick William I became the city's ruler as Elector of Brandenburg (the latest in a long line of Hohenzollern titles). A man of enormous energy, he was undaunted by the parlous state of his capital city, and threw himself into its reconstruction, laying out the boulevard that would become Unter den Linden in 1647, and establishing new suburbs at Dorotheenstadt and Friedrichswerder. In 1671, he also invited Jewish people – who had been expelled in 1571 – back to Berlin, and by the Edict of Potsdam in 1685 allowed French Huguenots, then persecuted in their native country, to settle. More than 9,000 came, many of them bankers, industrialists and others with expertise in the weaving industry – all of which helped establish Berlin as not only a royal capital, but a manufacturing and financial powerhouse.

Frederick William's successor, Frederick I, had himself declared king of Prussia, and built a lavish palace at Charlottenburg, west of the city. He was every inch the enlightenment monarch, creating an Academy of Arts in 1696, one of Sciences in 1700, and founding the city's first hospital, the Charité, in 1710. Yet he was also a spendthrift (employing 24 royal trumpeters), and his son Frederick William I obsessively cut back on unnecessary outlays, reducing the feed ration to the royal horse stables. Beggars were rounded up and put to what the king regarded as useful work, and even Berlin's last convicted witch, Dorothea Steffin, was sentenced in 1727, not to death, but to a life-term of weaving in Spandau prison. Yet Frederick

William still oversaw the expansion of the army to 90,000 soldiers, giving Berlin, by 1740 a city of 98,000 people, the air of a garrison town.

The next Hohenzollern, Frederick II, earned himself the nickname "the Great" through his tactical brilliance during the Seven Years' War (1756–63), though not without his capital suffering the indignity of two foreign occupations (by the Austrians in 1757 and Russians in 1760). Frederick continued the enlightenment tone of his predecessors' rule by encouraging innovations such as water pumps and steam engines, and investing in a new cannon foundry and porcelain factory. He also permitted a free press and set up training schools for teachers.

Frederick's proud boast to his sister Sophia Wilhelmina was that "we are emerging from barbarism", but it could not last. Toleration went only so far, and even a leading German Enlightenment figure such as the philosopher Moses Mendelssohn (1729–1786), being Jewish, was denied membership of the Academy of Sciences.

One of Frederick's building projects had been the Brandenburg Gate, inaugurated in 1791, and it was through this that Napoleon marched in October 1806, loosening the grip of the Hohenzollerns on power. Society became more diverse, and the urban population poorer, leading to the revolutionary spasm of 1848, in which soldiers only barely put down the uprising.

A railway line to Potsdam opened in 1838, and Berlin's famous U-Bahn began operating in 1902, providing access to the centre from the sprawling suburbs of a city that had 1.3 million inhabitants by 1880. Meanwhile a sewerage system, begun in 1874, dampened the water-borne diseases, such as cholera, that had become an increasing blight. Thoughts of liberalisation were staunched by the regime of Otto von Bismarck, chancellor from 1871, who balanced the infant democratic politics of the newly formed German Empire with the demands of his royal masters (now emperors). Those demands, though, helped propel Germany into its disastrous defeat in the First World War, in whose aftermath the monarchy fell, and the Spartacist Revolution in 1919 nearly installed a communist regime in Berlin. The city got instead a restored, but unstable, democracy, rampant inflation in which the price of a loaf of bread soared to 3.6 million marks, and the disenchantment which helped Adolf Hitler's Nazi Party secure significant representation in parliament. Then, in 1933, in the aftermath of a fire in the Reichstag (parliament building), allegedly set by a left-wing radical, the party dismantled democracy completely.

Berlin's official 700th anniversary celebrations were held under the shadow of a regime that had already begun to persecute its Jewish population, whose synagogues were burnt and thousands of whom were arrested on Kristallnacht in November 1938. During the Second World War, almost all the remaining 90,000 Jewish residents of Berlin were deported to concentration camps and murdered. The city itself was targeted by major Allied air raids from early 1943, which within a year had rendered half a million Berliners homeless. By spring 1944, thousand-bomber raids were pulverising the centre, and then on April 16, 1945, the advancing 2.5-million-strong Soviet Red Army launched a last, massive assault on the city. In two weeks of brutal street-fighting, what was left of the city centre was practically obliterated, leaving around 100,000 Berliners, civilian and military, dead.

The Berlin that emerged on May 2, 1945, was as shattered as its ancestor had been in 1648 at the end of the Thirty Years' War. Yet now it faced division, and in large part Soviet occupation. Having endured Nazism and now the apocalyptic capture of their city, Berliners could have been forgiven for thinking that, for them, enlightenment was forever at an end.

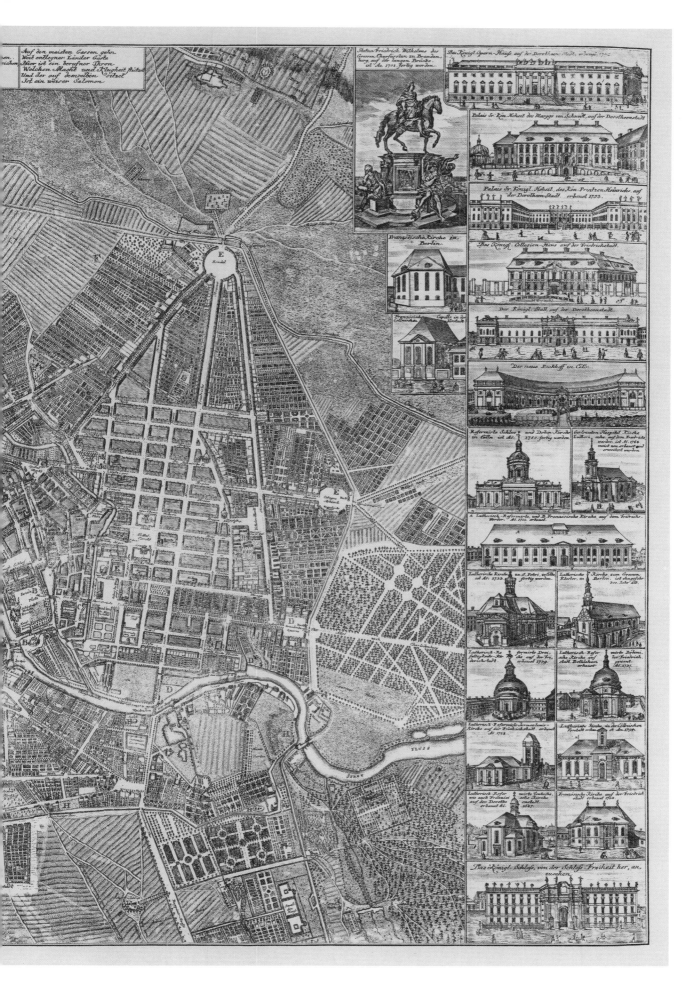

A PLAN
OF
BOSTON,
and its ENVIRONS.
shewing the true SITUATION of
HIS MAJESTY'S ARMY.
AND ALSO THOSE OF THE
REBELS.
Drawn by an Engineer at Boston.Oct.r 1775.

REFERENCE.

A { Copse Hill, a Battery of 8 Pieces of Cannon, Mortars &c&c Erected to
favour the Troops Landing on y. 17 June & to set Fire to Charles Town.
B { North & South Batteries, built by the Province for the defence of y. Harbour,
they are in a ruinous State.
C. Town Hall.
D. Fanuil Hall.
E. Two Batteries Erected on Wharfs against Dorchester Neck.
F. Fort Hill, a proper Place for constructing a Citadel.
G. Fortification now constructing for the immediate defence of the Town.
H. A Block House & 2 Strong Batteries pointing on part of Dorchester Neck.
I. Lines to defend the Boston Neck.
K { A Hill from whence the Enemy annoy y. Centries & Officers with small
Arms, but seldom do any Execution.
L { Roxbury Meeting House, upon a Hill from whence y. Enemy often Fire Cannon
into the Lines.
M { A Strong Post of the Enemy Fortified in appearance with great Judgment,
& much Elevated, from whence with a 24 Pounder they can just reach
the Lines.

EXPLANATION.
The Works shaded Green, shew those constructed
by His Majesty's Troops.
The Works shaded Yellow, shew those thrown up
by the Rebels, as they appear from Boston.

S ISLAND

HOG
ISLAND

Yards or Half a Mile

Cradle of Revolution

Boston, 1775

The map shows a settlement under siege by the revolutionary forces of George Washington's Continental Army, which eight years later would emerge as the victorious army of the new United States. Its draughter was a soldier on the opposing side, Lieutenant Richard Williams, who had reached Boston on June 11, 1775, to join his regiment, the 23rd Foot, bottled up in the city following the British army's retreat southwards after the battles of Lexington and Concord in April. Williams was known to be a cartographer, and so his superiors asked him to map the district, including elements of military importance. From the top of Beacon Hill, he could spy the rebel lines in the distance across the Charles River and commented sadly in his diary, "What a country we are come to, discord & civil wars began & peace & plenty turn'd out of doors."

The Boston that Williams mapped was very different to today's version, with the core of the city essentially an island, joined to the mainland only by the "Boston Neck" – which caused a stalemate as the Continental Army could not storm the fortifications there, nor could the British escape – while the Charles River debouched into marshy flatlands that made military manoeuvres difficult.

It was into this swampy landscape of the Shawmut Peninsula that Boston's first European settler, the Reverend William Blackstone, arrived, moving from a failed colony at Weymouth, to the south, in 1625. However, he found the isolation uncongenial and four years later invited a group of Puritans from nearby Charlestown to settle. Initially led by Isaac Johnson, his contemporary at Emmanuel College Cambridge, but then under the more redoubtable leadership of Governor John Winthrop, they made their base in September 1630 close to springs on the northern edge of Beacon Hill. Three years later, there were nearly 4,000 residents, and within a further three they had founded North America's first institution of higher learning at Harvard. New migrants were encouraged by William Wood who, in his 1634 *New England's Prospect*, remarked that Boston was "very pleasant" and did not suffer from "the three great annoyances of Woolves, Rattlesnakes and Musketoes".

A touch of intolerance entered the early settlement, as the Puritan strand of Anglicanism took firm hold, driving away the hapless Blackstone and leading to the persecution of religious dissenters, such as the Quaker Mary Dyer who was hanged in 1660. The colony though, prospered, adding the region's first circulating library in 1765, and weathering trials such as the regular outbreaks of smallpox – including one in 1721–22 that killed 844 people (almost one in twelve of the population) – and a fire that incinerated 350 buildings in March 1760.

There were a few early signs of the independent-mindedness that would place Boston among the first ranks of revolutionary cities – although with nowhere near the reputation for agitation that Paris, with uprisings in 1789 and 1848, or St Petersburg with its two world-upending revolutions in 1917, achieved. In 1689, Boston's church and civic leaders arrested the royal governor Sir Edmund Andros and frogmarched him into a prison cell.

That action did not stop the British crown folding Boston into the Province of Massachusetts Bay in 1691, but the sense that the colonists' interests were being ignored festered and exploded in spectacular fashion some 80 years later. Measures such as the 1765 Stamp Act, which imposed a duty on all printed goods, were resented in highly literate Boston, and the increasingly provocative actions of the hardline governor Francis Bernard aggravated tensions. In October 1768 he had 4,000 British troops stationed in the city and then, on March 5, 1770, an argument between apprentice wigmaker Edward Gerrish and a British army officer, over an unpaid bill, exploded into violence, during which five colonists were shot dead.

The Boston Massacre marked a turning point and when a British-imposed tax on imported tea further raised tempers, on December 16, 1773, the Sons of Liberty, part of the mix of increasingly anti-British radicals, dumped 342 chests of tea into Boston Harbour as a protest. Two years later, the revolution had broken out; the British found themselves fighting a desperate fight for survival at Bunker Hill to the northwest of Boston and were then penned into the city. The siege lasted nearly 11 months, before the British gave up and evacuated the garrison to Nova Scotia. Ironically, Williams' map was printed just a few weeks before the surrender, rendering it redundant.

Williams did not live, either, to see his side's final defeat in 1783, as he fell ill, returned to Britain and died in late April 1776. The Boston which he had mapped developed slowly, taking time to heal the scars of the Revolutionary War. Its harbour brought it prosperity, profiting from the Triangular Trade, one leg of which was the trafficking of enslaved Africans to the New World, but in Boston's case involved the refining of sugar from plantations in the Caribbean into rum and molasses.

By 1810, Boston's population had reached 34,000, almost double that at the end of the war. Although fashionable new streets started to be built to the east of Boston Common, the open space which the settlement had somehow preserved, there was still an air of the bucolic, as the town's council levied a cow tax on the animals that still grazed on the Common (limiting the number of animals to 119 in 1823, and levying an annual fee of $5 per beast). The cows were only finally banned in 1830.

Boston formally became a city in 1822, allowing the new authorities to take more concrete steps to improve conditions in the increasingly crowded centre. A proper water supply finally arrived in October 1848, carried along 15 miles of aqueduct from Lake Cochituate. The opening ceremony was a carnival, with seven black horses ceremonially pulling large cast iron water pipes, accompanied by odes composed by Temperance campaigners (very much in favour of water as a beverage).

The Back Bay had been dammed in 1818–21, allowing the city ultimately to reclaim hundreds of acres of land which by 1880 had joined the old island of Boston to the mainland in one continuous conurbation. The extra space was needed, as new Bostonians flooded in, drawn by the textile mills and other light industry established in the suburbs, their number swelled by Irish migrants fleeing the effects of the Great Famine of the 1840s, creating the large Roman Catholic presence it has had ever since. The railways arrived in the 1830s, and in 1897 Boston received its first subway on Tremont Street, assisting movement in a city which by now had absorbed previously independent settlements such as Roxbury, Dorchester and Charlestown.

These acquisitions meant that by 1875, the city's population had reached 341,000, close to half its size today. In the century that followed, Boston would undergo many vicissitudes: earning unwanted fame as the hometown of the swindler Charles Ponzi in the 1920s, whose inventive scheme raked in $15 million in eight months and lent his name to the whole genre of pyramid frauds. It also experienced one of the more unusual disasters in urban history on January 15, 1919, when an explosion at a factory in the North End sent a flood of boiling molasses surging down the street at nearly 60 kilometres an hour, crushing and burning 21 people to death.

Through it all, though, Boston continued to adapt and grow, in 2007 completing the "Big Dig", one of the largest infrastructure projects in urban history, which placed the Central Artery highway underground. No longer a revolutionary city, Boston still knows how to do things on a grand scale.

Back to Nature

Seoul, c 1795

The city is encircled by nature, the Dobongsan and Bukhansan mountains framing the small urban grid of Joseon-era Seoul, depicted in full overleaf with an intricated pattern of waterways and the main royal palace, the Changdeokgung, set in a wooded area as also shown on the map extract to the right. The *tosongdo* (map of the capital) forms part of a tradition of pictorial landscape maps popular in Korea and this one was probably made for royal use, as it is oriented with south at the top to reflect the direction the king would look out from his palace while attending to matters of state. It probably dates from the 1790s, during the reign of King Jeongjo (reigned 1776–1800), as it depicts the Royal Guards Garrison which was instituted in 1785, but abolished in 1802.

Seoul began as Wiryeseong, the capital of the ancient Baekche state in 18BC, and by the mid-7th century AD had been annexed into the Silla Kingdom and provided with its first set of walls, with a small summer palace being added in 1104 during the Goryeo dynasty. Then called Hanyang, it remained a small provincial town until chosen in 1394 by King Taejo to be the royal capital of his new Joseon dynasty. The pace of construction was rapid: within a year the Gyeongbokgung Palace had been built, together with the Jongmyo, a Confucian shrine to hold the memorial tablets for Taejo and his royal descendants. A year more, and the imposing set of 6-metre- (20-foot-) high fortress walls that defined the limit of the city for around 600 years had been added, punctuated by four grand gateways, principal among them the Donhwamun, which led into Changdeokgung Palace, another royal residence, built in 1412.

By now officially called Hanseong, the city acquired the popular nickname Seoul (or "capital") during the years of Joseon rule, remaining the epicentre of political and administrative power but growing relatively slowly – from 100,000 people in 1429 to around 250,000 in 1910. Modernisation came in the late 19th century as foreign trade increased, and the beginnings of industrialisation occurred with electric power reaching the city in 1899, when Jongno Street became the first to be illuminated and an electric streetcar service began, all sponsored by the reformist King Gojong, who also promoted western-style schools and hospitals.

The first of the upheavals which Korea, and Seoul with it, would endure in the 20th century came in 1910 when the country was annexed by Japan. The new rulers rechristened the city Gyeongseong and clamped down on any expressions of Korean culture. Although the Japanese paved roads and built a new sewage system there, deprived of its political raison d'être, Seoul shrank, retracting once again within the fortress walls. The liberation from the Japanese in 1945 opened only a small window of hope. The country split into a communist-aligned North and a South that looked to the United States, with Seoul, now South Korea's capital,

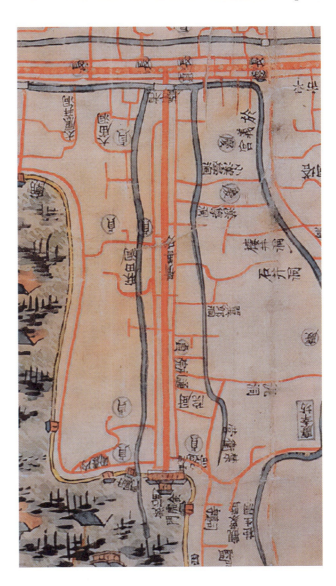

perilously close to the border between the two. Within five years the Korean War had broken out, during which the city changed hands four times, leaving it utterly ruined when UN forces finally entered it in March 1951.

Reconstruction was slow at first, but gathered pace in the 1960s as South Korea's industries experienced an export-led boom, at first focused on iron and textiles and then diversifying into light consumer goods and electronics. The city borders expanded as Seoul absorbed neighbouring Gwangju-gun, Sheung-gun, Gimpo-gu and, most importantly Gangnam-gu, south of the Han River, which became Seoul's most fashionable quarter. The construction of the Hannam Bridge (1966–69) and Gyeongbu Expressway (1968–70) accelerated the shift of gravity of the city towards Gangnam, but the rapid development came at a cost of pollution, congestion and the growth of informal settlements around the periphery.

Recognising the problems, Seoul's metropolitan authority embarked on a programme of regeneration, widening roads, building new housing in the incipient slums, and opening seven new subway lines. By the time Seoul hosted the Olympic Games in 1988, its population had plateaued at 10 million, but it had begun to get to grips with resolving many of the issues that blighted rapidly growing cities in countries whose economies were not growing as strongly as that of South Korea.

By the 2020s, South Korea was ranked among the world's 15 largest economies, with around a fifth of the population and most of its financial institutions based in Seoul, a city which buzzed with the country's new-found talent for soft power, with K-Pop, K-Dramas and Korean cuisine among its astonishingly successful exports. The city had acquired a skyline filled with skyscrapers, the tallest among them the 555-metre (1,819-foot) Lotte Tower, the sixth highest in the world.

Yet it continued to work towards a more sustainable urban environment: the Cheonggyecheon Stream, a $900 million restoration project carried out between 2003 and 2005, involved dismantling an urban freeway and reopening the stream beneath it, which had long been covered over, and regreening the area with a strip of urban forest. This, together with other initiatives – such as the Seoul Urban Forest and the Seoullo 7017 "skygarden", which transformed a concrete flyover into a 983-metre- (0.6-mile-) long public walkway showcasing 228 species of plants – shows that the appreciation of nature so apparent in the 1795 map of the city is still present in its 21st-century citizens.

Like the bell in the Bosingak Pavilion on Jongno Street, which tolled the morning and evening hours for the closing of the fortress gates during the Joseon Dynasty (and still does so on New Year's Eve), the people of Seoul still appreciate tradition, but in a very modern form.

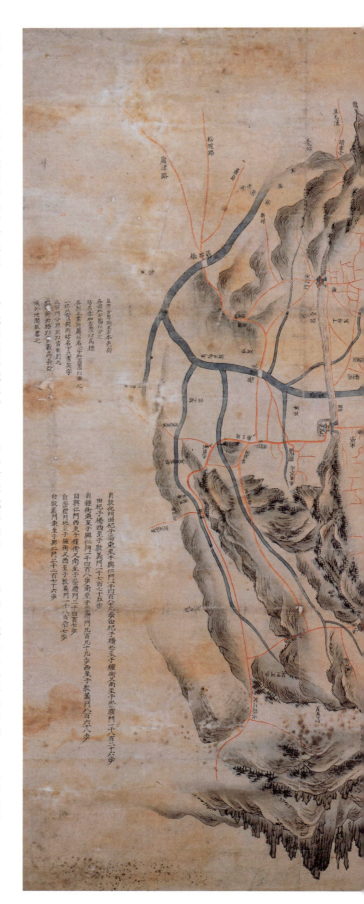

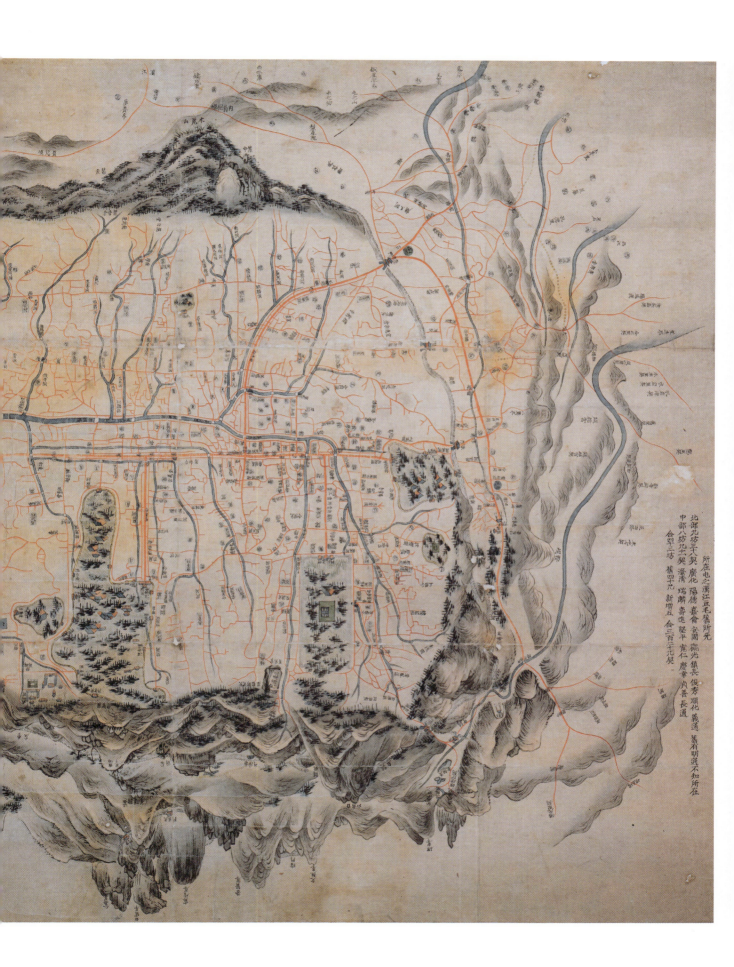

Birth of a Capital

Washington, DC, 1795

The first plan of Washington, DC after it became the national capital of the United States is almost the birth certificate of one of the world's most powerful cities. Shown in full overleaf, it was drafted by the British cartographer John Russell (c 1750–1829) and appeared bound in a later edition of John Reid's large-format *The American Atlas* (1796).

Many nations have gone in search of a new capital, often to move away from hotbeds of opposition – as the government of Myanmar did in building a showcase, but scarcely inhabited, new city deep in the jungle at Nay Pyi Taw in 2005 – or to rebalance power structures away from entrenched central areas, as Indonesia chose to do in 2024 in selecting a new capital city at Nusantara on the island of Borneo. Yet a new nation has a more obvious reason to search for a new capital, and for the United States, the need was pressing.

The capital had been provisionally established at Philadelphia, site of the First Continental Congress in 1774, but it decamped to Princeton, New Jersey, in 1783 following an army mutiny. There was rising sentiment in favour of a fixed capital, free from the influence of the state in which it was situated, leading to intense horse-trading by those states which felt that, nonetheless, immense prestige, and likely enormous revenues, would flow to whichever of them won the prize. Arguments raged over whether it should be in the northern states, with their greater population, or go to the south, creating a more even geographical balance. In the end, by dint of the southern states agreeing to take on some of the financial debt incurred by the north during the Revolutionary War, a slight southern tilt was achieved, with a site identified at the confluence of the Potomac and Eastern Branch (now Anacostia) Rivers on the border between Maryland and Virginia.

An initial survey was carried out by Andrew Ellicott and the African American surveyor Benjamin Banneker, which confirmed the area's suitability. On July 16, 1790, Congress passed the Residence Act designating it as the future seat of the Federal Government. The French-born engineer Pierre Charles L'Enfant was tasked with designing the new city. His vision laid the template for the urban landscape, with a strong grid pattern, wide diagonal boulevards (named after the original states, most famously Pennsylvania Avenue, which links the White House and Congress), with streets on the east–west axis of the grid named in alphabetical order, and those on the north–south numerically. And when initial government attempts to sell lots of land in the new city in October 1791 fell flat, he drafted the very first official plan of Washington to encourage investors.

By 1800, something like the nucleus of a city was in place. The "President's House" (the first version of the White House) was completed three years too late for George Washington to move in, so the first residents were John Adams and his wife Abigail. The first 131 federal employees had arrived in June that year, making up the bulk of the initial population and beginning the tradition that the city would, for good or for ill, always be dominated by the machinery of government.

The city struggled to get into gear, with Congress more interested in matters of national import than in funding what it saw as local projects. The first school did not open until 1806, while a surging crime wave was barely contained by Washington's single policeman, who also had to act as a health inspector and supervise the fire service. The "solution" in 1811, to double the police force to two, hardly helped.

The city soon had worse things to worry about, as in August 1814 the British captured it during the War of 1812, and engaged in a five-day campaign of arson during which the Presidential House, the Capitol (whose original plan in 1793 had won a $500 prize for its designer Dr William Thornton), the Arsenal and the Treasury Building were all burnt. In the aftermath of the inferno, an alarmed Congress nearly mandated a move back to Philadelphia, with the motion to do so defeated by only 83 votes to 74.

Washington rose from the ashes, with reconstruction of the Capitol completed in 1819. The Library of Congress, whose collection had also gone up in smoke, was reinvigorated by the purchase of Thomas Jefferson's library of 7,000 volumes for the princely sum of $23,950. The mid-19th century saw steady growth for the city, whose population burgeoned from 14,093 in 1800 (including 3,244 enslaved people) to 51,687 in 1850 (with 3,687 enslaved). An increasing number of civil servants made up much of the growth, though in 1847 the city actually shrank in size after the voters of Alexandria on the outskirts of Washington had second thoughts and opted to return to the state of Virginia (but Georgetown, on the city's western fringe, at the highest navigable point on the Potomac, opted to remain loyal).

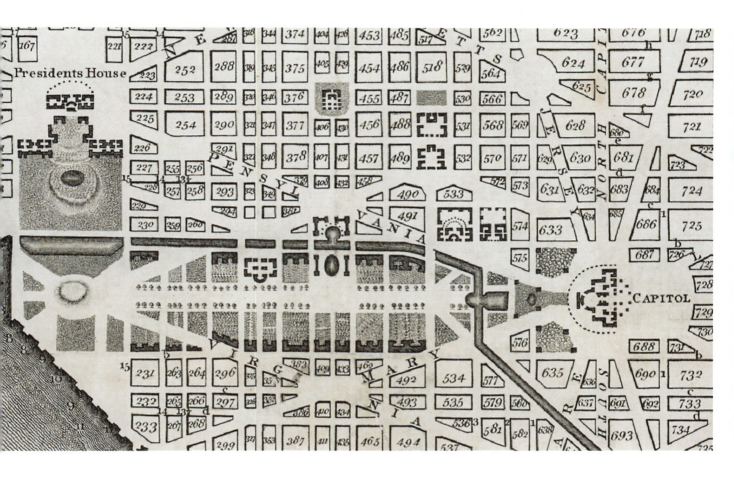

The Civil War brought a large military contingent to the city, which grew even further, reaching over 130,000 by 1870. The arrival of the Baltimore to Ohio Railroad in 1835 had alleviated the city's transportation problems (supplemented by the addition of the Baltimore and Potomac Railroad in 1872), but attempts by the city's governor Alexander Robey Shepherd to improved Washington's creaky infrastructure led to unsustainable overspending, and to Congress abolishing the local government of the District of Columbia (the larger area in which Washington lay) in 1874 and appointing commissioners to run it directly.

It was an issue that would bedevil Washington for the next century and a half. Named after the leader of a revolution whose basis had been that there should be no taxation without representation, it was a city that had no representation in Congress, and now not even its own city government. Martin Luther King's March on Washington on August 28, 1963 (during which he gave his "I Have a Dream" speech), was in a city which had only just received three electoral college votes two years before (and so having some say at least in presidential elections). The city did regain the privilege of its own directly elected mayor in 1973, though urban decay, in part caused by the move of much of the middle class from the city centre, left it almost bankrupt by 1995 and again suffering the indignity of the federal government running its finances. The movement for the District of Columbia, and with it Washington, DC, to become a state, or at least have representation in Congress and the Senate, is very much alive. The accolade of capital of the free United States had come at a price that still, over two centuries later, was being paid.

GEORGE TOWN

PART OF VIRGINIA

WITHIN THE TERRITORY OF COLUMBIA

ROCK CREEK

POTOMACK RIVER

Presidents House

PLAN
of the CITY of
Washington,
in the Territory of Columbia,
ceded by the States of
VIRGINIA AND MARYLAND
to the
United States of America,
and by them established as the
SEAT of their GOVERNMENT,
after the YEAR
1800.

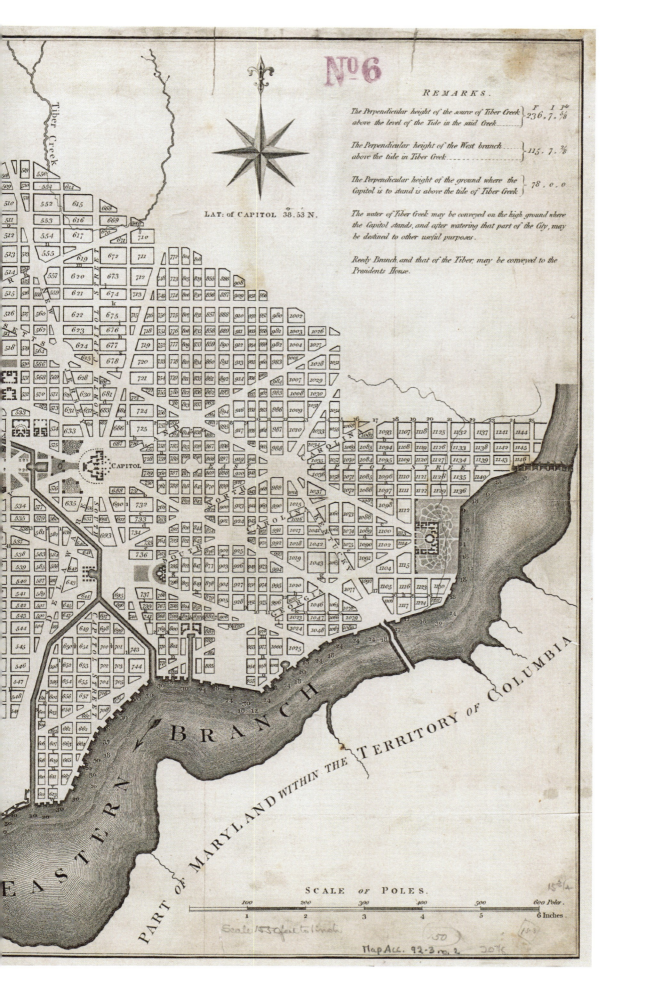

Tiber Creek

LAT: of CAPITOL 38.53 N.

REMARKS.

The Perpendicular height of the source of Tiber Creek
above the level of the Tide in the said Creek .... } F I I.
236.7. ⅜

The Perpendicular height of the West branch ......
above the tide in Tiber Creek .... } 115. 7. ⅜

The Perpendicular height of the ground where the
Capitol is to stand is above the tide of Tiber Creek } 78. 0. 0

The water of Tiber Creek may be conveyed on the high ground where
the Capitol stands, and after watering that part of the City, may
be destined to other useful purposes.

Reedy Branch, and that of the Tiber, may be conveyed to the
Presidents House.

CAPITOL

EASTERN BRANCH

PART OF MARYLAND WITHIN THE TERRITORY OF COLUMBIA

SCALE OF POLES.

100   200   300   400   500   600 Poles.

1   2   3   4   5   6 Inches.

Scale 153 feet to 1 inch

Map Ac. 92-3 no. 2

From Garden to City

Cape Town, 1795

References
A. *Table Mountain.*
B. *Lion's Head, or the Sugar-loaf.*
C. *Lion's Rump.*
D. *Devilsberg.*
E.E. *The Company's Garden.*
F. *The Church.*
G. *Hospital.*
H. *City Hotel.*
I. *Apartments for the Slaves.*
K. *Governor's House.*
L. *Company's Cove.*
M. *Corn Magazine.*
N. *Battery of 4 Guns.*
O. *Batt.º of 9 Guns.*
P. *Batt.º of 11 Guns.*
Q. *Batt.º of 8 Guns.*
R. *Batt.º of 8 Guns.*
S. *Batt.º of 22 Guns.*
   All the Guns are of
   small Calibres.
T. *New Barracks for 3000 Men.*
U. *New Justice.*
W. *The Governor's Garden.*
X. *Powder Magazine.*
Y.Y. *Store Houses.*

TABLE BAY

the Anchoring Ground

A PLAN of the TOWN of the CAPE of GOODHOP and its Environs, taken by Mons.ʳ Bourset, in December 1770.

LONDON: Published with some Additions and Emendations, By Wᵐ FADEN, Geographer to THE KING and to H.R.H. THE PRINCE of W. Charing Cross, Nov.ʳ 25ᵗʰ 1795.

Some cities were never intended to be cities. Cape Town, now a metropolis of nearly 5 million people, began as something of a fortified vegetable patch. The map, by the English cartographer William Faden (1749–1836) – who in 1783 became official geographer to King George III, and published the first Ordnance Survey map in 1801 – is dominated by three features. The thick contour lines denote Table Mountain, its 1,085-metre (3,560-foot) summit, bounded by Lion's Head and Lion's Rump ridges, providing a stunning visual theatre. Below it are the two star-shaped forts and gun batteries, placed to protect the "gardens" – the company's and the governor's – which were the raison d'être of the settlement.

Other cities, too, have had unlikely starting points: Eridu, in Mesopotamia, began around 4500BC as a shrine to the creator god Enki, believed to reside in an underground spring there; Vienna was founded as a Roman legionary fortress in the 1st century AD; while Sydney was originally intended as no more than a penal colony. Cape Town owes its existence to being a convenient stopping point for ships coasting Africa on their way to the spice islands of the East Indies. The Portuguese navigator António de Saldanha was the first European to land at Table Bay, in 1503, though a defeat by the Khoi, the region's indigenous people, in 1510 halted ventures inland.

Glowing reports of the area's potential given by survivors of the 1647 shipwreck of a Dutch vessel, the *Haarlem*, encouraged the Dutch East India Company (the VOC) to send Jan van Riebeeck to establish a provisioning station there in 1652. It was very much a company settlement, with a fort, a few streets parallel to the shore and a main thoroughfare, the Heerengracht (named for the canal in Amsterdam), that led to the vegetable garden, the most important part of "De Kaap", as the Dutch called it. The first enslaved people arrived in 1654, transported from East Africa, Madagascar and Bengal, bringing with them Islam to add to the complex mix of cultures that eventually emerged. Free White farmers followed in 1657, as van Riebeeck decided that the site deserved, in his opinion, a grander future, though this earned him a rebuke from the VOC's directors, who warned, "We have remarked that you are gradually tending toward the building of a town … this idea should be abandoned."

Fortunately for Cape Town, van Riebeeck had his way. The Castle of Good Hope – South Africa's oldest extant building – was completed in 1679, while the first non-Dutch settlers, Huguenots fleeing the persecution of Protestantism in France, arrived in 1688. By 1731, the population had reached a still modest 3,157, with around a third still VOC employees,

585 "free burghers" (the White European farmers and their families) and the rest largely enslaved Asians and, increasingly, Black Africans.

As Dutch commercial power waned, the French intervened, sending a garrison in 1781 to ward off possible British occupation and adding a touch of French flair to the "Cape Dutch" colonial style of high gables and whitewashed walls. Cape Town bounced between the British and Dutch in the Napoleonic Wars: occupied by Britain in 1795 at the time of Faden's map, it was only definitively removed from Dutch control in 1814.

British rule brought freedom for the enslaved in 1834, and it also sent 10,000 Dutch families north and east from 1836, as they left British territory in the Groot Trek ("great trek"). The municipality of Cape Town, formally established in 1840, was run by a board of commissioners elected by those owning property valued at £10 or more, so effectively excluding Africans, even though Cape Town's political atmosphere had long been, in theory, more tolerant than other parts of South Africa.

Gradually the city spread southwards down the Cape Peninsula, spawning new suburbs such as Woodstock, Rondebosch and Kalk Bay. The opening of Alfred Dock in 1870 brought larger ships and more migrants, particularly after the discovery of large diamond deposits in 1870 and gold in 1886. The city acquired all the trappings of a European colonial town, including a literary society in 1829 and a university in 1918. What it did not acquire, under the independent Union of South Africa from 1910, and particularly under the National Party governments after 1948, which implemented the discriminatory structures of the apartheid regime, was equality for the majority of "non-White" residents.

By the 1950s, Cape Town was highly mixed, with intermarriage between Europeans, Khoi and Black Africans and the presence of many "Cape Malays" (mainly descendants of enslaved Asians) creating a very diverse population. The apartheid regime was as harsh as elsewhere, declaring the mixed District Six area as "White only" in 1966 and removing 60,000 inhabitants, though "non-Whites" could still vote and hold office in Cape Town until 1971. It was an involuntary Cape Town resident that finally brought an end to apartheid. Nelson Mandela, South Africa's first Black African president, was imprisoned on Robben Island in Table Bay for 18 of the 27 years that he was incarcerated, before being released in 1990. Only then did Cape Town complete its transition from Dutch garden to a city open to all.

Let There Be Light

London, 1807

The London of Islington engraver Benjamin Baker's map, shown in full overleaf, is comparatively small, with locations now firmly within its centre, such as Islington and Chelsea, still mere villages around its periphery. All that was about to change. The population, around a million in 1807, surged to 2.2 million by the time Baker died in 1841 (having risen to become chief engraver to the Ordnance Survey), as the urban leviathan digested ever more land to create new suburbs.

The city changed in another crucial respect: it became light. Until the 19th century, the hours of darkness were precisely that – although some cities, such as medieval Cordoba, had a few roads and buildings illuminated by oil lamps, the light they cast was dim, and nighttime streets were largely the domain of the desperate, the criminal, or the well-guarded. Work that could not be done by the light of flickering oil lamps ceased at sunset, and good folk hurried home before darkness (or in many cases, curfew) arrived.

It fell to a German migrant, Frederick Winsor (1763–1830), to bring light to London. It had long been known that coal produced a gas that, when heated, produced a luminous flame. In 1792, the Scottish engineer William Murdoch piped this into his house, and carried out the arguably rash experiment of igniting it to light his home.

Winsor's ambitions were greater: on June 4th, 1805, he placed lamps powered by gas on a wall outside his house on Pall Mall to celebrate King George III's birthday. A bemused crowd watched the spectacle for several hours, and the display helped Winsor get permission for something even more eye-catching. He erected 13 lampposts along Pall Mall. The posts were topped with glass globes, into each of which three jets of gas were piped. The array was lit up on January 28, 1807, and burnt each night until April 16. The display was a resounding success: the gas lights on Pall Mall were made permanent in 1809, by the end of 1813 Westminster Bridge was fully lit by gas, and, ten years later, there were 39,500 gas-fired street lamps illuminating over 215 miles of London's streets.

A dash for gas ensued, as other cities scrambled to install the new-fangled devices. Preston came next, when a 12-metre- (40-foot-) high obelisk was erected in 1816, atop which a 56-centimetre (22-inch) globe lit up its market square. Bristol followed the next year, together with Baltimore,

which became the first gas-lit city outside Britain, when lamps were installed on Market Street. By 1828, Paris, too, had 10,000 gaslights, though New York was a comparative late adopter, with none in place until 1825.

Evening light opened up new vistas. As well as the obvious security benefits brought by the streets (at least the main ones) no longer being shrouded in inky blackness, middle-class Londoners now took to evening shopping in shops with large plate glass windows for browsing, and in whose interiors it was now possible to view the goods after dark. Theatres, too, changed, with the first to be lit by gas being the Lyceum, on August 6, 1817. Actors now no longer needed gaudy make-up or extravagant gestures as audiences could actually see them properly (though some grumbled that the lights were so bright that well-heeled theatregoers in the stalls suffered the indignity of being able to spot each other's servants in the upper tiers).

By the 1850s, gas was ubiquitous, with gas fittings even installed in the traditionalist bastion of Parliament. But there was an insurgent challenger: electricity. Electric-powered arc lights were briefly installed on the Place de la Concorde in Paris in 1841, on the Champs Élysées in 1856, and at the opening of the Clifton Suspension Bridge in 1864, but falls in the price of gas, and the invention of the von Welsbach mantle in 1891, which gave a brighter flame with less gas, meant electricity struggled to gain traction. Forty arc lights, though, were installed along Victoria Embankment between Westminster and Waterloo in 1879, and the opening three years later of the Edison Company Electric Light Station at Holborn, the world's first coal-fired power station, and another on Pearl Street in New York's Manhattan, provided reliable sources of electricity that boosted its attractiveness to customers.

Electricity reshaped the domestic and urban landscapes in ways even gas had not. The electric elevator, invented by Werner von Siemens in Mannheim, Germany, in 1880, allowed skyscrapers to become a practical proposition, while Edison's incandescent lightbulb, invented in 1879, gave light at the flick of a switch in people's homes.

Gas, though, did not die out. When the Eiffel Tower was completed in 1889 it was illuminated by 10,000 gas lamps, and in 1956 there were still 529,000 gas lamps operating in the United Kingdom. Even in the 21st century their use continues, but now rather as heritage devices: London

retained 1,500 of them in 2021, though operated on timers rather than by the time-honoured ritual of gas-lighters climbing up ladders to ignite or douse their flames at sunset and sunrise. And although in 2017 around 840 million people worldwide still did not have access to a regular supply of electricity, most of those were rural dwellers. For people living in cities, the banishing of darkness from the streets, an event whose novelty astounded the onlookers at Frederick Winsor's 1807 jamboree, seems an entirely natural occurrence.

A PLAN OF
LONDON,
WESTMINSTER,
AND
SOUTHWARK.

HACKNEY

HOXTON

Bethnal
Green

STEPNEY

Mile End Road

White Horse Lane

Rose La.

Brook Street

Ratcliff Cross

Upper Shadwell

Ratcliffe Highway

Cable Street

Rosemary L.

White Chapel

Ayliff Street

Good mans Fields

Wentworth S.

Montague Str.

Church Str.

Hare Str.

Church Str.

Cock Lane

Shoreditch

St. Agnes le Clare

Hoxton Road

Charles

Royal R.

Worship Str.

Chiswell Str.

Barbican

Old Street

Goswell Street

Brick Lane

White Cross

Bunhill Row

Brick Lane

Cheapside

Leadenhall S.

Cornhill

Bishopsgate Street

Tower Hill

East Smithfield

St. Catherines

East Smithfield

THAMES

Wapping

Redriff

Rotherhith

Paradise S.

Shipwright S.

Queen St.

Cherry Garden S.

Bermondsey Street

St. Olaves St.

Snow Fields

Queen St.

Peter St.

Red Cross St.

Kent Street

the Borough

Long Lane

Horsel Street

Grange Walk

Kings Road

Grange Road

WALWORTH

CUTTS

B. Baker sculp! Islington.

Map 265.3. [179-?]

6 3/8

Possession & Dispossession
Sydney, 1814 & 2024

The map overleaf, showing land grants in what is now the greater Sydney area, documents both acts of possession and dispossession. Drafted by J Burr, its publication by the London-based G Ballisat came just 26 years after British settlers arrived at the great natural theatre of Sydney Bay. The act of colonisation came with a double exercise of force, both directed at the more than 750 convicts transported against their will by the military guard aboard the First Fleet that arrived in January 1788, and on the 5,000 or so people of the Eora nation, on whose land the British had disembarked.

Captain Arthur Phillip, the commander of the fleet, justified his actions under the European legal notion of *terra nullius*, that indigenous people's claim to territory was deemed void if they were not "effectively occupying it". This largely happened by fixed settlements, neat territorial divisions and agricultural cultivation, all notions alien to the First Australians' concept of what it meant to live on the land and their traditional use of its resources. The place to them was hardly a "new world", as the ancestors of the coastal Eora people – the Darug people of the area inland from Parramatta to the Blue Mountains and the Dharawal people south of Botany Bay – had lived there for at least 30,000 years.

Their fate was to be a repetition of that of other indigenous peoples on whose land cities were founded by outsiders through the ages. In North America, the future site of New York was supposedly "bought" in 1624 by the Dutch trader Peter Minuit from local Lenape people for 60-guilders-(then around $24) worth of trade goods, beads and other trinkets, the acceptance of which the indigenous partners in the transaction could hardly have understood to mean that they had now lost all rights to their traditional lands. The very word "colony" derives from a notion of military occupation, coming from the Roman *colonia* of military veterans implanted in conquered lands to ensure their quiescence. Great cities such as Vienna (*Vindobonum*) or York (*Eboracum*) owe their origins to the displacement of others' rights.

Sydney, named for Thomas Townshend, 1st Viscount Sydney and British Home Secretary, who had recommended its settlement (in part to forestall any French move to do the same), almost failed at its outset. The initial settlement at the enticing-sounding Botany Bay proved to have little fresh water, and was moved within weeks. The new site at Port Jackson was hardly better and struggled with poor soil, leading to a near state of famine only alleviated by the arrival of the Second Fleet in 1790, and then the granting of parcels of land to former convicts on which to grow food (the type of allotments shown in the Burr and Ballisat map). Without the assistance of First Australians, it might have vanished altogether. Men like Bennelong, an elder of the Eora people, who acted as an interlocutor between the British and his people after his capture in November 1789, helped calm the tensions that arose as it became clear that not only was the European settlement permanent, but it was steadily expanding inland. Nonetheless, violence flared between 1795 and 1810 with the Darug people, and in 1814–16 with the Dharawal people, as settlers steadily encroached on their ancestral lands.

Yet Sydney survived, and prospered. Lachlan Macquarie, governor of what was now designated New South Wales from 1810 to 1821, oversaw its transition from a penal colony into an infant free society. He established a bank, hospital and the Royal Botanic Gardens, employing the architect and former convict Francis Greenway, who had been transported for forgery, to build a series of striking Georgian buildings, such as Hyde Park Barracks (1819), and to design a formal grid layout. That this was not too rigid, was applauded by the English novelist Anthony Trollope, who visited in 1875 and commented that the place was "not parallelogrammic and rectangular".

By 1836 there were 29,000 free settlers in "Sydney Town", and the move away from its convict roots accelerated after the end of transportation there in 1840. Despite its temporary eclipse as Australia's largest city by Melbourne, whose growth was fuelled by a gold rush from 1852, Sydney continued to expand: its population burgeoned from 95,000 in 1861 to 387,000 thirty years later, and it acquired grand new public buildings such as the Town Hall (1889) and General Post Office (1892). New suburbs such as Daceyville and Matraville sprang up after the First World War, the city knitted together by the steam trams that had begun service in 1879 and which by the 1930s boasted 1,600 cars in operation.

Sydney's iconic Harbour Bridge was completed in 1932, and its other most emblematic landmark, the Opera House with its dramatic sail-like roofs (containing over a million ceramic tiles), was added to the city's skyline in 1973. On the face of it, Sydney's transformation into a global city was complete with its hosting of the Olympic Games in 2000, and a population that reached five million in 2016 (around a third born overseas), the urban sprawl illustrated on the modern-day map below. Yet the contradictions inherent in the celebrations, in 1988, of the bicentenary of its foundation were still raw: it was only in 1962 that First Australians were given the right to vote in elections, and the doctrine of terra nullius persisted until the Mabo judgement in 1992 set it aside and gave them the right to exercise claims on their traditional lands. The divisions on Burr and Ballisat's map ran far deeper and longer than the lines on the page.

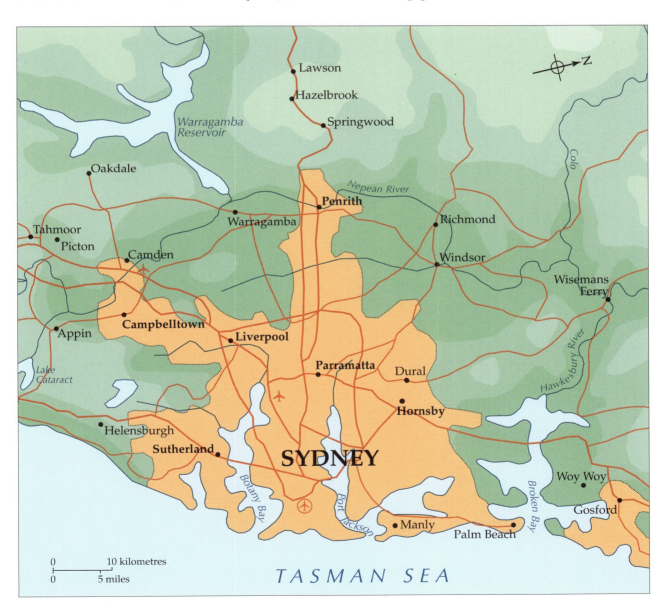

VIGILENTIA ROBUR VOLUPTAS

*Admiral Hunter,
Late Governor of
NEW SOUTH WALES,
This Plan is by Permission
most respectfully Dedicated
by His Obliged & Obed.t Serv.ts
J. Burr & G. Ballisat.*

REFERENCE to DISTRICTS.

A . *Northern Boundary*
B . *Liberty Plains*
C . *Banks Town*
D . *Parramatta*
EEEE . *Grounds reserved for Gov.t purposes*
F . *Concord*
G . *Petersham*
H . *Bulanaming*
I . *Sydney*
K . *Hunters Hills*
L . *Eastern Farms*
M . *Field of Mars*
N . *Ponds*
O . *Toongabee*
P . *Prospect*
Q . *Dundas*
R . *Richmond Hill*
S . *Green Hills*
T . *Phillip*
U . *Nelson*
V . *Castle Hill*
W . *Evan*
X . *Bringelly*
Y . *Cabramatta*
Z . *Botany Bay*
Æ . *Castlereagh*
Ƀ . *Upper Nelson*
Œ . *Cooks*
Ӡɛ . *Minto*
ƆC . *Cow Pasture*

E.
Nº 3.
29383 Acres

12300 Acres
Orphan Grant

9345 Acres
Common Lease

5860 Acres
Common Lease

BOTANY BAY

PORT JACKSON

Emu

Published Nov. 22d 1810 by the Proprietors

RIVER

97

New Acres
Common Grant

M.C.O'Connel
2500
Acres

R

S

Boolasbury

T
6150 Acres
Common Grant

U

5650 Acres
Common Grant

3500 Acres
Common Grant

B

E.
Nº 2.
34559 Acres

Second Branch

First Branch

Æ

HAWKESBURY RIVER

Swamp

Swamp

Plan
OF THE
ALLOTMENTS OF GROUND,
Granted from the Crown
In
NEW SOUTH WALES.

Shoal Water

Shoal Water

Granted to
Andw. Thompson

Acres

Sº Arm or PittWater

BROKEN BAY

North Arm

...shall Street and R.Wilkinson, Cornhill, London.

Engraved by Saml Neele, 352 Strand; near Wm. St Surrey.

Defenestrations & Liberations

Prague, 1816

Prague's position, sandwiched between the neighbouring leviathans of Germany, and (before its dissolution in 1918), the Austro-Hungarian Empire, and on the route of French armies marching eastwards or Russian ones advancing westwards, has condemned it to a constant struggle of asserting, and then losing, its freedom. Sometimes it has done so by hurling perceived oppressors out of windows.

Shown in full overleaf, Joseph Jüttner's map of Prague, the first of the city created using scientific trigonometrical techniques, suffered delays through one of these tussles. Jüttner was an engineer at the military Mathematics School in Prague. Commissioned in 1812 by Emperor Francis I to carry out a detailed survey of the city, Jüttner's work was only completed four years later, having been interrupted by the exigencies of the Napoleonic Wars (a cause dear to Ferdinand's heart, as he had been unceremoniously deposed by Napoleon as Holy Roman Emperor in 1806, leaving him with the unwieldy title of Emperor of Austria and King of Hungary, Croatia and Bohemia).

Bohemia, the larger region within which Prague was positioned, took its name from the Celtic Boii who established an *oppidum* (fortified settlement) near the city in the 5th century BC. In a foretaste of what was to come, they were displaced by Germanic peoples in the 5th century AD, who were then ousted by Slavs around a century later. By the late 9th century two castles had been built, at Vyšehrad and Hradčany, the latter just across the Vltava river from the Staré Město (Old Town), the nucleus of the city of Prague.

The settlement became the capital of the Přemyslid dukes of Bohemia, one of whom, Václav the Good (or Wenceslas), was murdered by his brother, Boleslav, in 935 and subsequently canonised (and immortalised in the Christmas carol *Good King Wenceslas*). His statue, marked on Jüttner's map, overlooks the square named for him, which was laid out in 1348, and is one of Europe's biggest (and certainly one of its longest), at 750 metres (nearly half a mile) in length.

A bishopric by 973, the city expanded slowly, its status as a trading post attracting a significant Jewish population (which established the Old-New Synagogue in 1270), while a new district, the Malá Strana (Little Quarter) was founded in the shadow of the Hradčany in 1257, becoming a centre for German merchants. Prague (and Bohemia) slid out of Přemyslid control with the death of the dynasty's last duke, Wenceslas III, in 1306. The Habsburg Duke Albert I sent his son Rudolph to seize the Bohemian crown, but he lasted only a year before being dethroned by Henry, Duke of Carinthia. He in turn was replaced in 1310 by John the Blind of the House of Luxembourg, whose son Charles IV elevated Prague to the status of an imperial capital when he became Holy Roman Emperor in 1355. His reign saw the city become an archbishopric in 1344, and the foundation of Charles University in 1348.

The period of relative tranquillity did not last. In 1402 the radical Czech theologian Jan Hus began calling for reform of the Catholic Church. Although he was burnt at the Council of Constance in 1415 (having believed he had been given safe passage), he had gathered a large following in Bohemia. In 1419 a group of them attempting to free some Hussite prisoners held in the Town Hall stormed the building and threw the burgomaster and several members of the town council out of an upper storey window.

This first "Defenestration of Prague" sparked the Hussite Wars, which ravaged the Bohemian lands until a final Hussite defeat at the Battle of Lipany in 1434. Even then the crowning of George of Poděbrady, a moderate Hussite, sparked a crusade against Bohemia, which resulted in the installation of Matthias Corvinus of Hungary as king. Prague's dizzying procession of foreign rulers continued when he was supplanted by the Vladislav II, of the Polish Jagiellonian dynasty, in 1471. Vladislav's sudden death in 1516 after eating a rotten fig (there were dark rumours of poisoning), left his young son Louis as king. Seven years earlier, Vladislav had taken the precaution of arranging a coronation to ensure a peaceful succession, at which the infant is reported to have cried when the heavy iron crown was place on his tiny head during the ceremony. His untimely death at the Battle of Mohács against the Ottomans in 1526, then led to another change of dynasty to the Habsburgs (as his sister had married Ferdinand, the son of Philip I of Spain).

The Habsburgs would rule Prague for the next 392 years, but it was not to be a period of uninterrupted peace. A disastrous fire at the castle in 1541 allowed Ferdinand to remodel it on Renaissance lines and he built the Summer Palace, but his successors had a less sure touch. Prague was restored as an imperial capital by Rudolf II, and became a major cultural centre, with the astronomers Tycho Brahe and Johannes Kepler and the artist Giuseppe Arcimboldo amongst those whom his patronage attracted to the court (though the presence of the eminent astrologer John Dee led to mutterings about the emperor's unhealthy interest in magic).

The Bohemian crown passed to another branch of the Habsburg family in 1617, when Ferdinand of Austria was elected king, but it also led to another catastrophic uprising, as the predominantly Protestant nobility of Prague protested against the staunchly Catholic Ferdinand. They promptly defenestrated members of the pro-Habsburg town council, chose the safely Protestant Frederick V of the Palatinate as king and sparked the Thirty Years' War, a devastating continent-wide conflict.

By the time the war was over, Prague's population had fallen from 60,000 to 20,000. The slow process of rebuilding was hampered by a major plague in 1713–14 that killed over 10,000 people. The city suffered brief occupations by the French (in 1742) and Prussians (in 1744) during the Austrian War of Succession, and then an unsuccessful siege by the Prussians in 1757 during the Seven Years' War. Although artillery bombardment during that last attack almost destroyed St Vitus's Cathedral, Prague recovered, its population reaching 80,000 by 1771, and the merging of the old municipalities of Staré Město, Hradčany and Malá Strana into one in 1784, helping consolidate its municipal consciousness.

As the 19th century progressed, that consciousness became an increasingly Czech one, as the Czech national revival took hold, and nationalists agitated for some level of autonomy. Although the Czech uprising during the 1848 year of revolutions was not as successful as those elsewhere in Europe, those aspirations were finally met in 1918, when the Austro-Hungarian Empire collapsed and Czechoslovakia became an independent nation with Tomáš Masaryk as its first president.

The crowds who cheered in Wenceslas Square little suspected that freedom would be short-lived, as Nazi Germany first seized the Sudetenland in the west of the country (where German-speakers predominated) in 1938, and then took the rest of Bohemia in March 1939. Nor did the uprising against German occupation on May 5, 1945, right at the end of the Second World War, herald freedom, as the "liberating" Red Army brought with it compliant communist politicians who soon stifled attempts at restoring democracy.

Czechoslovakia, and Prague, found itself on the wrong side of the "Iron Curtain", and the recipient of the world's largest Stalin Monument, the 15.5-metre- (51-foot-) high, 17,000-tonne statue atop Letná Hill that the city's residents derisively nicknamed "the meat queue". The student demonstrations in 1967 that prompted the Czech first secretary Alexander Dubček to declare a policy of "socialism with a human face" proved another false dawn, as Warsaw Pact tanks invaded on August 21, 1968, putting the brief flirtation with freedom to an end.

Only the political sclerosis of the Soviet Union, which released its grip on the satellite states two years before it finally imploded, gave Prague its freedom back. The Velvet Revolution in 1989 overthrew the communist regime and plugged Prague back into the European mainstream. Although Czechoslovakia fell apart in 1993 (into Czechia and Slovakia), Prague once again became a vibrant European cultural centre, where foreigners were no longer invaders, but tourists (8.4 million of them in 2017). After centuries of struggle, and two defenestrations, Prague can finally determine its own destiny.

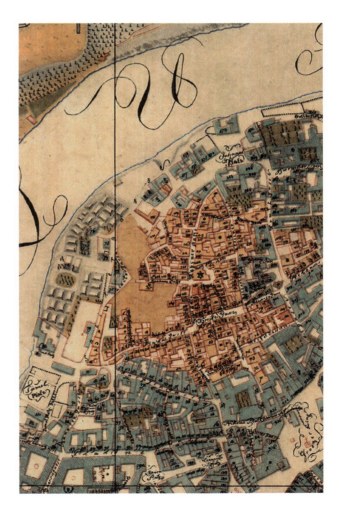

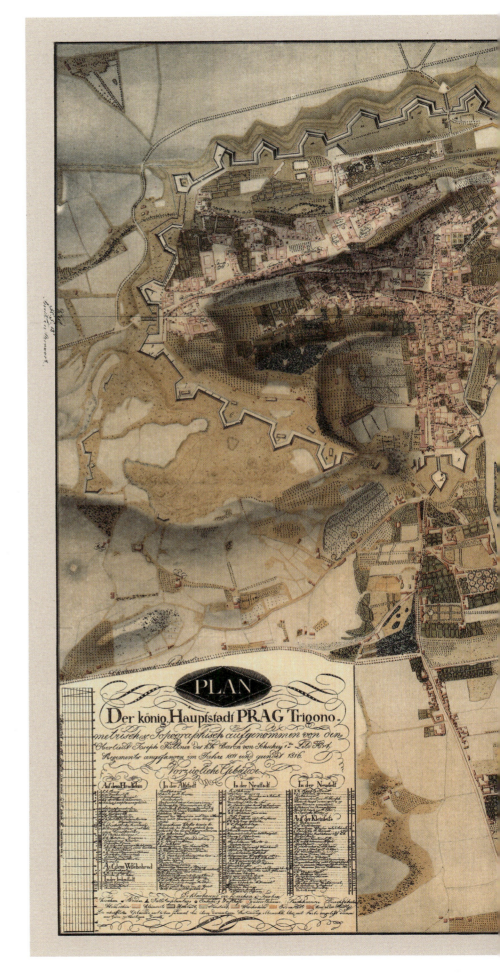

City of Parklands

Adelaide, 1837

Parks are a city's lungs, green spaces where its inhabitants can forget, if only for a moment, the myriad voices, the rushing traffic and the towers of concrete that are an inescapable part of their everyday lives. Adelaide, and the architect of its plan, Colonel William Light (1786–1839), were visionary in this respect, as this map, made just a year after the city's foundation as Australia's first major European settlement not based on convict labour, illustrates.

The grid pattern of 1,000 lots, each of 4,000 square metres (1 acre), north and south of the River Torrens, is apparent in the map drawn by the 16-year-old Robert George Thomas, who later became assistant to Adelaide's Town Surveyor and eventually Government Architect. Light surveyed the ground using the latest trigonometrical methods, batting off arguments from others who wanted the city built closer to the coast, but where there would be no fresh water. By March 1837, he had it complete, and Thomas's map was created as a means to get investors to buy lots which would in turn fund the passage of the free labourers and craftsmen needed for the new colony to prosper.

The most striking feature of Light's design for Adelaide was the Park Lands, 9 square kilometres (3.5 square miles) of green, which were to be reserved for public recreation. Although such urban parks are commonplace now and badges of civic pride, with New York's Central Park, Rome's Villa Borghese and Moscow's Gorky Park among the more famous, in the first half of the 19th century the idea was revolutionary, as most large green spaces were the domain of the nobility: London's Regent's Park, in origin a royal hunting park, was only opened to the public in 1841.

Light was not thanked, being summarily demoted in June 1838 when he refused to accelerate the survey of lands outside the centre using less rigorous techniques. By then, the city had acquired its name, after Adelaide of Saxe-Meiningen, the wife of King William IV. The streets, too, had been named, following a session of the 12-strong committee, which included all the senior colonial officials, including Governor John Hindmarsh who, another participant recalled, "brought a pocket full of royal and naval heroes" as a prompt. No one thought to ask the local Kaurna people what they thought of this appropriation of their traditional lands, and in the end the committee named much of the city after themselves and members of the South Australia Company that had been formed in London in 1835 to promote the colony.

Governor Hindmarsh's name was attached to one of the wider avenues, and Edward Wakefield, who had dreamt up the whole idea of a free colony funded by land sales while reflecting on his fate as a prisoner in Newgate Prison (sentenced for marrying an under-age heiress) was similarly honoured. Another recipient, Robert Gouger, appointed South Australia's first colonial secretary, wrote a series of letters home in 1837 that indicated the challenges and state of the fledgling city, counselling would-be emigrants to bring their own portable iron stove, locks and hinges and pickaxes (though most of the humbler sort would not have brought the "ten pairs of windows, seven feet high" that he included in his own baggage).

Adelaide's economic prospects picked up with the arrival of sheep from New South Wales in 1838, which formed the basis of a highly profitable wool industry. The second Governor, George Gawler, who also came that year, expanded and reorganised the recently established police force and built a jail, a hospital and a customs house, as well as a governor's residence for himself. The city was incorporated as a municipality in 1840, the first in Australia to administer itself, although this was abruptly revoked in 1842 after Gawler's spending spree almost bankrupted the colony. A copper boom in the 1840s help the population grow from 2,000 to 14,000 during the decade, but a slump followed as copper prices fell and workers left in droves for the recently discovered gold fields of Victoria.

Still, the city continued to receive new facilities, helped by South Australia becoming a self-governing colony in 1856, a pioneer of suffrage in 1861 when women – although only property owners – received the vote, and of labour relations when it was the first territory in the British Empire to legalise trade unions in 1876. A telegraph line to Melbourne opened in 1858, Adelaide Town Hall was built in 1866, and in 1867 the Botanic Gardens opened on a section of the Park Lands.

By the time Australia federated as a nation in 1901 (with South Australia one of its new states), the population had increased tenfold to 162,000, compared with half a century earlier, and was nudging 1.4 million by 2024. In all that time, and despite the loss of around a quarter of Light's originally designated area, Adelaideans have been fierce defenders of their green belt against successive attempts at encroachment. One of the world's largest urban parks, the Adelaide Park Lands is also one of the most cherished.

William Light's Plan of Adelaide, 1837

Drawn by 16 year old Robert Thomas to Colonel Light's draft

Migration Museum, History Trust of South Australia, Historical Relics Collection

The Power of Industry

Manchester, 1851

The map overleaf shows a city transformed by technologies that changed forever the nature of urban life. Manchester in the 1770s was a collection of villages with a population that barely reached 25,000. By the time James Tallis produced his plan of the city for R. Montgomery Martin's *Illustrated Atlas* – timed, with entrepreneurial flair, to be published for the opening of the Great Exhibition at Crystal Palace in 1851 – it had mushroomed into a metropolis of over 180,000 people.

It was steam that was the motor of this growth, whose rapidity was unlike anything seen before. James Watt's improved steam engine, developed in 1765, used the force of super-heated water to drive wheels, gears and pistons. It appeared alongside such devices as Richard Arkwright's water frame for cotton spinning (1769) and Edmund Cartwright's power loom (1785), which turned the production of textiles from a craft to an industry.

Towns that had access to abundant water, as well as proximity to the coalfields where the fuel needed to fire the engines was mined, and good transport links were ideal sites for the factories and mills which sprang up in imitation of Arkwright's first venture at Cromford in Derbyshire. Manchester had all of this, and by 1830 there were nearly 100 cotton mills there – their growth had prompted Arkwright to sue the Manchester cotton magnates for infringing his patent, but he lost his case in 1785, and the city's status as "cottonopolis", the cotton capital of Britain, was secured.

It had taken Manchester a long time to reach these heights. Founded in AD79 as the Roman fort of *Mamucium* ("breast-shaped hill") at the strategic confluence of the rivers Irwell and Medlock, it was upgraded to stone in about 200, before being abandoned after the Roman withdrawal from Britain in the early 5th century. The settlement emerged from the shadows as a frontier post between Anglo-Saxon Wessex and the Viking-controlled north – Edward the Elder sent a force to "Mamecaester" in 919 to strengthen its defences – and grew into a modest market town in Norman times, gaining the right to hold an annual two-day fair in 1223 (which only ceased operation in 1876).

The parish church of St Mary, constructed in 1215, was rebuilt as a collegiate church in 1421. Now the cathedral and one of the vignettes shown on Tallis's map, its most famous warden was the alchemist Dr John Dee in 1595. By then there had been an influx of Flemish weavers into the town, refugees from the war between Spain and the Netherlands, who helped established the town's reputation for textile production on which its future greatness depended.

The modestly prosperous town's famous Grammar School was founded in 1515, and in 1653 Humphrey Chetham established Britain's first free public library. But the pace of change quickened in the 18th century, with the opening in 1761 of the Bridgewater Canal that connected Manchester to the nearby coalmines at Worsley. As cotton mills opened, rural workers flooded into the city which by 1801 had a population of 70,000, and, a decade later, over 20,000 people employed as either spinners or weavers. Many newcomers arrived from Ireland, driven by the Great Famine of the 1840s, with 47,000 reaching Manchester in 1847 alone, and making a quarter of the population Irish-born by 1871.

The growing city acquired new facilities: the Manchester Institution (eventually to become the Art Gallery) was founded in 1823, and in 1851 the textile merchant John Owens endowed Owens College, which over time evolved into Manchester University. The railways came, too, with the Liverpool to Manchester Railway, the world's first passenger line, setting up its Manchester terminus at Liverpool Road in 1830 (now the world's oldest surviving railway station). Lines to Leeds and Birmingham followed with their terminuses shown on the Tallis map at Victoria (1844) and Store Street (now Piccadilly, 1842).

The improved transportation helped move the huge increase in cotton exports from Manchester, with their value rising from £200,000 in 1764 to £19.3 million in 1830. This made the mill owners rich, but did little for the worsening plight of the urban poor. The Industrial Revolution's ability to promote economic growth far outstripped the country's capacity or willingness to deal with the accompanying social ills. Disease and malnutrition were rife in the jerry-built slums and fetid basements into which the workers were crammed. In 1837 it was estimated that the average life expectancy in the labouring classes was just 17. Ten years later, of the city's 47,000 homes, just 11,000 had a piped water supply, a situation that contributed to the spread of water-borne diseases such as cholera, an epidemic of which claimed 674 lives in 1832.

The industrial revolution literally changed the atmosphere of the city, causing Dr CG Carus, who visited in 1844 in the entourage of the King of Saxony, to remark that, "Nothing is to be seen but houses blackened by smoke and in the external parts of the town half-empty ditches between smoking factories." Token gestures such as the establishment of the first public baths in 1846 were woefully inadequate.

Radical politicians, appalled by the conditions industry had created, urged reforms to give the poor a voice and dignified working conditions. The Blanket March of unemployed weavers in 1817 unnerved the authorities, and when Henry Hunt, an advocate both for social and parliamentary reform (Manchester, despite its size, had no representation in parliament at the time) prepared to give a speech at St Peter's Field in 1819, the Manchester and Salford Yeomanry charged it. In the ensuing melee, around 15 people were killed.

After this "Peterloo Massacre", Manchester's reputation as a centre for radical ideals grew: the German revolutionary theorist Friedrich Engels wrote *The Condition of the Working Class in England* there in 1844, and the city was the birthplace of Emmeline Pankhurst (1858–1928), the inspiration behind the suffragette movement. But by the time real progress was made, the high tide of the Industrial Revolution had already begun to ebb. The number of cotton mills peaked in the 1850s, and although the city's population breached the half-million mark by 1900, and the opening of the Manchester Ship Canal in 1894 gave the city a direct outlet to the sea, competition from the United States, Germany and eventually India and China meant the mills gradually closed until the last one shut its doors in 1980. From being the first truly industrial city, Manchester became one of the world's post-industrial conurbations. Two massively successful football teams and a vibrant music scene, with bands such as the Stone Roses and Happy Mondays contributing to its nickname as "Madchester" in the late 1980s, offered an alternative vision of the future to the grime-blackened skies of the 19th century. What was the ninth-largest city in the world in 1900, knows it can no longer rely on the power of industry.

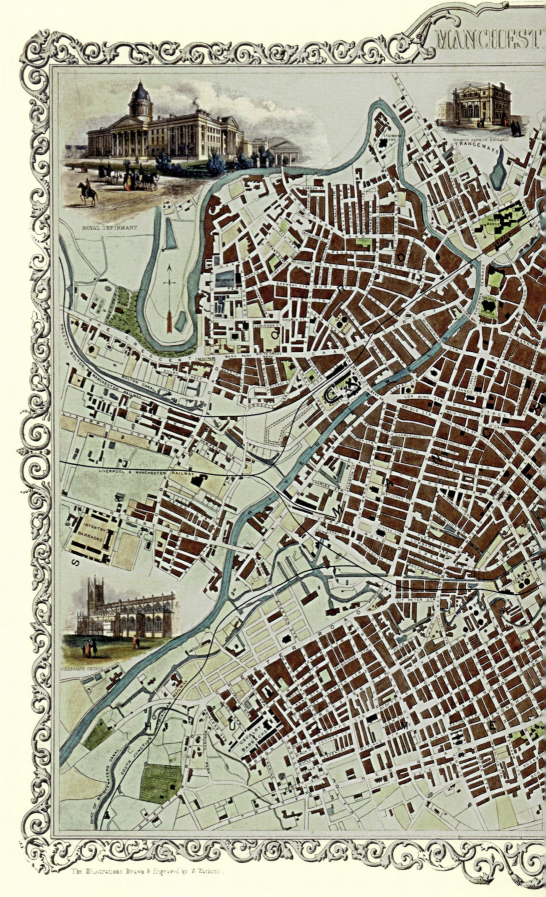

ROYAL INFIRMARY

COLLEGIATE CHURCH

STRANGEWAYS

INFANTRY BARRACKS

CAVALRY BARRACKS

MANCHEST

JOHN TALLIS & COM

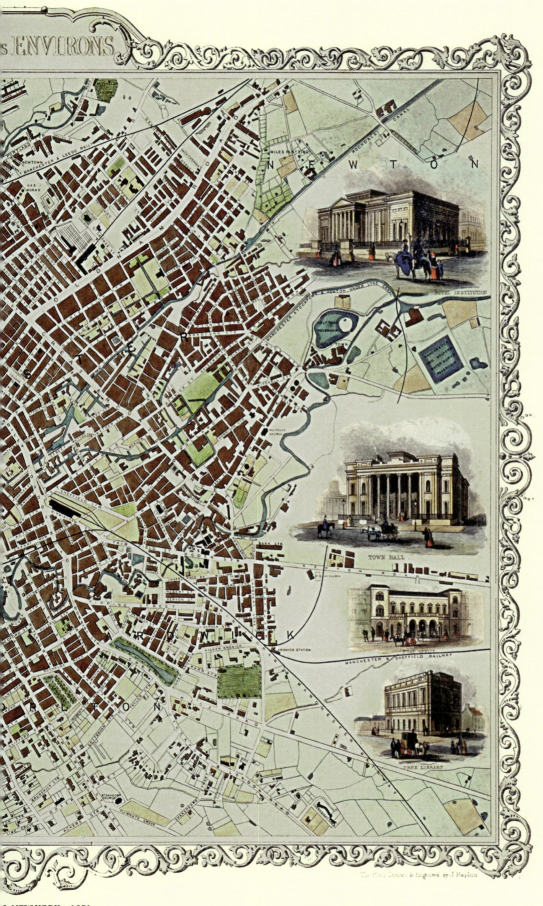

NEWTON

ROYAL INSTITUTION

TOWN HALL

MANCHESTER & SHEFFIELD RAILWAY

FREE LIBRARY

City on Top of the World

Bogotá, 1852

The map overleaf, republished in 1890 from an earlier version by the Italian revolutionary and cartographer Agustín Codazzi (1793–1859), shows the world's third-highest capital city, Colombia's Bogotá, situated at a heady 2,640 metres (8,660 feet) on the *Sabana de Bogotá*, an elevated plateau in the Andes and now home to seven million people. Codazzi's career was intimately linked with the early history of the young republics that broke away from Spanish rule in the first decades of the 19th century. In 1815, when hopes of an independent Italy seemed hopelessly distant, Codazzi offered his services to Símon Bolívar, the revolutionary leader, who employed him to make maps of the strategic southeastern area of Gran Colombia (which later broke up into Venezuela, Colombia and Ecuador) and then set him to work making an atlas of Venezuela. Elevated to the level of governor of Barinas province, Codazzi fled to Colombia in 1850, along with his mentor, the former president José Antonio Páez, dying nine years later while surveying around Espíritu Santo in the Colombian mountains.

The Andes, the epicentre of the revolts against Spain which began in 1810, is also home to the two capital cities even more elevated than Bogotá: Quito in Ecuador at 2,850 metres (9,350 feet); and La Paz in Bolivia at 3,640 metres (11,942 feet), which is equivalent to more than two fifths of the way up Mount Everest. It takes a descent to 2,350 metres (7,710 feet) to reach Ethiopia's capital of Addis Ababa, the highest outside South America. Life at such high altitudes carries significant health benefits. Those living in such oxygen-thin environments tend to have stronger lungs and suffer a lower incidence of

heart disease and many cancers. It also bears cost, in the additional effort required to perform any physical activity and the inconvenience of hauling building materials and other essentials to such heights, disadvantages in part balanced by the additional security such eyrie-cities enjoy: it is no accident that the Incas sited their capital at Cusco, at 3,400 metres (11,100 feet).

The altitude, though, proved no barrier to the expedition of the conquistador Gonzalo Jiménez de Quesada, which reached the region in 1537, encountering Meuqueta, the capital of the Muisca, a federation of Chibcha-speaking peoples. The *zipa*, the Muisca ruler, resisted doggedly, but after his death in battle, opposition to the Spanish collapsed, and on August 6, 1538, Quesada founded what he called Santa Fé, after his birthplace in Spain. A little settlement grew up, built around the nucleus of the later grid pattern so evident in Codazzi's plan. The roads running broadly east–west were called *calles* (streets) and those north-south called *carreras* (avenues), which all cluster on the map around the Plaza de Bolivar, complete with a statue of the Liberator and the main public buildings.

Santa Fé de Bogotá as it became known, incorporating the Chibcha word meaning "enclosed field", soon developed into an administrative centre, selected in 1550 as the seat of the Audiencia of New Granada. The archbishop who was appointed in 1553 suffered the indignity of his new cathedral, a mud-brick structure with a thatched roof, collapsing in an earthquake just seven years later. Although rebuilt, it fell victim to further tremors in 1785 and 1805, until the final version, shown in one of Codazzi's vignettes, was constructed in 1807. By then, Bogotá had a university, endowed by the Dominicans in 1580, and in 1717 the city's status improved still further, when it became capital of the Viceroyalty of New Granada, placing it, at least theoretically, on a level with the far larger colonial centres of Lima and Mexico City.

By 1789 the population had reached 18,000, but discontent with Spanish rule festered and in 1810 an uprising installed an independent junta. It took nine further years to finally defeat the Spanish, but in 1819 independence was secured as part of Gran Colombia, a federation of what is now Venezuela, Ecuador and Colombia, with Bogotá as overall capital. The unwieldy state fell apart in 1830, but Bogotá remained the capital of what was now called New Granada.

Although the city's population continued to grow (to over 30,000 by the 1820s), acquiring new buildings such as the Public Library in 1823, and transport links improved with the arrival of the trams in 1884, Bogotá's later 19th-century history was a troubled one. An army rebellion in 1833 and a civil war sparked in 1840 when General José María Obando tried to overthrow the government were symptomatic of a chronic state of political instability aggravated by rivalry between the Liberal and Conservative Parties. This culminated in 1899 with the War of a Thousand Days, sparked when a downturn in coffee prices caused the Conservative government to print money, provoking a disastrous inflationary spiral. By the time it was over in 1902, around 100,000 Colombians were dead, Bogotá was in ruins and Panama, previously a province of Colombia, had seceded.

Reconstruction was slow but steady, marred by outbreaks of labour unrest in the 1920s, but by 1938, the city's 400th anniversary, it had 330,000 people and a railway (built in 1909). But then Bogotá suffered yet another setback when the assassination of the popular presidential candidate Jorge Eliécer Gaitán in April 1948 led to "el Bogotazo", a spasm of violent rioting in which 3,000 were killed and many government buildings, schools and churches razed. It also marked the start of La Violencia, another civil war between Liberals and Conservatives, this one lasting ten years and costing the lives of 200,000 Colombians.

The country, and Bogotá with it, was plagued through the 1970s and 1980s by violence associated with drug cartels and left-wing insurgencies, notably that of the M-19 movement which attacked the Palace of Justice in November 1985, leading to the death of 100 people, including 12 Supreme Court Justices, when government forces stormed the building to take it back.

Bogotá is more tranquil now: a final peace deal was signed with the FARC, the largest group of insurgents, in 2016, and the city government can concentrate on the more regular problems of streets choked by traffic, with major investment in public transport, of providing new services, such as the three large public libraries that opened in the 2010s, and of improving conditions in the extensive *barrios*, or informal districts, which cluster around the centre. Even in the absence of revolution, civil war or insurgencies, life at high altitude has its challenges.

PLANO

Levantado

AGU

Arreglado

Contiene las mejora

Las ilustraciones

CALLES
de Occidente á Oriente

Antioquia	2y3E	Mompos	4y5EF
Ayacucho	4 H	Marquitero	2 B
Banco	3y4C	Neiva	3y4CD
Bárbula	1y2C	Occidente	3y4DE
Barinas	1y2C	Oriente	2y3E
Boaachica	2y3C	Panamá	3á5EF
Bogotá	3y4D	Palaré	4y5CD
Bolivia	2y3F	Perú	4 E
Bombaná	4 F	Pichincha	5y4G
Calibío	3 F	Pitayó	4 F
Callao	4 H	Rinhacha	3y4CD
Cariaco	4y5FG	Sambrondón	3 G
Cartagena	3y4E	S.Andrés	4y5F
Casanare	2 D	S.Felix	3y4BC
Chire	2 D	S.Martin	3 F
Chiriguaná	2 A	S.Mateo	1 C
Chiriqui	2 D	Santamarta	3 D
Chocó	2y3F	Tacinas	4y5F
Ibarra	4 G	Tarqui	2y3B
Janin	5 G	Tenerife	2y3C
Mayngual	1y2CD	Trincheras	1 B
Margarita	1y2B	Tintama	2y3DE
Marviquita	3 F	Veragua	3 F
Matalemiel	1y2B	Yurumal	2 C
Maturin	2 B		

IGLESIAS

1 La Catedral
2 San Carlos
3 San Rosa de Vice
4 Santo Temple
5 Las Nieves
6 Santa Bárbara
7 La Concepción
8 S.Victorino
9 La Tercera
10 Santo Domingo
11 San Francisco
12 San Agustin
13 La Candelaria
14 San Diego
15 Santa Barbaela
16 Santa Clara
17 La Concepción
18 Santa Luis
19 El Carmen
20 El Sagrario
21 Del Sagrario

CAPILLAS

DISTRITOS PARROQUIALES
Catedral
Las Nieves
Santa Bárbara
San Victorino

A. CODAZZI
Población de Bogotá en 1890, 120,000 hab.

BOGOTÁ, fundada sobre las rui-
nas de la antigua capital de Cundi-
namarca...

3ᵃ CARRERA DE FLORIAN HÁCIA EL NORTE

CALLE 8ᵃ
AL. NORTE

BANCO DE COLOMBIA

3ᵃ CARRERA DE FLORIAN HÁCIA EL NORTE

COLÓN

S.CARLOS

S.BARTOLOMÉ

ESTATUA DE BOLIVAR

Grabado por Erhard hermanos, 8.Calle Nicole Paris.

BOGOTÁ

ngenieros

M. PAZ

erificadas hasta hoy
de Racines, BOGOTÁ

Ferrocarril de la Sabana
Tranvías del Norte

Los N.° y las letras con referencia al
plano, y combinadas entre sí, sirven para
buscar en el cuadro respectivo la calle ó
carrera que se necesite.

2ª CARRERA DE FLORIAN HÁCIA EL SUR

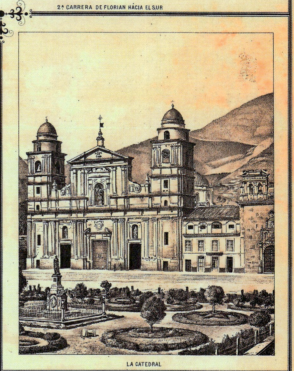

LA CATEDRAL

CAPITOLIO NACIONAL

CASA CONSISTORIAL

BOLIVAR

Remodelling a City

Paris, 1857

Europe's old-established cities made piecemeal attempts to transform themselves into something more rational, more modern, or at least more healthy. Sir Isaac Newton's grander plans for London in the 1660s went largely unrealised and Frederick the Great of Prussia's development of Berlin in the mid-18th century concentrated mainly on set-piece monumental buildings. What they both lacked was the vision and the impetus to reshape a whole city.

Paris in the 1850s had both these things, in Napoleon III – whose deft manoeuvrings elevated him from president to emperor, confirmed in his new role by a plebiscite in November 1852 – and the determination of Georges-Eugène, Baron Haussmann, appointed prefect of the Seine in 1853 with a brief to carry out a scheme of urban renewal ordered by the new emperor.

Shown in full overleaf, the map by the engraver and publisher Alexandre Vuillemin (1812–80) depicts the city in the first throes of this project, described by Napoleon III in 1858 as one of "Paris responding to its highest calling" with "major arteries opening, populous areas becoming healthier ... poverty diminishing through better organisation of relief".

Paris had experienced its fair share of tumult since 1789: from the Storming of the Bastille that lit the touchpaper of revolution on July 14 that year, through the violent overthrow of the monarchy and the Terror that followed it. There were then lesser outpourings of revolutionary fervour in 1832 and 1848, the last of which contributed to the ascent of Napoleon III. But it remained a fundamentally medieval city: Napoleon III's uncle, Napoleon Bonaparte, had begun the construction of the Arc de Triomphe in 1806, and the comte du Rambuteau, one of Haussman's predecessors as prefect of the Seine between 1833 and 1848, had paved quays along the River Seine and partly redeveloped the Marais district. But the centre of the city remained a labyrinthine warren, so unhealthy that the political economist Victor Considérant described it as "a great manufactory of putrefaction" in 1848, the same year in which a cholera epidemic claimed the lives of nearly 20,000 Parisians.

The key to Haussman's plans was the building of a *grande croisée*, a grand cross of wide, intersecting avenues to make transit north–south along the new Boulevards Saint-Michel, Sébastopol and Strasbourg, and east–west along an extended Rue de Rivoli and Champs-Élysées,

both more rapid and far more graceful. Cutting through desperately crowded neighbourhoods, whose residents were bought out with cut-rate compulsory purchases and shunted off to distant suburbs, the first section, along the Rue de Rivoli, was completed and opened in March 1855. It needed 3,000 labourers working day and night to get it done, and at its peak, the whole project required ten times that number, imported from départements such as Creuse in central France.

By 1859 the north–south axis, too, was complete. Almost 20,000 old buildings had been demolished – Haussmann tactlessly described himself as a "demolition artist" – and 350,000 Parisians had been displaced. The next phase was even more ambitious, involving the construction of a further 26 kilometres of boulevards, including the boulevard Malesherbes, new railway stations at the Gare du Nord and Gare de Lyon, the new Opera House, and the redesigning of the Place de L'Étoile around the Arc de Triomphe to produce a dramatic effect of spoke-like avenues radiating from the square.

Yet this was not all. His plans for the city were so comprehensive that afterwards people spoke of "Haussmannisation", as if Paris had been remade in his image. He swept away almost all the private houses on the Île de la Cité, the ancient heart of Paris, turning it into an administrative zone (save for Nôtre-Dame Cathedral), gave the city two new green spaces in the Montsouris and Buttes Chaumont parks, and enlarged the Bois de Boulogne and Bois de Vincennes, totally rebuilt Les Halles market, and together with his chief engineer Eugène Belgrand, installed a modern sewerage system beneath his new boulevards. The apartment blocks erected alongside these avenues – lined with over 100,000 trees – were all designed to a single plan, no higher than five storeys, with wrought iron balconies on the second and topmost levels, lending the centre of the city a new unified appearance. Even the street furniture, including kiosks, and public toilets, were all "Haussmannised". Finally, in 1860 he enlarged Paris by annexing outer suburbs into a system of 20 arrondissements (there had been previously only 12) which has remained in place until this day.

Through this, and natural growth, Paris's population reached 1.7 million. But its debt grew too. The massive series of projects had cost over 2.5 billion francs, and allegations of corruption in the means used to finance

it led to Haussmann's downfall in 1870. Not everyone had in any case been enamoured of his changes. A mob stormed the city hall in September 1870 and tore to pieces the copy of Haussmann's original plans which were on display there. Others commented more eloquently, if less directly, as the poet Charles Baudelaire who lamented in his 1857 poem *Le Cygne* ("The Swan"), "The old Paris is no more". That old Paris may have been swept away by Baron Haussmann, but the new one that he created still defines the Paris of today.

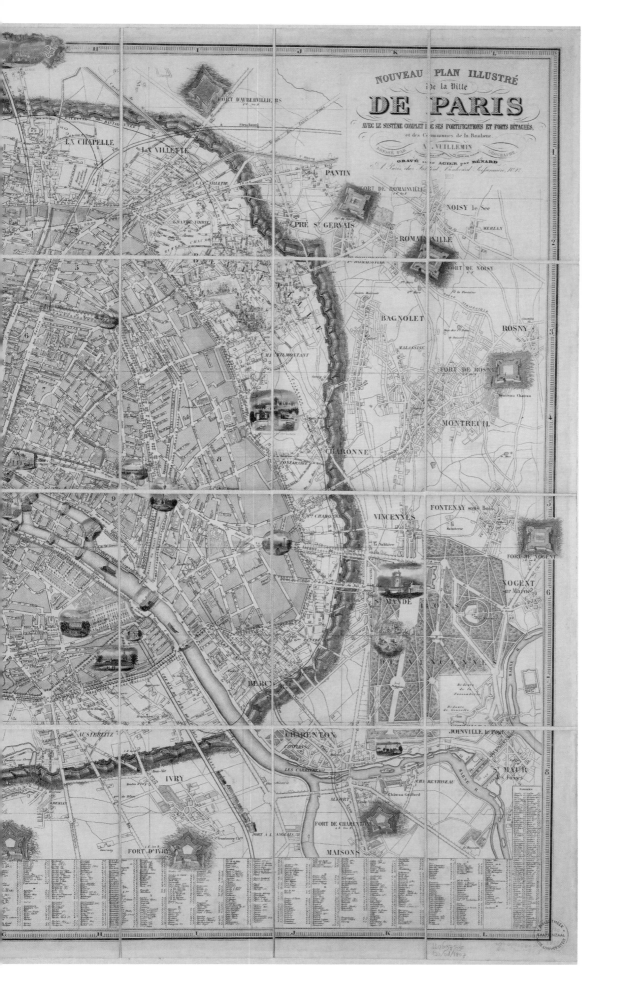

Africa's Largest City

Lagos, 1887 & 2024

The transformation is startling. From a small, neat town of around 60,000 people on the northwest tip of an island in Lagos Lagoon on the Bight of Benin in 1887, the spreading orange blob of Lagos in the modern map has consumed swamp and marshland and sent its tentacles onto the mainland. Now a tumultuous, chaotic, congested metropolis of over 23 million people (in the wider urban district), it jostles with Cairo for the title of Africa's largest city, and with its explosive growth rate may soon far outpace its Egyptian rival.

There is a certain irony in the drafter of the earlier map being Elisée Reclus (1830–1905), a French anarchist, opponent of state control of marriage and early exponent of the importance of conserving nature. He drew it for his *La Nouvelle Géographie universelle, la terre et les hommes* ("The new universal geography, the earth and the people"), while in exile in Switzerland for his support of the 1871 Paris Commune. Decidedly not a supporter of colonialism, Reclus might have recoiled in horror at some of the paths that Lagos was later forced to tread.

The first settlement in the area was by Yoruba-speaking Awori fishermen who moved in the 14th century to Iddo, one of the four main islands of the lagoon (the others being Lagos, Victoria and Ikoyi). Finding it too small as their numbers grew, they transferred to the northwest tip of Lagos Island. They called their home Oko (which may mean "lagoon"), and by the 16th century it had become a frontier outpost of the kingdom of Benin (who called it Eko, or "encampment"). The arrival of the Portuguese in 1472 led to the involvement of local rulers in the trade in enslaved people, with Eko becoming the largest enslavement port in the Bight of Benin: one French visitor in the early 18th century noted that it had over "5,000 souls". Rule by Benin was replaced by that of Oyo, and when that empire dissolved between 1817 and 1836, the local *obas* (rulers) emerged, who held sway over smaller regions, including one based in Eko.

The abolition of the trade in enslaved people in the British Empire in 1807 and the activities of the British West African Squadron sent to suppress it corroded Portuguese influence over what they termed *Lagos* (or "lagoons"). The deposition of Oba Akitoye, who opposed enslavement, by his brother Oba Kosoko, who wished to continue profiting from the trade, brought British intervention in 1851 and a temporary occupation of Lagos, which in 1861 became permanent.

The British administered Lagos in a shifting pattern of west African colonies: as part of the Gold Coast Colony from 1874 to 1886, then as a separate entity, and only finally becoming part of the Protectorate of Southern Nigeria in 1906. Finally, in 1914, Lagos became capital of a unified colony of Nigeria. In the meantime, it had been equipped with a suite of colonial buildings, such as the Colonial Secretary's Office (1895) and the first version of the Anglican Cathedral of Christ Marina (begun in 1867, but substantially remodelled between 1924 and 1946), though its architectural heritage was enriched by the arrival of African Brazilians in the 1840s, whose spending power was lavished on baroque-style suburban villas. Electric power reached the town in 1898, and terrestrial connections improved with the arrival of the first railway, from Lagos to Ibadan, in 1901.

The town grew steadily, still focused on the tip of Lagos Island, reaching a population of 60,000 by 1872. Nationalist sentiment grew gradually, too. There were intermittent revolts, such as one against the alienation of indigenous land in 1911, while the foundation of the Nigerian Youth Movement in 1933, and the growing organisation of labour – which resulted in a massive rail strike in June 1945 in which 200,000 workers took part – all fed into a stream of demands for independence.

That independence, which came in 1960, brought hope, but it also carried a surge of rural migrants seeking to escape poverty into the city, where they found instead crowded and increasingly slum-like conditions. A troubled political history of military rule and corruption, aggravated by oil wealth from the Niger Delta, meant that investment in infrastructure was absent or misdirected. In 1974, a building boom caused the government to purchase massive amounts of cement at inflated prices, leading to hundreds of cement-laden ships choking the harbour for over five years (and doing little to ease the city's housing shortage).

The "Cement Armada" was symptomatic of a city struggling to cope with vertiginous growth in its population, as land reclamation joined together the islands and the city seeped into new areas such as Apapa, Ebute-Metta, Yaba, Festac Town and Satellite Town. By the 1990s, Lagos's population was increasing by 300,000 every year, with a rapid pace of urbanisation that turned new housing estates into slums and left the city's historic core, on Lagos Island, as a dilapidated district from which the middle-classes had long fled. Even the transfer of Nigeria's federal capital to Abuja in 1991 did nothing to halt Lagos's growth.

There were signs of hope. The development of the Nollywood film industry in 2000, tech startups in the Yaba district, the opening of a new deep-sea port and a section of suburban railway in 2023 showed that Lagos, for all its deep-rooted problems, is still a vital, creative place. In 1911, the Edwardian journalist ED Morel had worried – at a time when the city only had 80,000 inhabitants – whether "the already crowded and circumscribed areas of Lagos can possibly prove equal to the demands on it". With a population now 200 times that level, a century later, that question is even more pressing.

The Power of a Name

Beijing, 1888

Beijing has had many names, by some accounts fifteen, in its long history. And for over 750 years it served, with occasional breaks, as the capital of six dynasties. Always at the centre of each was an imperial palace, itself the symbolic centre of China (and thus of the world). The most famous of these lay at the heart of the Zijincheng, the "Purple Forbidden City" (the colour is associated with bravery), constructed under the Ming from 1406, but the image overleaf is of another palace, to the northwest of the city.

Here, the Qing emperor Qianlong laid out the Yiheyuan (the "Nourishing Peace Garden"), a complex of palaces, lakes and waterways to act as an escape from the oppressive summer heat of Beijing. Completed in 1764, and shown here in a view from 1888, it was sorely needed; Lord Macartney, the British envoy who visited the Qing court in 1793 wrote of Beijing that "the air is so filled with dust that the sun appears in a fog, a red disk showing dimly through the thick dense atmosphere". It was indeed a haven of tranquillity, covering around three square kilometres (just over one square mile), with at its centre the 60-metre- (200-foot-) high Longevity Hill covered in halls and pavilions on one side, and with a more rustic view of forest and hills on the other. The site was dominated by the more than two square kilometres (0.75 square miles) of the artificial Kunming Lake with its three large islands that provided even more privacy for the emperors.

Unfortunately, the Summer Palace, as it became known, though well suited to brief rural idylls, was utterly impractical for the business of running the government and so, despite the enormous expense, the Qianlong emperor and his successors rarely spent more than a night at a time at the Yiheyuan. Instead, the imperial court was largely based at the Forbidden City in the heart of Beijing. The area had been inhabited since prehistoric times – remains of Peking Man, a subspecies of *Homo erectus* dating to perhaps 500,000 years ago, have been found at Zhoukoudian – and there was a city on the site since at least 1000BC, when, as Ji, it was capital of a state of the same name. But it was only in 938 that it became capital of China when the Khitan-Liao renamed it Nanjing (which means "southern capital", as the true Liao powerbase was far to the north, at Shangjing in what is now Inner Mongolia).

The Khitan were the first of a succession of invaders from the steppelands who conquered northern China (and sometimes the south, too), becoming assimilated to Chinese culture before being displaced by yet more northerners. For each of them, Beijing, close to their traditional heartlands, was a logical choice as capital. So, in 1125 it fell to the Jurchen, who called it Yanjing, and made it their capital (with yet another name change, to Zhongdu) in 1152. In 1215 it fell to the remorseless power of the Mongol army of Genghis Khan, whose grandson Kublai Khan completed the conquest of China and made the city its unified capital, now called Dadu (though often referred to as Khanbalik, "the khan's city").

In each of these iterations, Nanjing, Zhongdu and Dadu, what is now Beijing had an imperial palace, growing increasingly in size and grandeur, all of them oriented on a north–south axis according to the Chinese principles of feng shui, with the main buildings facing southwards, the most auspicious direction. The next change of regime was almost its downfall. The Ming, who overthrew the Mongol Yuan dynasty in 1368, had their roots inside the imperial frontiers, rather than being northerners from beyond its boundaries, and at first they chose Nanjing (the city in eastern China) as their capital. But then in 1403 the Yongle emperor, not feeling secure there, as the city had been a powerbase of his nephew whom he had just toppled in a civil war, returned the capital to Beijing (or Beiping as it had been called under the early Ming). He ordered the construction of the most extravagant palace complex yet, which took 14 years to build, allegedly required the work of a million labourers, and which was reputed to have 10,000 rooms (though the true number is closer to 8,700).

At the centre of this Forbidden City stood the Imperial palace compound, measuring some 960 metres (1,050 yards) north to south and 750 metres (820 yards) east to west. At its heart was the Hall of Supreme Harmony, the ceremonial centre of imperial power, with a massive coiled dragon carved in wood on the ceiling. Here, all foreign envoys, having passed through the Meridian (or Wu) Gate of the city, were required to prostrate themselves three times before an audience with the empire. Further in stood the Halls of Central Harmony and Preserving Harmony, and then an Inner Court which housed the imperial residence with the Palace of Heavenly Purity for the emperor and the Palace of Earthly Tranquillity for the empress.

The Forbidden City weathered the change of regime from Ming to Qing in 1644, though the last Ming emperor hanged himself from a tree just outside the imperial compounds. All around it the city of Beijing grew, reaching a population of 1.3 million in 1825. It was not long before the outside world impinged again, this time not in the shape of northern steppes peoples but in the form of the British, who in the Opium Wars (1839–42 and 1856–60) exploited their technological lead in weaponry and superior military organisation to enforce a series of humiliating treaties on the Qing court, which opened up a number of Treaty Ports (including Hong Kong) in which the British and other Europeans could trade free of Chinese jurisdiction. The British came to the Yiheyuan too, in 1860 pillaging the pavilions and ransacking the palaces (although they damaged the nearby Old Summer Palace even more, burning it to the ground). The destruction was only repaired by the Dowager Empress Cixi in 1884–95 by diverting money that was supposed to be used for the modernisation of the Qing fleet. The effort was in vain, because the Eight-Nation Alliance (which included Japan and the United States as well as six European nations) that attacked Beijing in 1900 to relieve its embassies under siege during the Boxer Rebellion, once again attacked and damaged the Summer Palaces.

The long era of imperial palaces as the centre of Chinese power was by then almost over. The Xinhai revolution in 1911 toppled the last Qing emperor, the six-year-old Puyi, although he was able to remain ensconced in the Forbidden City until finally evicted in 1924. The same year, the Yiheyuan was turned over to the state as a public park. Beijing was occupied by the Japanese in 1937, after which it had several more transformations to undergo. The first was into the capital of the People's Republic of China, declared in 1949; the second in its name, which was changed from Peking when China adopted the pinyin method of transliterating Chinese characters into the Roman alphabet in 1979; and the last into a modern city of over 20 million inhabitants, none of whom were alive when an emperor passed his summers in the Yiheyuan.

City of Angels, City of Dreams

Los Angeles, 1891

The map is a piece of propaganda, designed by the Southern California Land Company to entice newcomers to invest in all the empty acres in clear view beyond the city boundaries, at a time when the growth of Los Angeles had been, frankly, stuttering. The bird's-eye view and the vignettes of stately buildings such as the City Hall, a Romanesque set-piece erected in 1888 (and the municipal authorities' fourth home), the well-appointed businesses and the High School, were all calculated to induce a sense of an established, orderly, prosperous place.

Of course, that the map's publication came just three years after a major property crash, and that the Land Company stood to gain handsomely from the sale of all those extra-suburban acres, were not matters the map's makers cared to comment on. They were instead peddling a dream, something Los Angeles has done right from the start, and continues to do today.

Originally home to the Tongva people, the area around Los Angeles was claimed for Spain by Juan Rodríguez Cabrillo in 1542. The Spanish were very slow to settle it, and it was not until September 1781 that the region's colonial governor, Felipe de Neve, established an outpost on the site of the Tonga village of Yaanga, with 44 settlers drawn from 14 families. El Pueblo de Nuestra Senõra la Reina de los Ángeles de Porciúncula ("The Town of Our Lady the Queen of the Angels of Porciúncula"), named for the chapel near Assisi where the Franciscan order of friars was founded, then remained scarcely more than a village under Spanish, and then Mexican rule from 1821.

Passing to the control of the United States by the Treaty of Guadalupe Hidalgo in 1848, Los Angeles was incorporated as a municipality in 1850, and began to draw migrants in increasing numbers after the Southern Pacific railroad reached the city in 1876, to be joined by the Santa Fé railroad nine years later. The land boom that ensued ended in bust, but the population had already reached 50,000 and the discovery in 1892 of oil by Edward Doheny at Inglewood (near the present-day LA Dodgers baseball stadium) gave the city a much-needed shot in the arm.

Recovering from yet another financial crisis in 1893 (during which 500 banks failed nationwide), Los Angeles had breached the 100,000 population mark in 1900. In the dry climate of Southern California, the city could scarcely get any larger without the securing of an adequate water supply and without a firmer hand on the city's hitherto unplanned expansion. In 1905, the municipal authorities passed an ordinance that no building could be over 46 metres (150 feet) in height, a rule which they broke in allowing themselves the 138-metre- (454-foot-) high, 28-storey new City Hall constructed in 1928, but which meant that in contrast to the other major cities on the west coast, Los Angeles has always remained a comparatively low-rise metropolis (the ordinance was only finally repealed in 1957). In 1913, the city finally got an aqueduct, which piped in fresh water from the Owens Valley, but whose $24 million cost caused huge arguments: when it finally opened on November 5 that year, its engineer William Mulholland simply declared, "There it is, take it!".

Long in the shadow of San Francisco, with only one-sixth its rival's population in 1890, by 1920 Los Angeles had finally won the demographic race, with 577,000 inhabitants against a shade over half a million for San Francisco. It had done so in part by absorbing surrounding municipalities, in 1910 annexing a rather unassuming suburb that later became Hollywood. There had already been one film partly made there (*The Count of Monte Cristo* in 1908), but the climate and lack of unionisation made it attractive to investors, and in 1910 the director DW Griffith made the short film *In Old California* in Hollywood. By 1911 there was a full-time film studio, Nestor Motion Picture Company, and in 1915 Cecil B DeMille shot one of the first great epic movies, *Birth of a Nation*, there.

Los Angeles was suddenly glamorous, Hollywood's Sunset Boulevard the haunt of acting greats such as Douglas Fairbanks and Mary Pickford, as the film industry there entered its golden age after the release of *The Jazz Singer*, the first feature-length "talkie", in 1927. The city also acquired its iconic 13-metre- (44-foot-) high "Hollywood" sign in the hills around 1923 (although it originally read

"Hollywoodland", being yet another land promotion, and the final four letters were only removed in 1949).

The dreams Los Angeles sold included sporting success, as it hosted the Olympic Games in 1932 when morale was sorely in need of a boost during the Great Depression. The home crowds thrilled to Babe Didrikson winning gold as she smashed the 80-metres hurdles world record, and repeated the feat for the javelin, and satisfaction was high as the United States topped the medal table by a healthy margin. By the time the summer games were next held in LA, in 1984, the atmosphere in the city had become more gloomy. The population had reached 3.5 million and large areas of the city centre were blighted by pollution, poverty and crime. The Watts riots in 1965 had highlighted the chronic interracial tensions those problems aggravated, with the beating of African American Rodney King in 1991 by members of the LA Police Department leading to protests that turned to violence, during which 63 people died and $1 billion-worth of damage was caused.

An earthquake in 1994 – like much of California, Los Angeles lies along the San Andreas fault line – caused 72 deaths and losses worth $12.5 billion, and impatience with the problems of the larger metropolis caused Hollywood to try to reverse its 1910 amalgamation with Los Angeles, and to secede.

The move was defeated in a vote by a margin of more than 2 to 1, and so Los Angeles remains firmly in the centre of a metropolitan area of 13.2 million people. More than 200 times the size it was when the Southern California Land Company commissioned its map to encourage outsiders to buy into the city, it is an outcome of which they could scarcely have dreamed. Yet Los Angeles' continued appeal as a setting for movies – by some counts it has featured as the backdrop for over 540 feature films – and that it is scheduled to hold the Olympic Games once more in 2028 (one of only three cities in the world to be awarded the honour for a third time) shows that the City of Angels remains a City of Dreams.

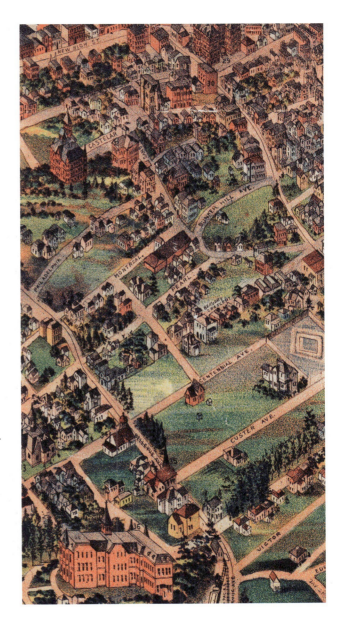

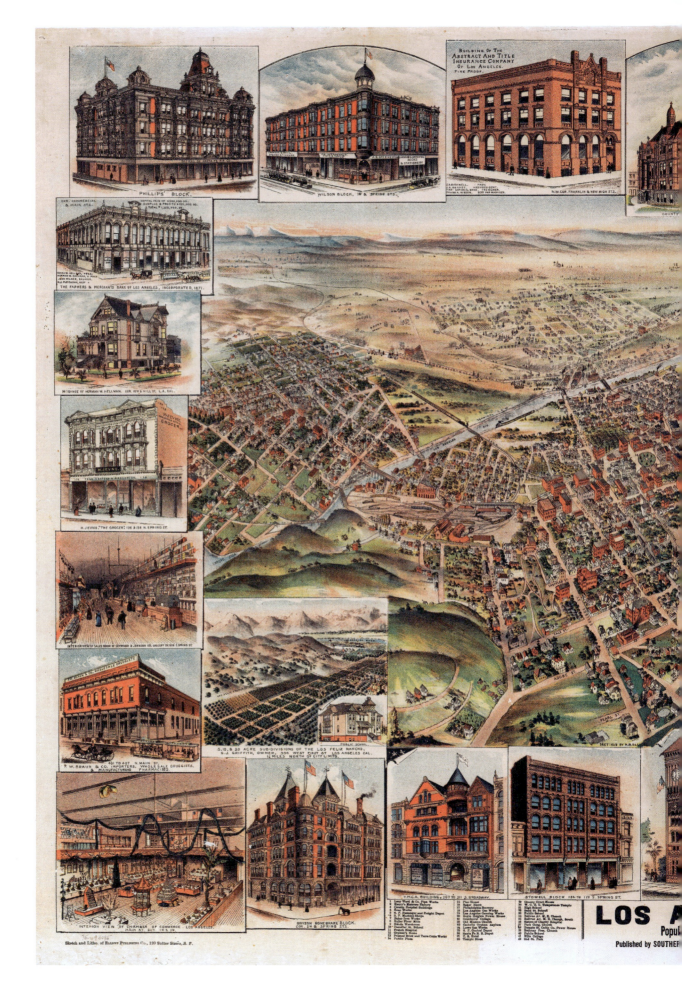

"THE HOLLENBECK" AMERICAN & EUROPEAN PLAN, COWLEY, BAKER & CO. PROP'RS, SPRING.

TEMPLE BLOCK.
JUNCTION, SPRING & MAIN STS.

JOHN C. PLAYER, PRES.
ROBERT S. BAKER VICE PRES.
ONE A. STEWART CASHIER.

1852   BAKER BLOCK   1890
WELLS, FARGO & CO'S EXPRESS
Express Carrier of Money, Jewelry, Valuables and Freight between all points, North, South, East and West.
WELLS, FARGO & CO'S MONEY ORDERS.
Cheap, Safe and Convenient. Issued for any amount up to $50, and payable at over 15,000 places in the United States and Canada.
RATES.

HOFFMAN HOUSE, NOS. 411 TO 417 N. MAIN ST.

NORMAL SCHOOL.

HIGH SCHOOL BUILDING, CASTELLAR ST.

GERMAIN FRUIT CO. WHOLESALE HOUSE, LOS ANGELES ST.

FIRST NATIONAL BANK, 226 & 228 NORTH MAIN ST.
E. F. SPENCE, PRES.   J. M. ELLIOTT, CASHIER.

"TEMPERANCE TEMPLE" W. C. T. U. BUILDING, COR. BROADWAY & TEMPLE STREET.

C. F. HEINZEMAN, DRUGGIST & CHEMIST, 222 NORTH MAIN ST.

SOUTHERN CAL. FIRE INS. CO. 345 N. MAIN ST.

PACKING HOUSE, ALAMEDA ST.

NURSERY DEPARTMENT, GERMAIN FRUIT COMPANY, COR. 4TH & LOS ANGELES STS.

LES. CAL.
Environs 65,000.
344 N. Main Street.   1891

Skyscraper City

Chicago, 1892

Like a phoenix from the ashes, the 12-storey Home Insurance Building graces Chicago's skyline in the panorama, shown overleaf, by the New York printmaker Currier and Ives, whose lithographer-founder Nathaniel Currier specialised in illustrating notable events in American history. One such was the devastating fire that broke out in the O'Leary's barn on DeKoven Street on the night of October 8, 1871. Although stories that a grumpy cow knocked over a kerosene lamp, setting the barn ablaze, are probably apocryphal, the fire that took hold, fanned by winds that blew burning brands and embers to create nine separate blazes that merged into one massive conflagration, devastated Chicago. Three hundred people died, 17,500 buildings – around a third of the city – were razed and 100,000 Chicagoans rendered homeless. Matters were made worse by the boom town's predominant building material being wood, and a dry summer that had left its streets tinderbox dry.

Amidst the ruins, the abolitionist poet John Greenleaf Whittier gloomily wrote that "The City of the West is dead", though the day after the fire the *Chicago Tribune* declared that "Chicago Shall Rise Again". The newspaperman proved to be a better prophet than the poet, and Chicago did rise. With land values at a premium in the business district, and in a hurry to recoup lost time, the city rose upwards.

It was not the first city to do so. Ancient Rome had its *insulae*, the urban slums of the inner city, which climbed to six or seven storeys, the upper ones bereft of water or sanitary facilities, and all of them death traps when the frequent fires broke out. In Yemen, the 16th-century mudbrick residential towers of Shibam rose to a precarious ten

storeys, giving it the later nickname of the "Chicago of the Desert". What, though, made Chicago's Home Insurance Building unique was iron. Its architect, William Le Baron Jenney, used recent advances in cast iron technology to create an inner skeleton of the metal (and, on the upper storeys, the even lighter steel) which had the dual virtue of being both light, while bearing a heavy load, and fireproof. It allowed him to send his creation soaring to a vertiginous ten storeys and 42 metres (138 feet), with a further two stories and 13 metres (42 feet) being added by the time of Currier and Ives' panorama. It remained an iconic part of the city's skyline until its demolition in 1931.

This, the world's first skyscraper, was the crowning act of Chicago's "Great Rebuilding", which transformed a city of wood into a metropolis of stone, brick, marble and steel. It also marked the end of a long journey from the indigenous settlements of the Meskwaki, Sauk, Potawatomi and Miami people sited on the shortest portage distance between the Great Lakes and the Mississippi River network. Chicago derives its name from *shikaakwa*, the word for a type of wild garlic in the language of the Miami people, who can have had little idea that the first Europeans they encountered – French explorers in the 1673 Marquette and Joliet expedition – would eventually number in their millions.

In 1803 the US army established Fort Dearborn on the Chicago River, but it was evacuated nine years later, and by 1840 the infant city – which had acquired a charter three years before – had only 4,000 inhabitants. It was transport links that made Chicago. The building of the first railroad out of the city in 1848, linking into what would become the Union Pacific transcontinental railroad in 1862, and the opening of the Illinois and Michigan Canal, also in 1848, sealed Chicago's position as the Midwest's main transportation hub.

The city pulled in migrants: first Scandinavians, Irish and Germans; and later Italians, Czechs and Poles, as well as Jewish people. They were attracted by jobs in enterprises such as Cyrus McCormick's pioneering mechanical reaper factory, established in 1847 with $25,000 seed money from Chicago's mayor William Ogden, but above all by the grain elevators, which handled 60 million bushels in 1870 alone, and the massive stockyards, such as the Union Stock Yards which could house 20,000 cattle, 75,000 hogs and 20,000 sheep.

The city's population surged to 300,000 in 1870. The devastation of the 1871 fire proved a mere hiccough, as by 1880 it had reached 503,000, making Chicago the United States' second largest city. Its massive expansion aggravated an already chronic hygiene problem – in 1850 the *Gem of the Prairie* newspaper had commented on "the gutters running with filth at which the very swine turn up their noses" – but Chicago proved equal to the task. The solution was the Chicago Sanitary and Ship Canal, which opened in 1900, as part-transport conduit and part-receptacle for the city's sewage.

Late-19th-century Chicago was a hotbed both of radicalism – its growing industrial base led to labour unrest and outbreaks such as the Haymarket Riot in 1886, in which a bomb killed seven policemen – and of innovation: the 1893 World Columbian Exposition drew 27.5 million visitors to its "White City" of plaster, which sprang up on reclaimed marshland along the lake shore. Then, the gradual clogging of its industrial arteries caused Chicago's blazing pace of development to falter.

The city did receive a new shot in the arm after the First World War, with a growing workforce of African Americans and Mexican Americans who moved up from the southern states. The inner city, though, became the domain in the 1930s of gangsters such as John Dillinger and Al Capone, as the prohibition era gnawed at the bonds of social order. After the Second World War, the long reign of the Democrat mayor Richard J Daley, from 1955 to 1976, kept a firm, if perhaps clientelist, grip on affairs, as stockyards and mills closed one by one.

Chicago has experienced a Renaissance of sorts in recent decades, with new public housing projects and a diversification of its economic base. It acquired new skyscrapers, including the Sears (now Willis) Tower, which at 443 metres (1,450 feet) and 110 storeys was the world's tallest building between 1973 and 1998. Yet its supremacy was then toppled by Malaysia's Petronas Towers, which in turn lost the title in 2010 to Dubai's Burj Khalifa. At 828 metres (2,716 feet) and 160 stories, this is almost twenty times taller than the Home Insurance Building. Although Chicago pioneered the skyscraper city, its imitators have far outpaced it.

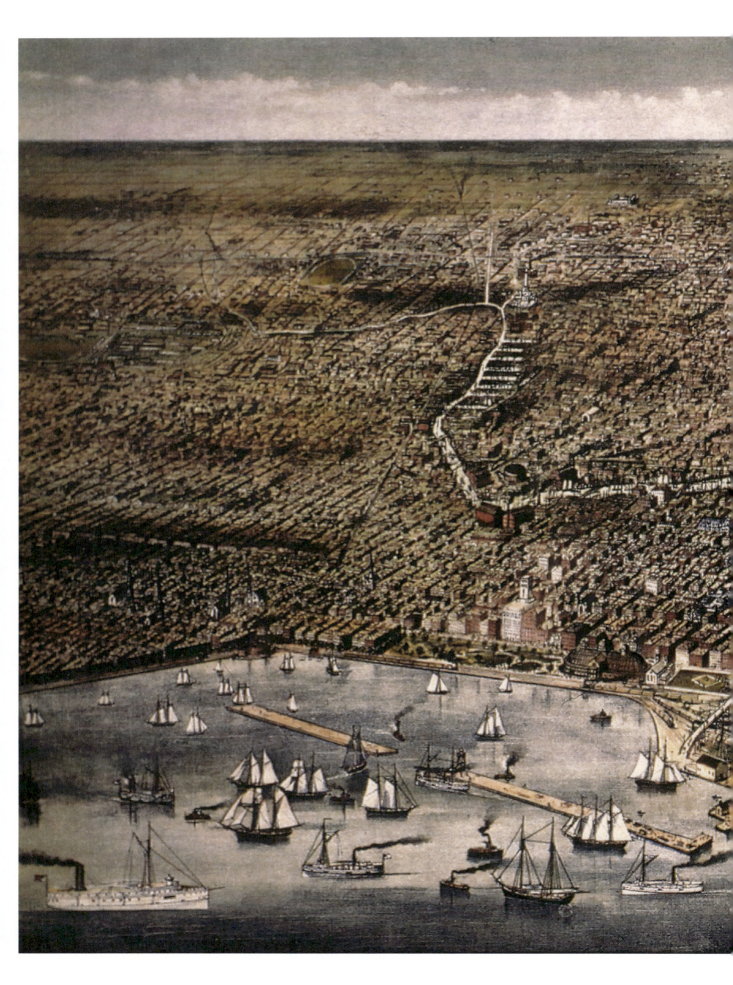

Fever Dreams

Rio de Janeiro, 1895

Produced by Brazil's Federal Health Institute, the map overleaf shows a city afflicted by fever, specifically yellow fever. Its victims are indicated by the black dots which cluster tightly in the older part of the town by the port, and are less densely spread in the healthier, new suburbs to the northwest and around Sugarloaf Mountain, Rio de Janeiro's magnificent backdrop, to the southeast.

It had been a bad year for fever. Although Rio's Sanitary Report dated January 11, 1897, noted that "on the whole it is rare to have so healthy a time in January", with just five deaths from yellow fever, 1896 had seen 3,789 cases of which 2,090 were fatal. Yellow fever was hot news, its causes debated in vitriolic exchanges in the city's press between physicians who contended that it either arose from "miasma" (bad air), and those who championed the theory that it spread through contagion between sufferers. Only in 1901 was it proved that bites from infected mosquitoes were responsible and once this was known, Oswaldo Cruz, Rio's director general of public health, engaged in a campaign of extermination of the insects that led to a massive fall in incidence.

Large cities have a terrible habit of appearing on the type of swampy ground which characterised early Rio de Janeiro. Heat, humidity and stagnant water have created an insect's paradise in a belt from Lagos to Jakarta that carries a heavy public health cost in malaria, dengue fever and other insect-borne diseases. Even further north, the Pontine Marshes outside Rome were a reservoir of malaria until finally drained by the Italian Fascist regime in the 1930s, and Philadelphia suffered a major yellow fever epidemic in 1793, which killed 5,000 people, around a tenth of its population.

The Portuguese first reached the area of Rio de Janeiro in January 1502 (the month giving the city its later name). A further expedition under Estácio de Sá, which established Portugal's first settlement there in 1565, had little inkling of its unhealthy nature: its more immediate concern was La France Antarctique. This French outpost, lodged there since 1555, threatened Portugal's claims to the eastern seaboard of South America and was only finally evicted in 1567 after the feuding of rival Huguenot and Catholic factions undermined its defence.

The early town amounted to just three streets along the shore by 1648 (although these housed some 3,000 people) and it was only the discovery of gold and diamonds in nearby Minas Gerais, with Rio the obvious port to ship them to Europe, that made the city's fortunes. Fresh water came in through the Arcos aqueduct, built in 1723, and the swamps were partially drained to open new areas for building, so that by 1763 Rio had grown to 46 streets housing around 24,000 people. Even though the headquarters of Brazil's colonial administration were transferred there that year, the city might have remained a sleepy backwater but for an accident of European politics. In 1807 Napoleon invaded Portugal, angered at support for Britain's opposition to his occupation of Spain. The Portuguese court, including the Prince Regent João, fled across the Atlantic to Brazil, accompanied by around 15,000 nobles and hangers-on.

The effect on Rio was electrifying. The city suddenly found itself capital of a European empire and, within a short time, had been equipped with a suite of grand buildings, including the Royal Military Academy, The Royal School of Sciences, Arts and Crafts, and a neoclassical National Library. It also gained its first newspaper, the *Gazeta do*

Rio de Janeiro, the more suitably to report on royal doings. Foreigners were impressed. In 1832 Charles Darwin, in the middle of his *Beagle* voyage, was moved to remark that Rio was "more magnificent than anything any European has ever seen in his city of origin". Other British visitors noted more mundane improvements, such as the merchant John Lubbock who in 1813 wrote that compared to his first visit five years earlier "it was no longer difficult to get a horse shod".

In 1811 João decreed tax incentives for building houses on land reclaimed from the marshes. The trick worked, and by 1821 the city had 113,000 inhabitants. Congestion became so bad that ox-carts were banned from the main streets in 1828. In 1858 the railways arrived, and two years later the city acquired gas lighting. By then, too, it gained an even more crucial transportation link with the first steamship services opening up to Europe. Instead of a journey lasting months, now it was possible to cross the Atlantic in just over a week, bringing fresh waves of migrants, including over a million Italians who settled in Brazil between 1880 and 1920.

With Brazil having declared independence from Portugal in 1822 (though still ruled by emperors of the Portuguese house of Braganza), Rio increasingly made its own way. The reformist emperor Pedro II (reigned 1831–89) oversaw the introduction of the telegraph in 1874 and brought back a telephone gifted to him by Alexander Graham Bell on a visit to the Centennial Exposition in Philadelphia in 1876. The end of his reign saw the final abolition of enslavement in Brazil in 1888, freeing around 700,000 enslaved people, but causing a temporary economic dislocation that led to the monarchy's overthrow in 1889.

Republican Rio continued to grow, with the construction of the Municipal Theatre, inspired by Paris's Opera House, in 1905, and the elegant two-kilometre- (1.1-mile-) long Avenida Central (now Avenida Rio Branco), in 1912, also modelled on a Parisian boulevard. The 20th century brought troubled times politically, with the installation of the authoritarian Estado Novo regime of Getúlio Vargas, who ruled the country from 1930 to 1945, and 1951 to 1954. The city did, though, acquire one of its signature landmarks in 1931, the 30-metre- (98-foot-) high statue of *Cristo Redentor* (Christ the Redeemer), which presides over the city from the top of Mount Corcovado to the south and is the world's biggest art deco sculpture.

By 1960, Rio had lost its position as Brazil's capital to the new-build city of Brasília. Pride aside, it scarcely mattered as the city's population ballooned from around 3.3 million to over 11 million in the early 21st century. Rio was the site of the 1992 Earth Summit, which made a series of landmark declarations on sustainable development, and in 2016 was the first South American city to host the Olympic Games. Yet even so, as Rio continued to grow, a worrying scourge returned. Although the city had last seen an epidemic of yellow fever in 1942, in 2006 the disease re-emerged, with an outbreak in 2016–19 causing 759 deaths nationally, concentrated around the city. Rio de Janeiro has not yet seen the end of fever dreams.

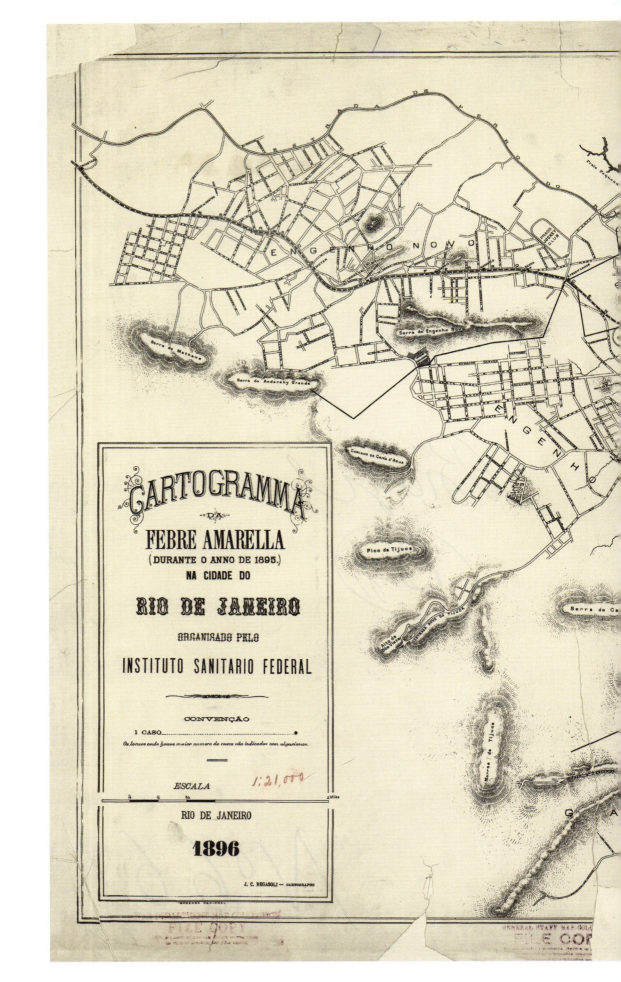

CARTOGRAMMA
·DA·
FEBRE AMARELLA
(DURANTE O ANNO DE 1895.)
NA CIDADE DO
RIO DE JANEIRO
ORGANISADO PELO
INSTITUTO SANITARIO FEDERAL

CONVENÇÃO

1 CASO.................................•

Os locaes onde houve maior numero de casos vão indicados com algarismos.

ESCALA 1:21,000

RIO DE JANEIRO

1896

J. C. REGASOLI — CARTOGRAPHO

New for Old

Delhi, 1912

It is a city on the edge of a transformation, the projected buildings of a planned new imperial capital for India shown outlined in red on this map from the 1912 edition of the *Encyclopaedia Britannica*.

The new city, to be built in the shadow of the 250-year-old Red Fort, was announced with great fanfare by the King-Emperor George V at the Delhi Durbar in December 1911. The glittering event was laid on to emphasise Britain's continuing firm control over India at a time of growing tensions caused by the Viceroy Lord Curzon's attempt to weaken nationalist opposition by partitioning Bengal in 1905. It required a city in itself, with 24 new railway stations built and 233 tent camps erected for the 200 ruling Indian princes who were expected to process past the British sovereign's dais. One visitor was moved to remark that the nighttime scene of campfires was "as if a million giant fireflies had settled on the plain".

The announcement they heard was startling. Aside from the amnesty for almost 10,000 prisoners, George V proclaimed that Delhi was henceforth to be India's capital (removing this from Kolkata, where it had been since 1772). Barely was the proclamation made than a scramble was on to establish planning committees and select an architect to build a suitably imperial city. In 1912 the main committee co-opted Edwin Lutyens, an architect previously better known as the designer of stately homes for the British aristocracy, but with the compelling advantage that he was the son-in-law of a previous viceroy, Lord Lytton.

To create a new capital in the face of so much tradition was certainly a challenge. Suggestions that Delhi's site lay on that of Indraprastha, a city mentioned in the *Mahabharata*, an epic dating to the first centuries BC, are not archaeologically provable, but it had certainly become a royal centre by 1020, when the Rajput Tomara ruler Anangpal II established a base there. By 1206, it was capital of the Delhi sultanate, which held sway over much of northern India until its defeat by the Mughal Babur in 1526. Although the early Mughals preferred Agra as their royal capital, in 1648 Shah Jahan, the dynasty's fifth ruler, transferred his court to Delhi. The city then enjoyed its glory days, politically and architecturally, with the erection of the magnificent Red Fort and the Jama Masjid mosque, which formed the centrepiece of Shahjahanabad, the emperor's new city, and the core of Old Delhi, the still magnificent historic district with which Lutyens' new conception had to compete.

His first design, inspired by Haussmann's Paris and the New York city grid, was all 90-degree angles, until Viceroy Hardinge pointed out that the high winds and sandstorms to which Delhi was subject would render such wide, straight boulevards intolerable. Instead Lutyens came up with a revised plan, with diagonal streets creating a complex pattern of triangles and octagons. It all centred on the Rajpath, a ceremonial avenue leading past the 42-metre-(138-foot-) high India Gate – a memorial to the 80,000 Indian solders who perished in the First World War – and ending at the lavish residence constructed for the viceroy.

The 340-room building, only completed in 1930, was equipped with 37 fountains and took several million tonnes of stone and 7,500 tonnes of cement to build. Its design had provoked arguments between Lutyens, his fellow architect on the scheme Herbert Baker, and Viceroy Hardinge, who felt some deference to Indian tastes was needed. Hardinge got his way, as Lutyens developed a hybrid neoclassical style mixed with baroque and elements of Indian architectural style.

Many, including the British travel writer Robert Byron, felt that it was an improvement on traditional British colonial buildings in India, noting in 1931 that, "The nineteenth century devised nothing lower than the municipal buildings of India. Their ugliness is positive, daemonic." The inauguration that year was much lower key than the 1911 Durbar, and, though British India had its new capital, (officially renamed New Delhi in 1927), it was the last hurrah of the Raj. Indian nationalist opposition grew inexorably, and in 1947 former British India achieved independence as the two new nations of Muslim-majority Pakistan and Hindu-majority India, the latter with Delhi as its capital.

In the years since, the population has grown to 12 million in the urban core, and nearly 28 million in the larger metropolitan agglomeration. The rows of neat white bungalows which Lutyens designed for colonial officials have become a rather ambivalent reminder of the colonial past, under threat of demolition or unsympathetic remodelling. In 2019 a new plan was unveiled to deal with the "Lutyens Bungalow Zone" and the 26 square kilometres (10 square miles) it occupies in a city where space is ever at a premium. It is said that Delhi has gone through seven different versions in the past, and Lutyens' New Delhi, which imagined itself the eighth and final, now finds itself the "old", in danger of being replaced by a different "new".

DELHI

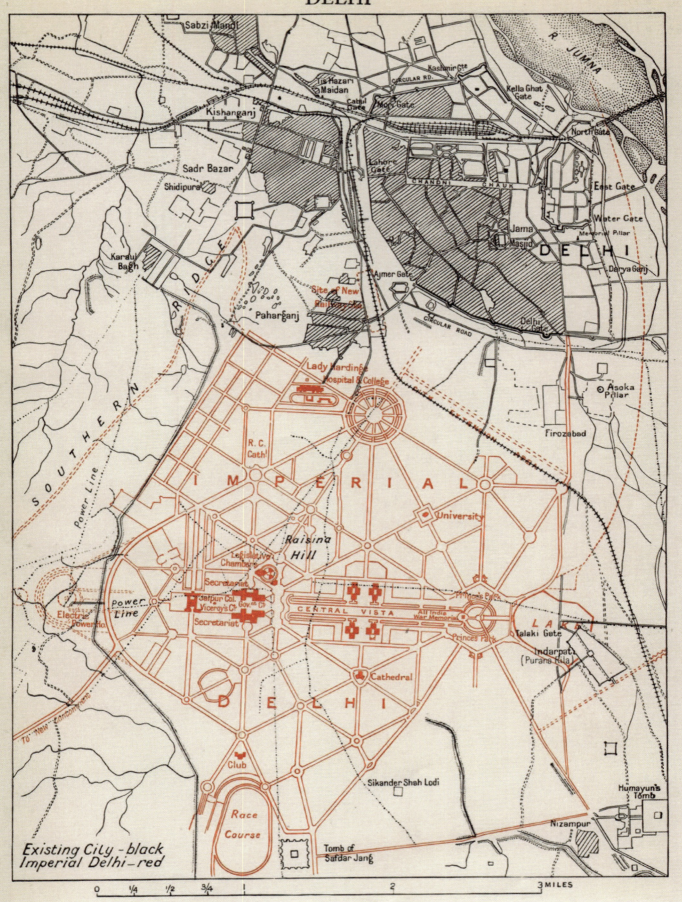

Existing City - black
Imperial Delhi - red

0   ¼   ½   ¾   1   2   3 MILES

Caught Between Two Worlds

Kyiv, 1914

The map shows a city trapped between two worlds. Kyiv, included in the guidebook publisher Karl Baedeker's 1914 publication *Russia with Teheran, Port Arthur and Peking* would, within four years, break free of Tsarist Russia to the east, be invaded by Germany to the west, assert independence again, and then be summarily annexed by the Soviet Union. It then saw the process repeated in 1941–43. Only in 1991 did Kyiv, and the Ukrainian state of which it is the capital, achieve full independence, an identity still bitterly contested by its Russian neighbour.

Baedeker's high-quality maps were the signature of a publishing empire whose red-bound pocket-sized volumes became ubiquitous by the early 20th century, with around a thousand editions on the market, in German, French and English, a dominance hardly suggested by the first humble edition, covering the Rhineland from Mainz to Cologne, published in 1832. Baedeker's great rival, the English publisher John Murray's 1868 guide to Kyiv, calls it the "Jerusalem of Russia" and explains its three districts: the Old Town (or Staryi Kyiv, shown as "Starokiewskaja" on Baedeker's map), the site of the first fortification and of governmental buildings; the religious centre of Pechersk ("Petscherskaja"), with its 11th-century cave monastery of Kyiv-Pechersk Lavra, both either side of a high ridge on the right bank of the Dnipro river; and, by itself on lower ground, the commercial district of Podil ("Podolskaja").

This tripartite division between state, church and enterprise has characterised Kyiv almost from the start and bedevilled its development. Those beginnings are obscure in the extreme: although the city celebrated its 1,500th birthday in 1982 in honour of its alleged foundation by three Slavic brothers, Shchek, Khoryv and Kyi (from the last of whom the city is said to derive its name), there is no real archaeological trace until at least the 7th century.

A tradition in *The Russian Primary Chronicle* relates that around 862 the Slavs, who were then settled at Kyiv, invited two Scandinavian brothers, Askold and Dir, to protect them as they were under attack from nomadic tribes, who had captured their ruler. Whatever the truth of these origin stories, by 882 there was a town large enough to attract the attentions of Oleg, the Swedish-descended ruler of Novgorod, who captured it that year.

Kyiv became the centre of a state called Rus, a fusion of Slavic and Viking Norse culture which, with the admixture of Greek Orthodox Christianity when Grand Prince Volodymyr converted in 988, became the dominant force in the region. Kyiv experienced a golden age under Yaroslav the Wise (reigned 1019–54), under whom the magnificent St Sophia Cathedral and the Lavra were built, but thereafter the state fragmented, as other rival principalities gobbled up parts of its territory. In 1169 Kyiv suffered a sack at the hands of Andrey Bogolyubsky of Suzdal, the first of many in a dark period in the city's history that culminated in December 1240 when it was comprehensively destroyed by Batu Khan's Mongol horde. The khan was afterwards said to have remarked, "I will tie Kyiv to the tail of my horse."

The Old Town lay almost in ruins for a century after yet another sack by the Crimean Tatar Khan Mengli-Giray in 1482. A weakened Kyiv found itself pulled into the orbit of Lithuania and then Poland after the two countries merged under the Union of Lublin in 1569. Its merchants, based in the Podil district, had recovered some of its prosperity, and were granted fiscal and limited legal autonomy under the Laws of Magdeburg – an early version of an international free-port system – around 1495. But the Grand Duchy of Muscovy, which became Tsarist Russia in 1547, pressed relentlessly from the east. A brief spark of independence was ignited when Bohdan Khmelnytsky's Cossacks took the city in 1648, using it as the base for their Hetmanate state, but the Poles retook it, and in 1669 conceded Russia a two-year occupation by Poland under the Treaty of Andrusovo, a grant made permanent in 1686.

Although the resulting stability brough prosperity, with Greek, Armenian, Jewish and Russian merchants crowding the alleys of the Podil, and new buildings such as the rococo Magistracy Hall, built in the 1690s (with an inscription declaring, "God watches over the city of Kiev"), other freedoms were curtailed, and the Magdeburg laws abolished in 1835. More and more incomers arrived from Russia, so that while the census of 1874 had four times as many Ukrainian speakers as Russian, that of 1897 recorded 58 per cent Russian speakers to only 23 per cent Ukrainian. In 1863 almost all publications in Ukrainian were outlawed, further marginalising the language.

The city (by then referred to as Kiev, its Russian form) did grow, from 23,500 inhabitants in 1817 to 247,000 by 1897. New industries sprang up, helped by the transportation possibilities offered by the Dnipro, and by the 1840s the city had 49 sugar refineries, while its annual Contract Fair brought in tens of thousands of merchants each year (to add to the 50–80,000 pilgrims who came to visit its churches and monasteries). The first modern bridge over the river was built in 1848–53, and Kyiv acquired a university in 1834 and gaslighting in 1872.

None of this, though, could mask a growing movement for Ukraine, finally, to assert its own identity. When finally the Tsarist empire began to break apart under the pressures of the First World War, Kyiv took its chance, with the declaration of a Peoples's Republic by its Rada (Assembly) in November 1917. Although evicted by the Russian Bolsheviks early in January 1918, a new Ukrainian state was declared just two months later after the Communists were ejected by the advancing German army. Kyiv changed hands several times between Germans, Ukrainians, Pro-Tsarist White Russians and Bolsheviks before finally being incorporated into the Ukrainian SSR in 1922.

Ukrainian identity was further suppressed in the 1930s, when the region suffered massive mortality from a famine in 1932–33 and the Soviet regime took St Sophia's Cathedral into state possession and simply demolished many other churches. The city was almost entirely destroyed during the Second World War, as the retreating Red Army set off a massive series of booby-trap mines as it retreated in 1941. The job of reconstruction in 1945 was massive, though amid the rebuilding of the old, the city did receive its first metro service in 1960.

Long submerged nationalist currents revived as the Soviet Union frayed and then collapsed in 1991. The new Ukrainian state which declared its independence still struggled to find a safe pathway between East and West. The city's Maidan Square became the scene of demonstrations against what was seen as the fraudulent election of the pro-Moscow politician Viktor Yanukovych as president in December 2004, and then again in 2013–14 when Yanukovych, by now president, sought to stop an association agreement with the European Union. Then, in February 2022, Russia's president Vladimir Putin, as unable to tolerate an independent Ukraine as his Tsarist or Bolshevik predecessors had been, ordered a full-scale invasion. Though Kyiv resisted the initial onslaught, it was clear, that for the city on the Dnipro, finding its own destiny amid the ambitions of its eastern neighbour continued to be a matter of life and death.

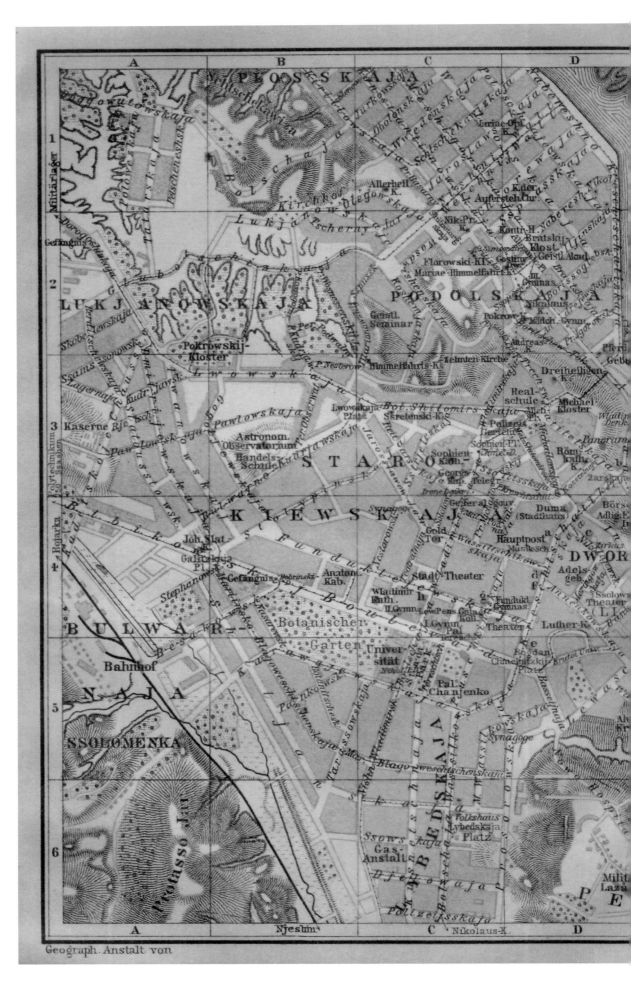

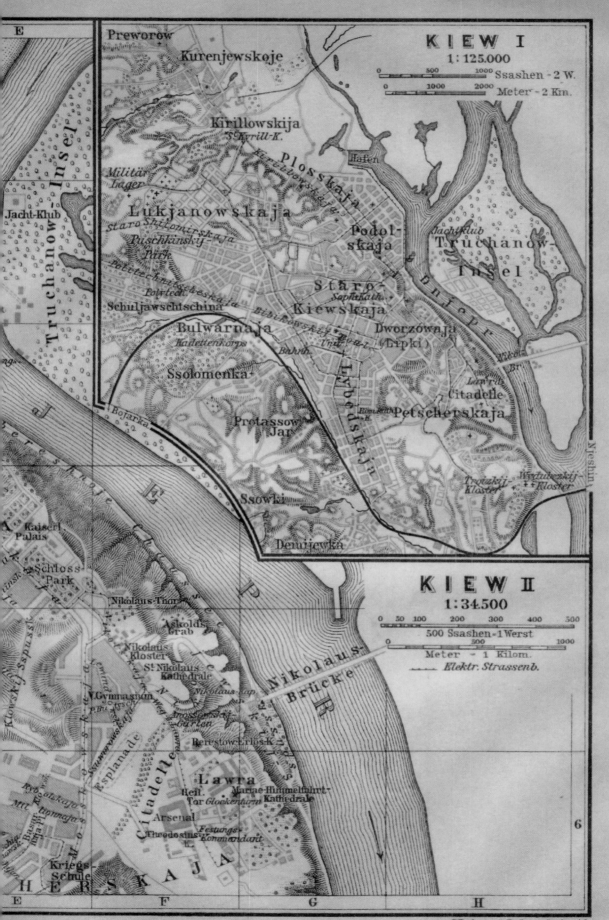

KIEW I

1:125.000

0 500 1000   Ssashen - 2 W.

0 1000 2000   Meter - 2 Km.

Preworow

Kurenjewskoje

Kirillowskija

St. Kyrill-K.

Plosskaja

Hafen

Militär Lager

Lukjanowskaja

Staro-Shitomirskaja

Puschkinsky-Park

Polytechnicheskaja

Schuljawschtschina

Podol-skaja

Truchanow-Insel

Staro-Kiewskaja

Sophia-Kath.

Dworzowaja

(Lipki)

Bulwarnaja

Kadettenkorps

Bahnh.

Ssolomenka

Lybedskaja

Bojarka

Protassow-Jar

Citadelle

Petscherskaja

Trotzkij-Kloster

Wydubenkij-Kloster

Ssowki

Demijewka

Truchanow-Insel

Jacht-Klub

Jachtklub

Dnjepr

Njeshin

KIEW II

1:34.500

0 50 100 200 300 400 500

500 Ssashen-1 Werst

0   500   1000

Meter - 1 Kilom.

Elektr. Strassenb.

Kaiserl. Palais

Schloss-Park

Nikolaus-Thor

Askolds Grab

Nikolaus-Kloster

St. Nikolaus-Kathedrale

Nikolaus-Kap.

Nikolaus-Brücke

V. Gymnasium

Berestow-Erlos.-K.

Esplanade

Citadelle

Lawra

Heil. Tor

Glockenturm

Mariae-Himmelfahrt-Kathedrale

Arsenal

Theodosius-K.

Festungs-Kommandant

Kriegs-Schule

ERSKAJA

E   F   G   H

6

Wagner & Debes, Leipzig.

The Plan Meets Reality

Brasília, 1960 & 2010

The contrast between Lúcio Costa and Oscar Niemeyer's plan for a new capital for Brazil and the 2010 satellite image of the city is stark. The neat lines and orderly divisions of the modernist city envisaged by its creators as "a cross on the landscape" or, in more secular mood, as an airplane or bird with outstretched, curved wings, are submerged in the urban sprawl and the dozens of satellite settlements which grew up in the intervening decades. By the measure of the sheer population attracted to a city, the plan worked, but its encounter with the realities of a growing city was only a limited success.

Brazil had been on the hunt for a new capital as far back as 1822, as a means to avoid the political centre of gravity tilting too far towards the coastal urban leviathans of São Paulo and Rio de Janeiro, and to encourage the development of the country's vast forest-swathed hinterland. It was not until a federal commission identified a general site in 1955 in the interior state of Goiás, on savannah land in Brazil's central plateau, that much progress was made. It needed, though, the inauguration of Juscelino Kubitschek as Brazil's president in January 1956 for the idea to spark into life. Kubitschek's "Fifty Years in Five" plan to promote the country's rapid industrialisation and urbanisation made him an enthusiastic supporter of the notion of a new capital, and a competition was rapidly set in train for its design.

The winners, urban designer Costa and architect Niemeyer, came up with a plan of deceptive simplicity based on the *Ville Radieuse* (Radiant City) theories of the French master architect Le Corbusier. Brasília, as the new capital was to be called, would separate out the housing and leisure sectors of the city, which were placed in the curved "wings", from the administrative and governmental functions at its head, with the cultural, religious and transport centres being in the body. A long *Eixo Monumental* (Monumental Axis), which would run broadly north–west to south–east, was to be lined with federal buildings.

Work began rapidly, and the city was completed and inaugurated in a dizzyingly rapid 1,310 days. The presidential palace was the first to be finished, sited alongside the city's set-piece, the Praça dos Três Poderes ("Square of the Three Powers"), so named for having the headquarters of the country's executive, judiciary and legislature all bordering it. The city was a modernist architect's dream of concrete and curves, brutal yet surprisingly graceful. Its highlights included the Metropolitan Cathedral, inaugurated in

1970, whose 16 concrete pilasters curved and twisted into the shape of a crown at its apex, the twin towers and white concrete dome of the Palace of Congress, and, less obviously, the *superquadras*, the six-storey housing blocks squatting atop pylons which were supposed to reduce social differentiation and encourage civic cohesion by dint of all being the same design. Every facility of a modern city was considered, including the University of Brasília, which opened in 1962, and the whole enterprise cost $1.5 billion, leaving a legacy of debts that still hung over the country decades later.

The city was intended to house 500,000 people and its designers believed that they had built in plenty of room for growth as the population slowly increased – new capitals take time to capture the public imagination and encourage any but the civil service to move in. But the reality soon began to deviate from the plan. A military coup in 1964 brought new leaders who considered some of Costa's plans too "Marxist" and so they were scaled back or adapted (the Ministry of Justice was given a marble façade more redolent of Mussolini than Moscow). Weak control of planning regulations and the lack of its own elected officials – the governors of the province in which it sat were appointed by the Brazilian president until 1990 – meant that the work encampments set up during the city's construction turned into more than two dozen satellite cities, none of them remotely envisaged in the original plan.

The growth in population – to 2.8 million by 2022 – overwhelmed Brasília's transport infrastructure and left Lake Paranoá, which it overlooked, highly polluted until a water treatment programme was introduced. The concrete surfaces of the main plaza and roadways cracked, and the lower-quality residential housing deteriorated dramatically, leaving it in danger of becoming a futurist slum. Recent moves to regenerate the ecosystems that supply the city's water indicate a growing realisation that something must be done before Brasília expands any further and the problems facing the city become even more intractable. Approaching the second quarter of the 21st century, Brasília is now almost half the size of Rio de Janeiro, the city it was in many ways designed to supplant, and whose overcrowding, poor conditions, pollution and congestion it was intended to avoid. Yet by now it is clear that no urban plan can be frozen in time, an inflexible template that dictates the tides of a city's development. In a contest with reality, the plan will always lose.

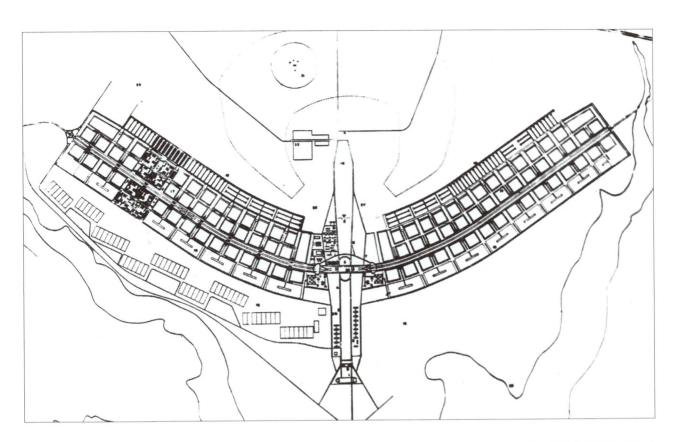

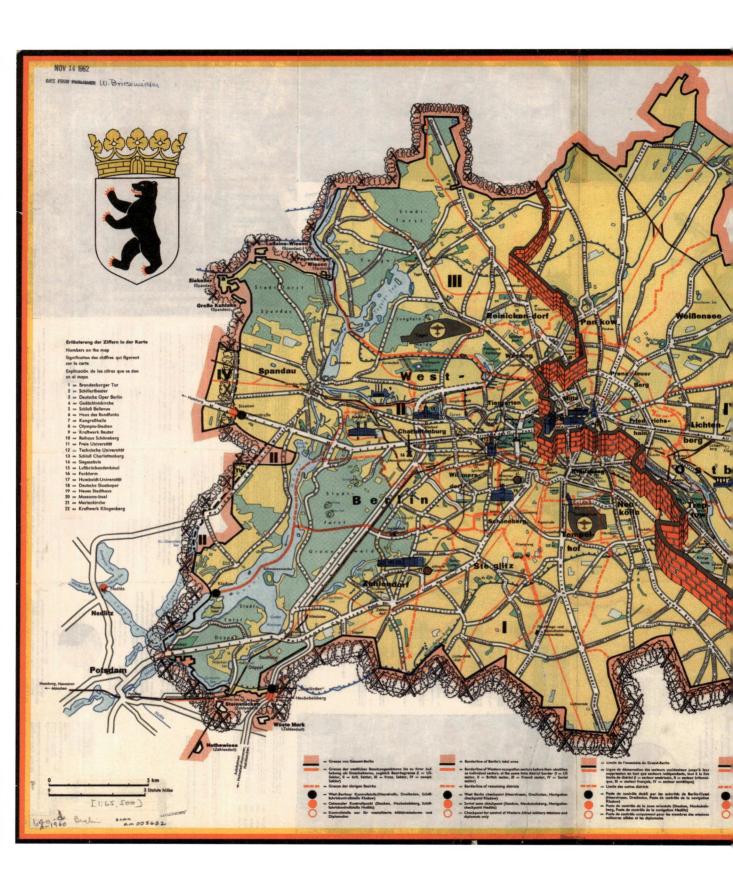

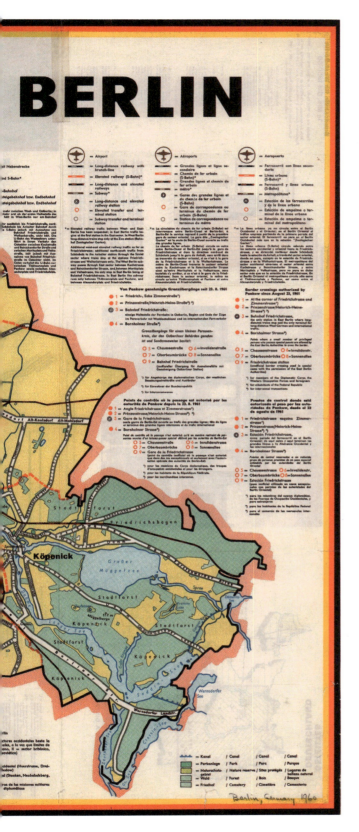

The map image shows the detailed railway and transit map of Berlin, with legends in German, French, and Spanish, and is labelled "Berlin, Germany 1960".

Divided Cities

Berlin, 1961 & Nicosia, 1974

The two cities bear scars, psychological and physical, marked by the lines that bisect them. For Berlin, it is the red bulk of the Berlin Wall, erected by the Soviet-dominated government of East Germany shortly before this plan's publication in 1961, and for Nicosia, the capital of Cyprus, the rather more ghostly green zone which from 1974 divided the Turkish Cypriot north of the city from the Greek Cypriot south, dramatically silhouetted against the city's star-shaped 16th-century Venetian fortifications.

There are many examples of cities that have found themselves divided when new borders sprang up, such as the Texas town of El Paso, sundered by the 1848 Treaty of Guadalupe Hidalgo from Ciudad Juárez across the frontier in Mexico, or the very special case of Rome and the Vatican City, the papal enclave which remained independent while nestled inside the larger city at the unification of Italy in 1871. A few cities, though, have found themselves divided by war or geopolitics, and remained separated for decades, creating problems of administration, security, supply and the gradual divergence of the identities of the communities either side of the dividing line.

Those lines and barriers go by various, often euphemistic names. Beginning in 1969, the Belfast "peace walls" were erected by the authorities to separate flashpoints along the dividing line between predominantly Catholic West Belfast and the largely Protestant east. Even after the 1998 Good Friday Agreement brought an end to the Northern Ireland conflict, many of the concrete barriers, complete with murals expressing competing views of Ireland's history, remained in place. Some, including Nicosia's, were called "green lines", a term allegedly deriving from the colour of the pen used by the United Nations officers who drew the 1949 ceasefire line between Arab and Israeli forces in Jerusalem, one of the more intractable of divided cities.

Berlin's division arose from irreconcilable differences between the Allied powers after Germany's defeat in the Second World War. The western Allies – France, Britain and the United States – saw Germany's future in a democratic and economic system broadly similar to their own, whereas Joseph Stalin's vision was of a neutral Germany, firmly under the thumb of the Soviet Union. The result was that the British, French and United States sectors of Berlin, which constituted the western 12 of the city's 20 districts, remained separate from the eight Soviet sectors to the east.

After initial attempts at a unified municipal council failed, the two parts of the city went their own separate ways administratively and politically. The Soviets tried (and failed) to throttle West Berlin with an 11-month-long blockade from June 1948 to May 1949, but a massive US-mounted airlift, which at its peak involved landing 13,000 tonnes of supplies each day, kept West Berlin alive, and Stalin relented. Increasingly though, those in the East were voting with their feet, making their way through the open border to the West. Soon, the German Democratic Republic (GDR), the East German state established by the USSR in 1949, was bleeding people, with 3.5 million residents defecting over the next dozen years.

On the night of August 12, 1961, East Berliners awoke to find legions of police and workmen lining the borderline between the two parts of the city. Streets were torn up and barbed-wire barriers erected to prevent any further flight to the west. In the first few hours, some escaped by climbing out of windows, but by the middle of next morning, the border was sealed. On August 24, East German border guards shot 24-year-old Günter Litfin dead as he tried to cross to the west, one of around 260 deaths the Wall and its guardians were to claim.

The barrier became more and more imposing, with a four-metre- (13-foot-) high double wall, guard towers, and a broad-section of no-man's land behind, partly mined and patrolled by dogs. The final version, complete in 1980, was composed of 45,000 separate concrete sections, but despite this, would-be escapees still tried to breach it by tunnelling, microlight plane, even by hot air balloon or simply trying to ram their way through in reinforced cars. Around 5,000 succeeded.

In the meantime, Berlin lived a curiously sundered existence. No citywide planning for sewage, water or transport was possible, direct telephone lines were cut in 1953, and crossing from east to west was impossible without a hard-to-acquire permit. The grand Brandenburg Gate, directly on the dividing line, acted as a very visible reminder of a city broken in two. Even the U-Bahn and S-bahn metro lines were divided: some terminated at the station nearest the Wall, three lines from the west crossed beneath the east without stopping, while others simply passed through the *Geisterbahnhöfe* (ghost stations), which were sealed. Only at the Friedrichstrasse Station did the two systems meet, one of the very few points (together with the nearby Checkpoint

Charlie, immortalised in dozens of spy films and novels), where authorised crossing was possible.

All this came to an end on November 9, 1989, as the East German government, destabilised by months of protests, began to implode. That evening, a careless choice of words by Günter Schabowski, East Berlin's communist party boss, gave the impression that restrictions on travel to the West had been scrapped, and tens of thousands of East Berliners made their way to the wall, overwhelmed the guards and surged into the west of the city. Once the dam was broken, it could not be plugged and East Germany, and with it the division of the city, was dissolved less than a year later. The Wall itself was dismantled by Berliners themselves, with hammers, chisels and mallets, as a symbol of the hated division of the city. Within a few years only a few preserved sections remained as a reminder of the damage an ideologically imposed division of a city can create.

Nicosia became a divided city in August 1974 after a series of breakdowns in relations between the Greek-speaking and Turkish-speaking communities, which looked to Greece and Turkey respectively for support. A coup by the Greek-Cypriot Nikos Sampson in July 1974, which aimed to achieve *enosis* (unification) with Greece triggered intervention by the Turkish army, at first limited to the area around Kyrenia, but then on August 14 extended to Famagusta and the northern part of Nicosia.

The line of control at the ceasefire two days later became ossified as a new "green line" which ran straight through the old town of Nicosia, where the forward positions of the two sides were in some places just metres apart. Patrolled by peacekeepers of UNFICYP (the United Nations Peacekeeping Force in Cyprus), the city was a symbol of a hopelessly divided community and constantly thwarted hopes of a peace settlement. As in Berlin, crossing between the two zones became next to impossible and the Ledra Palace crossing was used largely by diplomatic and UN personnel.

Easing of a sort happened in the early 21st century, as the Ledra Palace crossing opened to more general traffic in 2003, followed by a referendum on reunifying the island in 2004. That failed, as, though Turkish Cypriots voted heavily in favour, around three quarters of Greek Cypriots rejected it. Several rounds of peace talks since then have failed, and Nicosia remains Europe's only divided city. Half a century after its split, there are now fewer and fewer people who remember what life was like before the Green Line divided them from their former neighbours. A city, once divided, is a hard thing to reassemble.

Underground City

Tokyo, 1964

Produced in tourist-friendly fashion for the 1964 Summer Olympic Games held in Tokyo, the plan overleaf, with its spider's web of public transportation lines radiating out from the centre (and in particular the green feathery tentacles of the subway) illustrates an increasingly common feature of modern cities: they have an underground mass transit system. The number of these has grown relentlessly, so that now any municipal authority with pretensions to the status of a global city already has, is planning, or is busily extending its network.

Public transportation, or its lack, was a serious constraint on the growth of pre-modern cities. In 1994, the Italian physicist Cesare Marchetti devised a principle (known as the Marchetti Constant) that throughout history, people have in general been prepared to commute half an hour each way within a city to their place of work. In eras where walking was the only option this imposed a maximum urban radius of a couple of kilometres (1.5 miles). To grow, the only option for a city was to become denser. Hence, by the 17th century urban areas such as London and Paris had become nightmarish labyrinthine warrens of overcrowded housing mixed in with a few more prosperous suburbs.

The pioneer of public transport was the French mathematician and philosopher Blaise Pascal, who in 1662 gained permission from the French crown to run a horse-drawn service, with seven carriages each capable of carrying eight passengers. It does not require a genius for mathematics to work out that this hardly made a dent in early modern Paris's transportation crisis. Proper horse-drawn services only became more popular in the 19th century, with George Shillibeer's service from Paddington to Bank in London, which began service in

July 1829 (carrying 20 passengers for the not inconsiderable sum of a shilling a ride). Although the Shillibeer service ultimately folded (not helped by the entrepreneur's failing to pay road taxes and being imprisoned for smuggling French brandy), horse buses, or omnibuses, caught on and by the late 19th century London's fleet was operated by 25,000 horses.

Although people could now travel more quickly – as much as doubling the radius their half hour would carry them – this brought other problems, quite apart from that of cleaning up after all those horses. The streets were now congested with carriages, private and public, once again reducing transport to a crawl. Horse-drawn trams helped a little, but the golden prize of devising a transport system that ran quickly and did not clog up the road network remained elusive.

The solution came from the dream of London solicitor Charles Pearson to build an urban rail system, and the ingenuity of John Fowler, chief engineer of the Metropolitan Railway Company, in devising it. Fowler's vision was for an underground railway, built by simply excavating downwards, installing the track, platforms and ticket halls and then covering it over. Sceptics thought the whole 5.5-kilometre (3.5-mile) route from Paddington to Farringdon would simply fall in on itself, but work began in 1860, and after three years of excavation by thousands of labourers, the line was finished. A ceremonial opening day journey on January 9, 1863, took 600 VIPs two hours to complete, as they stopped off to inspect each station, though one notable absentee was the prime minister, Lord Palmerston, who insisted that at his advanced age he wished to spend as much time above ground as possible.

The London Underground system had 35,000 travellers on its opening day and 9.5 million passengers in its first year. Subsequent lines were built by tunnelling underground rather than cut-and-cover, and initial problems caused by the choking fumes that the steam locomotives used to pull the carriages emitted in the confined spaces underground were overcome when electric trains began operating in 1890. The system expanded remorselessly, reaching, and to some extent creating, new suburbs in "Metro-land" to the northwest of London by the 1920s. Underground trains (or the "Tube" as Londoners nicknamed it) had allowed the city to burst its bounds.

Other cities took note. Budapest opened the first subway system in continental Europe in 1896, while the first 10-kilometre (6.2-mile) stretch of the Paris Metro, between Porte Maillot and Porte de Vincennes, opened in 1900. Boston was the pioneer in North America, inaugurating a 2.5-kilometre (1.5-mile) section of line in 1897, while on 27 October 1904 the first line of what would soon become the largest system in the world began running in New York. The first subway system in South America opened in Buenos Aires in 1913, and Tokyo became the first Asian country to join the ranks of "underground" cities in 1927, when the Ginza Line began operating between Asakusa to Ueno stations. The system, with two separate operators, is now even more extensive than it was during the 1964 Olympics, with a further ten lines having opened, and between them all they carry over nine million passengers daily (460,000 of them travelling through the Ikebukuro station alone).

Moscow's subway (officially named the VI Lenin Metro) was launched in 1935 and is almost unique in the world for the quality of its architecture, originally planned to showcase futurist Soviet art, but whose grand chandeliers, high ceilings and capacious hallways lined with artworks are the envy of many more purely functional metros. London, the grandfather of metro systems, can at least claim some contribution in that Frank Pick, chief executive of the London Passenger Transport Board, was a consultant for the design of the Moscow Metro.

The post-Second World War period brought even more regions into the metro club, with China opening the Beijing subway in 1971, India's oldest metro opening in Kolkata in 1984, the same year that the Philippines became the first South-East Asian country with a subway, soon followed by Singapore's Mass Transit system in 1987. That was the year that Africa acquired its first subway, with the Cairo Metro commencing service in 1987, though it remained alone until Algiers opened its network in 2011. Elsewhere in Africa, light rail systems prevail (a half-way house between conventional railways and subway systems) but the explosive growth of megacities on the continent means that new forms of urban railways are planned in locations as diverse as Port Louis on Mauritius, Lagos in Nigeria and Addis Ababa in Ethiopia.

By early 2024 there were around 200 cities with metro systems, 47 in China alone, with the most extensive in the world being Beijing's 815 kilometres (506 miles) of track, while Tokyo's, which carries nearly 4 billion passengers a year, was the busiest. Public transport has come a long way since the 1964 Tokyo Games and an even further distance since Pascal's first experimental bus service more than 350 years ago.

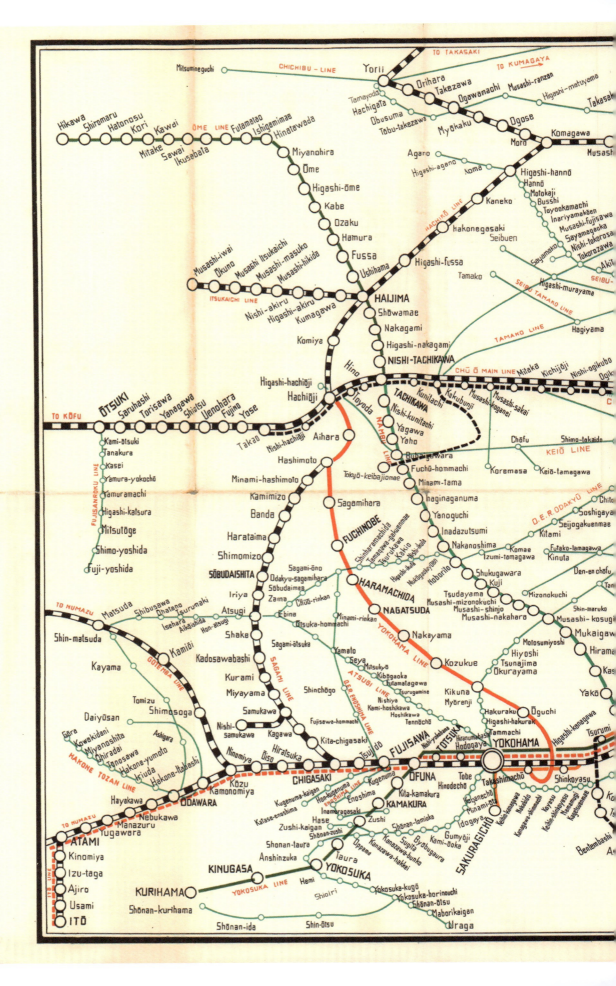

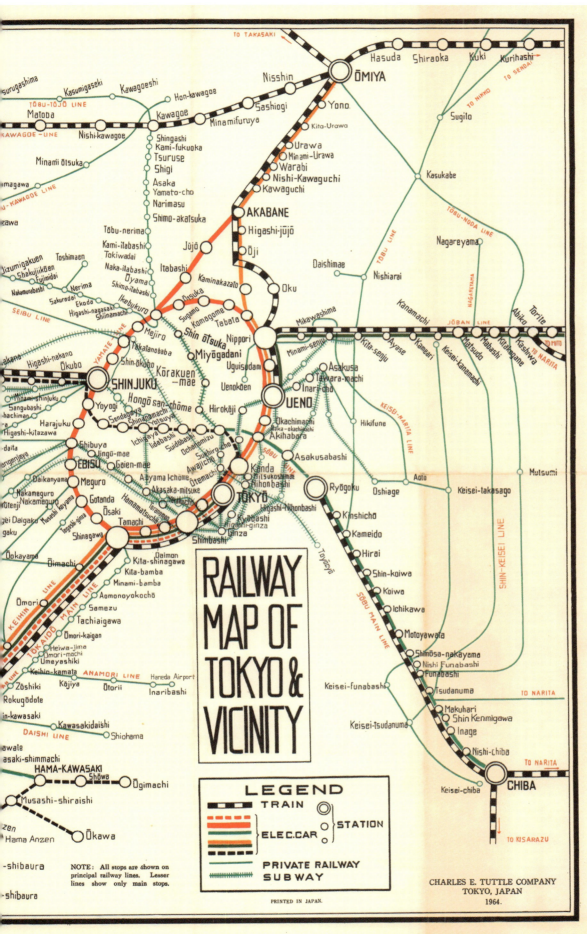

RAILWAY MAP OF TOKYO & VICINITY

LEGEND

TRAIN

ELEC. CAR

STATION

PRIVATE RAILWAY

SUBWAY

NOTE: All stops are shown on principal railway lines. Lesser lines show only main stops.

CHARLES E. TUTTLE COMPANY
TOKYO, JAPAN
1964.

PRINTED IN JAPAN.

Giant in the Desert

Dubai, 1984 & 2024

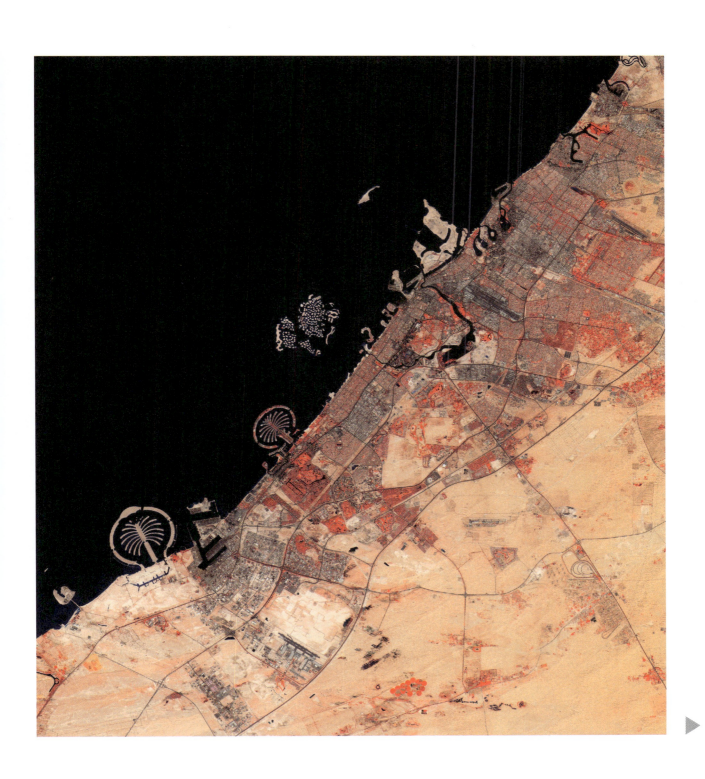

The two satellite images reveal an astounding story of urban growth in the unlikely setting of the Arabian Desert. The 1984 image has the city scarcely breaching the area immediately around the Dubai Creek, while that taken 40 years later shows a massively expanded urban footprint, complete with a series of artificial offshore islands including one (Palm Jumeirah) in the shape of a palm tree and another archipelago, the "World Islands", in the form of a map of the world.

This vast metropolis, now home to 3.6 million people, had even humbler origins. First mentioned by an 11th-century Arab traveller, it next enters the historical record (as "Dibei") around 1580 when Gasparo Balbi, the state jeweller of Venice, gave a description of temporary camps for the fishermen diving for pearls, an activity which long constituted the area's main industry.

In 1822 the area was surveyed by Lieutenant Robert Cogan of the Bombay Marine, at a time when British interest in the Gulf was growing – Dubai became a British protectorate as part of the Trucial States in 1820 – and he recorded a compact cluster of 25 buildings along the Creek's western bank and a few hundred inhabitants.

Those numbers were boosted in 1833 when an 800-strong group of the Al Bu Falasah clan, led by Maktoum bin Buti, whose descendants still rule Dubai, seceded from the neighbouring sheikhdom of Abu Dhabi and settled on the Creek. Sheltered under the British aegis, Dubai began a slow phase of growth, aided by the decision in 1900 of Sheikh Maktoum to establish a free port, exempt from taxes, which attracted merchants from all over the region and in particular Iran. By 1910 the population had reached 11,000, of whom 6,936 – virtually all the adult males – were engaged in pearling – and had extended to two new quarters: Al Shindagha, north of the Creek, and Deira to the east. But the industry collapsed during the Great Depression in the 1930s, aggravated by the Japanese invention of cultured pearls.

The prospects for Dubai, lacking the oil resources of its neighbours, were bleak, and it took the determination and vision of Sheikh Rashid (reigned 1958–90) to transform the city from a small desert settlement to a modern metropolis. Often acting against the wishes of more cautious advisers, he ordered the dredging of the Creek in 1959 to allow larger cargo ships to unload, and the building of Dubai's first airport the following year. The discovery of modest oil reserves at the Fateh ("good fortune") field in 1966 enabled him to diversify Dubai's economy still further, opening

the 15-berth Port Rashid in 1971 (extended to 35 berths in 1976 to make it one of the largest in the world). By 1985 Dubai had its very own airline, Emirates, and by 1980 the population had reached 276,000, its footprint sprawling to 84 square kilometres (32 square miles), sixteen times its size in 1960.

The pace of development was relentless. Dubai got its first skyscraper in 1979 – the 39-storey World Trade Centre – and strategic security was enhanced by the sheikh's negotiation of a merger with the other small states in the region (including Abu Dhabi) in 1971 to form the United Arab Emirates. His son, Sheikh Maktoum, who became ruler in 1990, propelled Dubai even further past regional rivals, building luxury hotels to promote tourism (where numbers rose from 600,000 a year in 1990 to 15.9 million by 2018). In 2002 he promulgated a land reform allowing foreigners to own real estate (previously they could only rent), bringing investment flooding in, particularly from Lebanon, India and the former Soviet Union. The population nearly doubled again between 1998 and 2008, the city acquired a metro in 2009, and in 2010 the Burj Khalifa, the world's tallest building at 828 metres (2,717 feet) and over 160 storeys, was completed.

New businesses were encouraged by the establishment of special economic zones – such as the International Financial Centre and Media City – which were partially exempt from local laws, making Dubai a regional centre for finance and technical services. All this did not come without a cost. Much of the old Dubai was swept away in the building frenzy, leaving only a small quarter around Bastakiyah, and although it is the world's most cosmopolitan city, with around 90 per cent of its population being foreign-born (and largely excluded from citizenship), the resulting social and economic imbalances present serious challenges.

The most serious threat, though, is environmental. The United Arab Emirates has been calculated to have the world's highest ecological footprint (at 9.5 global hectares per capita in 2008, compared to 5.3 for the United Kingdom) and one of its highest per capita water consumptions (at around 145 gallons per person per day). The continuing expansion of the city, with its ever-growing demands for electricity, water and food in a region ill-adapted to produce these on a large scale will stress that environment even further. Dubai has grown from minnow to giant in a few generations, but its ability to adapt to a less ecologically damaging way of operating will be a key indicator of whether today's rapidly expanding metropolises will become the sustainable cities of the future.

Informal City
Dharavi, Mumbai, 2011

The area north of Mumbai's peninsular core is mottled with red on the plan (shown in full overleaf), marking the location of the city's poorest areas, in which just over half of the city's population of over 12 million live. Largest of all, and one of the biggest slums in the world, is Dharavi.

Portrayed with brutal grittiness in the 2008 Oscar-winning film *Slumdog Millionaire*, the reality of life for its million or so residents – accurate counts are hard to make in such districts – is harsh. The 2.4 square kilometres (1 square mile) of close-packed housing is one of the most densely populated neighbourhoods in the world. People have been arriving there since the 1880s, when factories and low-quality housing were cleared out of the city centre by the British colonial government to make way for a building programme, and the leatherworkers and other residents moved to what had been the fishing village of Koliwada, perched on the edge of a mangrove swamp. Dharavi soon pulled in others, including potters from Gujarat and textile workers from Uttar Pradesh.

Such a diverse community of migrants is typical of many such settlements. They appear wherever urbanisation outpaces the ability or willingness of governments to provide adequate housing and facilities, creating vast cities-within-a-city such as Orangi Town in Karachi, Pakistan, with 2.4 million inhabitants, Ciudad Neza, east of Mexico City, with 1.2 million, and Kibera in Tanzania, with around 700,000. Their ubiquity is indicated by the vast range of terms used to describe them, from "slums" or "shantytowns" to *favelas* in Brazil, *villas miserias* in Argentina and *gecekondu* ("built in one night") in İstanbul.

Around 1.1 billion people currently live in slums worldwide, and although the proportion residing in them declined slightly from 25.4 per cent in 2014 to 24.2 per cent in 2020, this was simply because the cities themselves grew at an even greater pace. That around 183,000 people each day are added to the roll of slum-dwellers, whose total number is expected to rise by a further 2 billion by 2050, shows the challenge facing national and municipal authorities.

In general, they are unable to cope. Brazil and India have relatively well-resourced governments and levels of population, but when towns such as Dhaka (Bangladesh), Kinshasa (Democratic Republic of the Congo) and Lagos (Nigeria) all grew by 40 times between 1950 and 2006, and Nouakchott (Mauritania), Mogadishu (Somalia) and Bamako (Mali) exceeded the size of San Francisco, it was no surprise that the governments of poorer countries, whose infrastructure was already underdeveloped, had little capacity to cope with the burgeoning slums.

Slums are nothing new. Much of the centre of imperial Rome was one vast sea of *insulae*, low-quality multi-storey tenement-style blocks that lacked the most basic plumbing and were prone to disastrous fires. The development of London was piecemeal and largely unplanned, with the mass migration into the city in the early- to mid-19th century creating squalid districts graphically portrayed by writers such as Charles Dickens and whose clearance taxed the city's authorities into the middle of the 20th century (though arguably their solution in building vast, high-rise concrete blocks created slums of another sort).

Slums are the physical face of deep-seated economic and social inequalities, but they are not places without hope. Although Dharavi grew without planned housing, transport, sewage or education facilities, it has a vibrant economy, with over 5,000 business and 15,000 small factories and workshops producing goods worth around $1 billion annually. Around 60 per cent of all Mumbai's plastic recycling is carried out in the area, and Dharavi's traditional industries of leather, ceramics and textiles

continue to thrive. Arguments therefore rage as to whether the district is best rehabilitated by incremental investment, working with its residents to preserve some of its freewheeling, anarchic character, or by the type of wholesale clearances favoured by European governments in the 19th century.

For the moment, the latter approach seems to have won. In 2023 a contract was granted to an Indian property company to carry out a project costing over $600 million to provide new housing to the tens of thousands of families who can prove they have lived in Dharavi since before 2000, and to construct further housing for sale to others to finance the enterprise. Some local organisations worried that the complex ecosystem of Dharavi may collapse as the types of micro-industry that have thrived there are pushed out (just

as their ancestors had been in the 1880s), and that the 2000 cut-off date excludes a large proportion of its population.

Those red blotches on the map may move, if Dharavi is deemed to have reached a level of planning and facilities as to no longer merit the description of slum. But other informal settlements will spring up, as they always do in a period of rapid urbanisation. The UN established a Conference on Human Settlements in 1976 to examine the issue, but little progress globally has been made in the subsequent half-century. Only a concerted and sustained effort by governments, and a rise in incomes generally, will stem the tide of their growth. For some countries, whose economic growth itself is rapid, this may be attainable. For others, including large swathes of sub-Saharan Africa, it seems, at the moment, a distant hope.

The Power of Nature

Christchurch, 2011

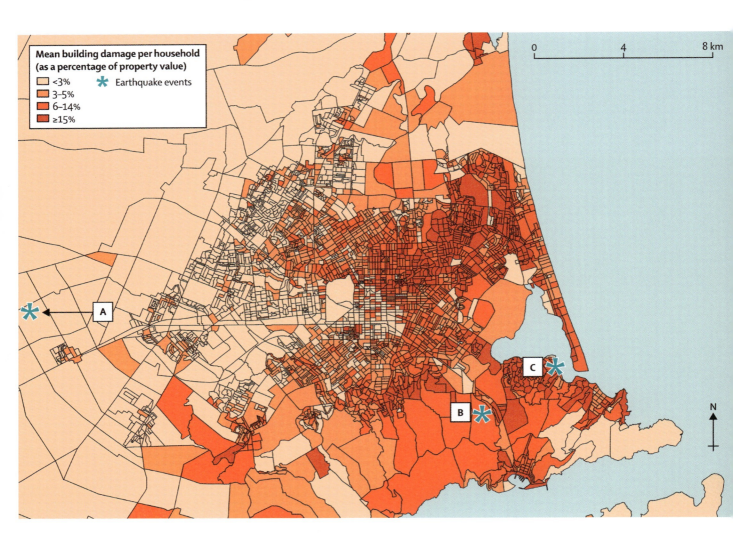

**Mean building damage per household
(as a percentage of property value)**

- <3%
- 3–5%
- 6–14%
- ≥15%

✳ Earthquake events

0   4   8 km

A

C

B

N

At 12.51pm on Tuesday, February 22, 2011, the New Zealand city of Christchurch was hit by a massive earthquake, registering 6.3 on the Richter scale. Buildings swayed as the earth below slipped, buckled and pushed, in some places literally liquefying as it sent jets of thousands of tonnes of silt upwards. No human agency could halt the destructive power of nature that, within less than a minute, severely damaged thousands of buildings and killed 185 people.

The map shows the pattern of that devastation, the deepest red indicating the highest proportion of buildings damaged (calculated according to their value), the worst-hit areas clustering around the epicentre of the earthquake, about 10 kilometres (6.2 miles) southeast of the city's central business district. The death and injury toll was worsened by it being lunchtime on a business day, and by a number of catastrophic building collapses, particularly that of the Canterbury Television Centre, in which 115 people died.

The largest city on South Island, Christchurch (named for the Oxford University college) was founded by the first large group of around 800 European settlers who reached it in December 1850 (Māori people had been there since at least 1250, eventually giving it the name *Ōtautahi*). Within a month Christchurch had a school, a newspaper (the *Lyttelton Times*) and a bank; by 1856 it had been formally designated a city (New Zealand's first) by royal charter. Eight years later, its Anglican cathedral was begun, and in 1868, with a population of 3,200, it was well on its way to becoming a modest-sized settlement.

Although the fault in the Earth's crust which moved that February day had been undocumented, Christchurch had had some prior warnings. The Anglican cathedral was damaged in an earthquake in 1888, when over seven metres (23 feet) of its spire fell off. Rebuilt, the spire toppled again in 1901 during another earth tremor, though this time it was replaced in timber and metal, rather than stone which is less flexible and so more sensitive to quakes. The cathedral stood firm in September 2010 when the region experienced the first in a series of shocks that heralded the February 2011 earthquake. Although some buildings were damaged that time, the scale was relatively minor and there were no recorded fatalities.

Christchurch was not spared five months later. The Anglican cathedral and its Catholic counterpart were severely damaged, and most of the central business district was so badly hit that it was closed off for months (only fully reopening in June 2013). Once the immediate search and recovery operation was completed, the government had to purchase around 8,000 properties which were unsafe and then demolish them. Among those to fall was the Hotel Grand Chancellor, the city's tallest building. As well as the human toll, the damage to the local and national economy was severe, and it was estimated that the total cost of reconstruction would be in the region of $40 to $50 billion.

That reconstruction was marshalled by the Canterbury Earthquake Recovery Authority set up in March 2011. As a relatively rich economy, New Zealand was able to rebuild, even in the face of what was deemed by seismologists to be a one-in-a-thousand-years event. Other countries have not been so lucky. Unable to afford the flexible steel and rubber bases on which modern buildings in earthquake zones are supposed to be built (to absorb the seismic waves), cities that have grown too rapidly with poor-quality concrete construction then suffer disproportionately when earthquakes strike.

In Turkey, the 2023 7.8-magnitude quake which struck the southeast of the country (as well as northern Syria) caused whole neighbourhoods to collapse like packs of cards, with as much as four fifths of the total housing stock in Antakya needing to be demolished. It was deemed to be the worst earthquake to hit the city since one in AD526, and killed around 53,000 people nationally (as well as 8,000 in Syria, where the equally ancient city of Aleppo suffered serious damage).

An earthquake in Haiti in 2010 which devastated the south of the country, and may have killed as many as 250,000 people, flattened large parts of the capital Port-au-Prince, leaving a government – already barely capable of addressing the almost intractable problems of one of the world's poorest nations – utterly ill-equipped to embark on the massive programme of reconstruction needed. Matters could have been even worse, though. The 2011 Tohoku earthquake in Japan was followed by a tsunami which damaged turbines at the Fukushima nuclear plant, causing the cooling systems to fail and very nearly a cataclysmic meltdown at the plant.

Cities will continue to exist (and even new ones be built) in zones known to be prone to earthquakes. San Francisco (which last had a catastrophic earthquake in 1906), Antakya, Aleppo, Christchurch and dozens of other cities situated along fault lines are not about to move (though Beichuan in China's Sichuan province was abandoned after an earthquake in 2008). Cities like Christchurch will continue to gamble, hope and pray that the next quake will be small, and that the measures taken to protect buildings will hold up. In the end, though, the power of nature will always prevail.

Megacity

Chongqing, 2023 & 1944

The contrast between the two photographs is stark. In that from 1944, Chongqing, in the Sichuan Basin of southern China, is a low-rise settlement clustered around the bend where the Yangtze river is joined by its Jialing tributary. In the 2023 image, the massively expanded city is dominated by dense clusters of skyscrapers. In between, the population of Chongqing's urban area, its tiny footprint shown in the 1945 map compiled by the British Royal Naval Intelligence Division, had risen from a million (a figure already swollen by its temporary role as the capital of China's Nationalist government) to around 22 million. Chongqing had become both a megacity and part of a megalopolis.

Right at the start of humanity's urban story around 6,000 years ago, cities such as Uruk in Mesopotamia might have counted as megacities, their population of 40 to 50,000 people ranking as the world's largest (in an era, granted, when there was little competition). The steady growth in city populations since then, accelerating after the Industrial Revolution and then going into overdrive in the late 20th century, prompted the United Nations to define a megacity as one having more than 10 million inhabitants. By 2018 there were something like 529 million people living in 33 such massive conurbations, itself a huge leap on the situation in 1970 when there had been just three cities (Tokyo, New York and Osaka) in the giants' league of over 10 million inhabitants.

By 2023, this number had surged to over 40, with the very largest – including Cairo, Mexico City, Beijing, Shanghai, Mumbai, Delhi and Seoul – having populations exceeding 20 million and Tokyo over 30 million. Into these ranks have ascended cities which were until relatively recently comparatively small in global terms: Ho Chi Minh City, Jakarta, Tehran, Kinshasa, Dhaka and Bogotá. Most of these cities are predicted to grow even further by 2050 (with the exception of Osaka and Tokyo in Japan, where low birth rates, ageing populations and modest inward migration will most likely see their numbers falling). By mid-century the population of Cairo may reach 40 million, that of Shanghai 50 million and Delhi a similar number.

The population of Seoul and Delhi today would have given them a place in the top twenty most populous countries in 1950. Over the next two decades there will be a radical shift, so that most of the world's megacities will be in Africa or Asia, and the populations of those continents, long principally rural dwellers, will become mainly urban.

Chongqing, a comparative minnow in 1938, with a population of around 250,000, now has an urban population within its metropolitan area of about 100 times

that number. Little in its long history would have suggested such heady growth. Said to have been the hometown of Tushanshi, the wife of the Yu emperor who founded the Xia dynasty – traditionally understood to have preceded the Shang, before around 1600BC – it became the centre of a state called Ba, before being subsumed into unified China in the 3rd century BC. Although it became a concessionary river port for trade with the British and Japanese from the 1890s, and had a brief moment at the centre of national politics as the capital from 1938 to 1946, it was only when its became a municipality separate from Sichuan in 1997, that its growth really began.

In 2010, Chongqing was designated one of China's "national central cities", intended to be at the forefront of urban development in the country (the others included Beijing, Shanghai, Wuhan, Guangzhou and Chengdu). Yet Chinese urban planning has gone one stage even further than this. In 2021, 19 regions were identified as being a megalopolis, a group of cities which have in effect merged into one continuous urban area, and for which a common planning framework is necessary.

Such urban mergers are nothing new in the history of cities (Budapest originally began as the separate settlements of Buda and Pest across the River Danube from each other), but the 21st-century megalopolis is on an unprecedented scale. Chongqing is included in the Chengyu megalopolis (which also includes Chengdu) to create an urban region of 185,000 square kilometres (71,500 square miles) – roughly the size of Syria or Cambodia – with a population of around 90 million in 2014 (more than Turkey or Germany have currently).

Other of the Chinese megalopolises are even larger: the Jing-Jin-Ji megalopolis, which includes Beijing and Tianjin, is 217,000 square kilometres in extent (a little more than Belarus) with a population of 130 million (on a par with Mexico or Japan); while the largest of all, the Yangtze River Delta, which incorporates Shanghai, is almost as large in area as Germany, with a population of 240 million (more than Brazil), and which would have it, if a country, vying for a place among the top five most populous nations.

Yet the megalopolis is not a phenomenon confined to China. Aside from the densely populated northeastern seaboard of the United States, which encompasses Boston, New York, Philadelphia and Washington, DC, and has around 50 million inhabitants, megalopolises are developing in Egypt, where Greater Cairo has around 22 million and the Nile Delta (centred on Alexandria) about 50 million, in

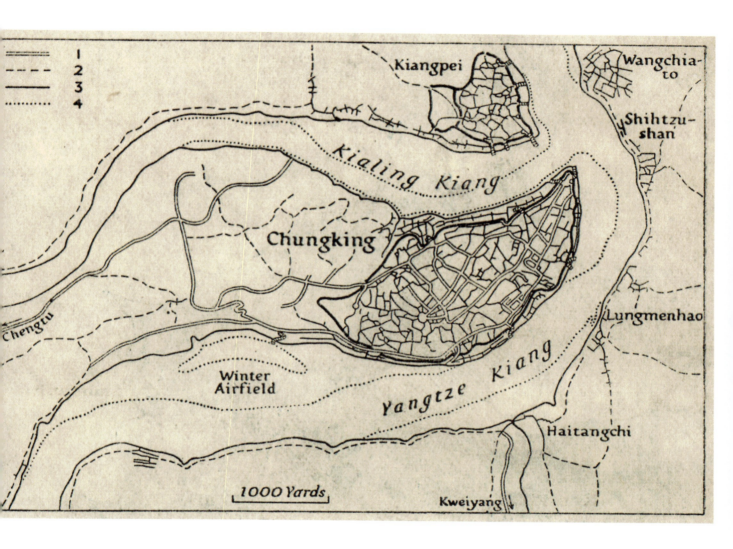

South Korea (where Seoul amounts to somewhere between 26 and 38 million depending on the region counted) and West Africa, where a corridor that links Abidjan, Lagos, Accra and Lomé is creating a cross-border megalopolis with around 27 million inhabitants.

The challenges of such developments are profound. Governing a metropolis the size of China's Greater Bay megalopolis (with 86 million inhabitants and a GDP equivalent to $1.64 trillion, around that of Thailand's PPP GDP), without the bureaucratic resources of a national government is difficult enough, but for developing countries where the infrastructure is already weak, and where there may be no formal co-ordination between the cities which have merged, it may be next to impossible. The authorities in the megalopolis of the future will have to cope with providing decent housing for the increasing numbers of slum dwellers, with supplying its citizens with clean water, coping with the pollution that will be emitted by the increasing quantity of cars (the number of vehicles in Delhi doubled between 2008 and 2020) and the sheer clogging up of transport arteries those cars will produce. Chongqing may be the blueprint for a future where cities engulf entire regions and provinces, making almost everyone a city-dweller, yet such giant-sized cities will come with giant-sized problems.

Future City

Oceanix Busan

It looks like a child's game, a brightly coloured mosaic of tiles arranged against a watery backdrop. But this is a city. Oceanix Busan, planned to be built off the busy port of Busan in South Korea, is described by its designers as the "world's first prototype of a resilient and sustainable community" planned around spaces for "sustainable, circular living".

With no roads, and composed of hexagonal modules each around two hectares in area and housing 300 people in a carbon neutral, community-friendly environment, Oceanix Busan is the dream of Marc Collins Chen, former tourism minister of French Polynesia, who realised that a third of the 118 islands in his home nation were due to sink beneath the waves in the next half-century due to global warming. Backed by the United Nations Human Settlement Programme he came up with a proposal for a modular city that can grow as needed (ideally into 36 units housing 10,000 people) and be built of bamboo (a material stronger than steel) which it could grow itself, be self-sustaining in food and, crucially, because it is a floating city, would be immune to rising sea levels.

Oceanix Busan is not the first such attempt at a maritime city. In the 1960s the American architect Buckminster Fuller, the inventor of the geodesic dome, was commissioned to build Triton City, a floating metropolis in Tokyo Bay which never got off the drawing board. More successfully, the Uros people of Lake Titicaca in Peru have been living on artificial floating islands for over 500 years, originally driven from their previous settlement on the mainland by the expanding Inca Empire. The impetus behind Oceanix Busan, though, is the remorseless rise in sea levels, which in 2018 were predicted to increase by 65 centimetres (26 inches) by 2100, putting huge numbers – including 90 per cent of the world's urban areas, which sit along coastlines – at risk of being inundated.

The world faces a perfect storm of land loss to the sea, water shortages, the exhaustion of non-renewable energy resources such as oil, changes in weather patterns that make feeding burgeoning urban populations even harder, and the rising demand for polluting cars, factories and buildings, which together mean the impact of cities on often already fragile ecosystems is becoming unsustainable. The response has been to dream up "sustainable cities" and "smart cities" with carbon neutral footprints, whose inhabitants need not stray more than 15 minutes from home in search of food, work or entertainment, and if they do so can do it on foot, bicycle or light rail systems.

Some of the future city plans are astonishingly ambitious. Saudi Arabia's Neom, a series of urban projects in the Tabuk region, could cost over a trillion US dollars if fully implemented. Its most show-stopping feature is The Line, a 170-kilometre- (106-mile-) long city intended to house 9 million people by 2030, which would be cantilevered hundreds of feet above the desert floor and have no cars, and not even streets, as residents got around by rail. Such gigantism, though, comes at a risk, not least implementing an urban paradise with a population density over five times that of Manila, the closest-packed urban centre in the world. The cost, too, may be prohibitive and in 2024 the plans for The Line were scaled back to a mere 2.4-kilometre (1.5-mile) length by 2030, to house 300,000 residents.

More utopian in conception is Telosa, an urban project to be established somewhere in the southwest of the United States that, its planners hope, "sets a global standard for urban living, expands human potential, and becomes a blueprint for future generations". This will be achieved by barring private ownership of property (everything will be leased and the income from this will fund housing, education and healthcare for the residents). In its centre will soar the "Equitism" tower, a skyscraper that will symbolise the city's egalitarian ethos. Intended to have a population of five million people by 2050, Telosa remains a dream of what might be achieved if only everyone agreed to get on.

More practical perhaps is China's Future City in Sichuan, to be built on a smaller scale with six zones of 5 square kilometres (2 square miles) within which no resident would have to travel more than ten minutes to reach services, or Mexico's Smart Forest City near Cancun that will have 7.5 million carbon-absorbing plants around it to reduce its carbon footprint to below zero, while being home to 130,000 people.

Yet all these future cities will barely dent the impact of the estimated two billion extra people who will live in urban centres by 2045. They may offer prototypes of approaches to resolve the growing environmental and demographic crisis of the world's cities, but they will only ever be lived in by a minority. For the rest of the world's city dwellers, a long, slow process of adaptation, of increasing access to public transport, of reducing the impact of pollutants such as cars and urban factories, and of not building in areas which impact on the food-producing land or water supplies, will be crucial. The majority of the cities of the future will be the cities of today.

Acknowledgements

Note from the author

Living in one of the world's great cities, it has been a privilege to look at London's history and that of more than 60 other metropolitan centres across all continents and 6,500 years and to examine the ways in which they have developed and been mapped over all that time. A book such as this is a highly complex one, and without the support of a dedicated and professional publishing team, could never have come about. I would like to thank Harley Griffiths and Robin Scrimgeour at HarperCollins for commissioning the book and steering it through its initial phases, to Gordon MacGilp for his beautiful interior design and Kevin Robbins for another striking cover design. My particular gratitude goes to Karen Marland for her eagle-eyed copy-editing, editorial project management and heroic efforts in keeping the author on schedule. Finally, I would like to thank the staff of the London Library, which contains a treasure trove of works on urban history and world cities.

Map and photo credits

While every effort has been made to trace the owner of copyright material reproduced herein and secure permission, the publishers would like to apologise for any omission and will be pleased to incorporate missing acknowledgements in any future edition of this book.

Front cover Science History Images / Alamy Stock Photo
p9 Images & Stories / Alamy Stock Photo
p10 *The Sigüenza Map*. [Place of Publication Not Identified: Publisher Not Identified, to 1599, 1500] Map. Retrieved from the Library of Congress, <www.loc.gov/item/2021668420/>. World Digital Library
p11 OCEANIX/BIG-Bjarke Ingels Group.
p12 From *The Indus Civilization* by Sir Mortimer Wheeler / © Cambridge University Press / reproduced with permission of the Licensor through PLSclear / Australian National University Archives: Basham Collection, ANUA 682-35, Mohenjo-daro: plans of Mohenjo-Daro citadel, heights in feet above sea level, 1968
p15–17 Chronicle / Alamy Stock Photo
p20–21 Antiqua Print Gallery / Alamy Stock Photo
p22 Armin von Gerkan, Griechische Städteanlagen. Untersuchungen zur Entwicklung des Städtebaues im Altertum, Berlin und Leipzig: Walter De Gruyter & Co., 1924, Abb. 9. Priene.
p26 Classic Image / Alamy Stock Photo
p27 Classic Image / Alamy Stock Photo
p29 Roma, Musei Capitolini, Museo della Forma Urbis / Archivio Fotografico dei Musei Capitolini / © Roma, Sovrintendenza Capitolina ai Beni Culturali
p31 The Print Collector / Alamy Stock Photo
p32 From the collection at the Harvard-Yenching Library of the Harvard College Library, Harvard University
p34 Gianni Dagli Orti/Shutterstock
p37 Science History Images / Alamy Stock Photo
p39 Magite Historic / Alamy Stock Photo
p41 © Collins Bartholomew
p42–43 Newberry Library, Chicago. VAULT Ayer 655.51 .C8 1524d
p45–47 University Library Vrije Universiteit Amsterdam, LL.06979gk
p50–51 The Picture Art Collection / Alamy Stock Photo
p54–55 Andrew Fare / Alamy Stock Photo
p56 Michael Jennings Antique Maps
p58 CPA Media Pte Ltd / Alamy Stock Photo
p60 GRANGER - Historical Picture Archive / Alamy Stock Photo
p63 CC-PD, https://commons.wikimedia.org/wiki/File:Hamburg_Braun-Hogenberg.jpg
p64 (top) Marzolino / Shutterstock
p64 (bottom) PAINTING / Alamy Stock Photo
p68–69 The Board of Trinity College Dublin
p71–73 ex. Photograph courtesy of the Main Library, Kyoto University - ローマ字タイトル: Heianjō tōzai nanboku machinami no zu

p74 & p76–77 Det Kgl. Bibliotek
p80–81 Paulus Swaen old maps & prints
p84–85 The Picture Art Collection / Alamy Stock Photo
p88–89 Heritage Image Partnership Ltd / Alamy Stock Photo
p91–93 From the British Library archive / Bridgeman Images
p96–97 From the British Library archive / Bridgeman Images
p99–101 The Picture Art Collection / Alamy Stock Photo
p103 From the British Library archive / Bridgeman Images
p106–107 © Giancarlo Costa / Bridgeman Images
p109 WStLA, Kartographische Sammlung, Sammelbestand, P1: 234
p112–113 Heritage Image Partnership Ltd / Alamy Stock Photo
p116–117 Courtesy of Geographicus Rare Antique Maps (http://www.geographicus.com).
p120–121 From the British Library archive / Bridgeman Images
p122–123 Penta Springs Limited / Alamy Stock Photo
p124–125 Antiqua Print Gallery / Alamy Stock Photo
p128–129 Topographical Collection / Alamy Stock Photo
p131–133 Reproduced with the permission of the National Library of Scotland
p136–137 Bridgeman Images
p138–139 The Protected Art Archive / Alamy Stock Photo
p141–143 Seoul National University, KYUJANGGAK INSTITUTE FOR KOREAN STUDIES 서울대학교 규장각한국학연구원
p145–147 Norman B. Leventhal Map & Education Center at the Boston Public Library
p148 Topographical Collection / Alamy Stock Photo
p151–153 Norman B. Leventhal Map & Education Center at the Boston Public Library
p155 © Collins Bartholomew
p156–157 From the collections of the State Library of NSW
p159–161 Andrew Fare / Alamy Stock Photo
p163 SLSA: b2557649, W. Light, Plan of the city of Adelaide, 1837
p166–167 Mary Evans Picture Library/Mapseeker Publishing
p170–171 Vicimages / Alamy Stock Photo
p173–175 University Library Vrije Universiteit Amsterdam, LL.06975gk
p176 (top) Antiqua Print Gallery / Alamy Stock Photo
p176 (bottom) © Collins Bartholomew
p180–181 Universal Images Group North America LLC / Alamy Stock Photo
p183–185 JJs / Alamy Stock Photo
p188–189 Granger / Bridgeman Images
p192–193 Geography and Map Division, Library of Congress
p195 Bridgeman Images
p198–199 Antiqua Print Gallery / Alamy Stock Photo
p201 (top) INTERFOTO / Alamy Stock Photo
p201 (bottom) NASA Archive / Alamy Stock Photo
p202–203 Kingdom of Maps / Alamy Stock Photo
p205 Paul Toal, Tara Florence, Cormac Maguire, Edwina Rusk, Claire Aiken, Laura Martin, Graeme Skelly, Adam Joyce, Kieran Dobbs, Emma Louise Matthews, Edelle Henry and Lindsay Totten (Authors), Queen's University Belfast / Professor Karim Hadjri
p208–209 © Tuttle Publishing / file supplied by Curtis Wright Maps
p210 PLANETOBSERVER / SCIENCE PHOTO LIBRARY
p211 Contains modified Copernicus Sentinel data (2024), processed by ESA
p213–215 PK Das & Associates, Mumbai
p216 Reprinted from The Lancet Planetary Health, Vol. 1, Issue 6, Andrea M Teng, Tony Blakely, Vivienne Ivory, Simon Kingham, Vicky Cameron, *Living in areas with different levels of earthquake damage and association with risk of cardiovascular disease: a cohort-linkage study*, Page e244, Copyright 2017, with permission from Elsevier
p218 sisi2017 / Shutterstock
p219 Everett Collection Historical / Alamy Stock Photo
p221 Antiqua Print Gallery / Alamy Stock Photo
p222 OCEANIX/BIG-Bjarke Ingels Group.